English Children and
Their Magazines, 1751–1945

ENGLISH CHILDREN
AND THEIR MAGAZINES, 1751-1945

Yale University Press · New Haven and London

Kirsten Drotner

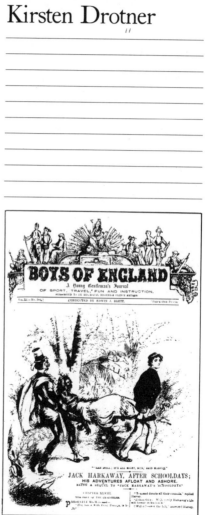

Published with assistance from the
Mary Cady Tew Memorial Fund.

Designed by Jo Aerne and set in Caslon
Old Face type with Forum I for display
by The Composing Room of Michigan.
Printed in the United States of America by
Vail-Ballou Press, Binghamton, New York.

Library of Congress Cataloging-
in-Publication Data
Drotner, Kirsten.
English children and their magazines,
1751–1945 / Kirsten Drotner.
p.   cm.   Bibliography: p.
Includes index.   ISBN 0–300–
04010–5 (alk. paper)
1. Children's periodicals, English—
History.   2. Youths' periodicals—
Great Britain—History.   3. Popular
literature—Great Britain—History and
criticism.   4. Children's literature,
English—History and criticism.
5. Young adult literature, English—
History and criticism.   6. Children—
Great Britain—Books and reading—
History.   7. Youth—Great Britain—
Books and reading—History.   I. Title.
PN5124.J8D72   1988   87–37156
052'.088054—dc19   CIP

The paper in this book meets the guidelines
for permanence and durability of the Committee on Production Guidelines for Book
Longevity of the Council on Library
Resources.

10 9 8 7 6 5 4 3 2 1

For Julie and Jonas, who taught me
the true meaning of childhood

CONTENTS

ACKNOWLEDGMENTS

This book has been a long time in the making. The first germs of interest were laid when as a nine- or ten-year-old I discovered Enid Blyton's and "Carolyn Keene's" serial excitements. My university studies, while not exactly nurturing an interest in juvenile literature, brought me together with fellow students, friends and colleagues who shared my enthusiasm for popular culture and helped me unearth my childhood dreams. I never suspected, however, that it would take three different jobs and the birth of two children before the results of this archaeological discovery materialized.

While the final arguments and conclusions presented in the following naturally remain my own responsibility, the book could not have been written without the support and assistance of a great many people. At the early stages of my research, Mary Cadogan willingly shared with me her large collection of interwar girls' papers and her intimate knowledge of their contents. Jean Mc-Crindle, Sheila Rowbotham, and Anna Davin all gave generously of their time, their professional insight and personal experience, and thus made my work seem meaningful at a time when I was least susceptible to understake it. I am grateful for their support. At Aarhus University, Assistant Professor Mette Kunøe was a source of encouragement, and Professor Johan Fjord Jensen made the theoretical groundwork shaping many of my ideas on popular literature. I appreciate his thoughtful criticisms of my work.

During the actual process of research and writing, I was helped in numerous ways. Thanks are due to the always helpful staffs at the Bodleian Library in Oxford and at the British Library in London, where the friendly provision of chairs at the stacks seemed of as much assistance as the professional information provided me by the librarians. Irene Whalley, head librarian at the Victoria and Albert Museum in London, clarified bibliographical and other uncertainties concerning nineteenth-century periodicals, while John F. Gore of the International Publishing Company, Gil Page of Fleetway Publications, and Martin Lindsay of D. C. Thomson and Company, helped out with missing details on contemporary papers. At Aarhus University, Professor Knud Sørensen and Steen Larsen offered me useful technical advice.

I appreciate the donation by the Danish Ministry of Education and the British

Council of a YRWIS travel grant, which enabled me to extend one of my numerous research trips to England. Also, the Danish Research Council for the Humanities and Aarhus University are acknowledged for financial assistance in the completion of my doctoral dissertation on which this book is based.

Part of chapter 13 appeared in an earlier version in *Feminist Studies* 9, no. 1 (1983): 33–52, and is reprinted here by permission of the publisher, Feminist Studies, Inc., Women's Studies Program, University of Maryland, College Park. Illustrations on pp. 19, 26, 30, 41, 52, 54, 69, 74, 82, 89, 96, 102, 110, 117, 122, 136, 146, and 155 are reproduced by permission of the British Library. Illustrations on pp. 164, 175, 186, and 211 are reproduced by permission of Syndication International, Ltd., and the British Library. Illustrations on pp. 196, 226, and 233 are reproduced by permission of Thomson & Co., Ltd., and the British Library. The illustration of p. 242 is reproduced by permission of *Just Seventeen*.

At Yale University Press, the professionalism of my editor, Gladys Topkis, bridged the Atlantic Ocean, and Carl Rosen as a meticulous manuscript editor is sincerely thanked for his helpful comments and suggestions.

Finally, I extend my warmest thanks to my parents and in-laws, who willingly displayed their expertise in baby-sitting, and, in particular, to my husband, Ole Mouritsen, who not only assumed all domestic chores and child-care responsibilities during my extensive periods of writing, but who also found the emotional strength to persuade me that it was all worthwhile.

PART ONE

Introduction

1

Juveniles and Popular Literature

W H Y D O children and adolescents dote on the weekly wonders of belligerent cats and orphaned ballerinas when they can have *Alice in Wonderland* or *Watership Down?* What made children living between the world wars prefer hair-raising escapades to the homely encounters favored by the young only a few decades before? Questions such as these concerning literary choice and fictional change have recurred over the years in my reading of children's literature. Some answers can be found in the analysis of the rise and fall of the juvenile magazine in Britain. Together with toys, these compound periodicals, with their mixture of reading matter and pictures, form some of the earliest examples of a commodity aimed specifically at the young. Historically speaking, the magazines are among the most important ingredients in the creation of what can be called juvenile consumerism. And Britain is their creator.

When thinking about childhood and youth today, we almost invariably include all the gadgets surrounding the young and shaping their lives. Cribs, bottles, and rattles for the baby, special cereals for the toddler, and comics, music tapes, and sports gear for older juveniles—all these have become integral elements of growing up, indeed almost a convention of childhood and youth. And yet both childhood, youth, and juvenile consumerism are historical constructs whose developments are closely connected. As early as the seventeenth century, childrearing began to take place in the nuclear family and often at school rather than through work in the field, the kitchen, or the workshop. The Puritans were the first to distinguish, if often imperceptibly, between educational works and leisure reading for their offspring. Written with the express intention of securing the spiritual welfare of the young, the few tales for children published during the seventeenth century are suffused with pious warnings and copious deathbed scenes. The following century saw the first transient attempts to promote a commercial juvenile literature, but only during the nineteenth century did these efforts begin to pay off. Along with the proliferation on the adult literary market of daily newspapers, weekly journals, penny-part novels, and cheap periodicals we find the first examples of popular literature intended

3

for the young—namely, juvenile magazines, or storypapers, as they are sometimes called.

These periodicals are popular literature, or mass literature, in two senses of the term. First, from early on the magazines were aimed at a mass reading public of juveniles. Second, the magazines were some of the first commodities in publishing to make use of the technical advances that facilitated mass production and national distribution.[1] Like other forms of literature, juvenile magazines existed in a tenuous balance between profits to the publishers and pleasure to the purchasers, whether these were the parents or, later, juveniles themselves. Since the mass-produced magazines have this balance adjusted every month or every week by the infallible workings of the market mechanism, they make particularly sensitive seismographs of taste and hence constitute unique objects for studying literary change. As fictional phenomena, these periodicals expanded enormously during the nineteenth and early twentieth centuries, to be overtaken by comics or transformed into picture storypapers in the years following World War II. As cultural phenomena, the juvenile magazines gradually merged into the lives of the young as natural aspects of their personal horizon. To trace the history of the popular juvenile periodicals is to prize open for analysis and revaluation an important element in the construction of modern childhood, an element that gains in importance along with the technological advances in contemporary entertainment industries.

It is the central argument of this book that the juvenile magazines must be understood and interpreted as emotional interventions into the everyday lives of their readers. More specifically, I claim that the juvenile magazines are aesthetic organizers of contradictory experiences. Childhood and youth as the phases of life we know today are based on a structural paradox: the young are brought up to adulthood at a remove from the social experiences and activities of their elders. The appeal of the magazines, and hence parents' or juveniles' incentive to keep buying them, depends on the solutions offered through reading. The contradictory needs and experiences of the young are felt consciously or unconsciously, and their modes of expression, dependent on class and gender, change over time. How the magazines are used varies accordingly. Hence, the magazines and their development can be interpreted in relation to the different ways in which they are read by girls and boys, by working-class and middle-class children and adolescents.

My interest in popular literature and in the relation between text and reader forms part of a general revaluation in cultural criticism and theory over the past fifteen years or so. When popular culture is debated and revalued—as in the

1. The terms popular culture and popular literature can also denote cultural products and expressions, such as traditional tales and rituals, that are shared by many people without being mass-produced (See Bennett 1980; MacCabe 1986).

1880s and in the 1950s, for example—the reasons are a complex mixture of economics, new audiences, and new technology. The continuous and sweeping transformations of culture that the advent of video, cables, and satellites has brought about have made it almost impossible for any academic or cultural critic to disregard popular aesthetics and the impact of popular culture on our lives. Especially if the critic is also teaching, he or she is faced by new generations of students who have been raised on rock music and television as integral aspects of their cultural horizons. Moreover, in the late 1960s and well into the 1970s, many of these students formed a critical and politicized opposition to the academic institution and its standard assumptions about research. Both empirically and theoretically, popular culture has affected academic disciplines such as literary studies, sociology, and psychology, just as it has been instrumental in shaping interdisciplinary fields like mass communications and cultural studies. The rapid innovation of popular culture itself, its increased impact on our lives, and changes in academia have brought about methodological and theoretical reshufflings that have called into question the cultural norms that have dominated criticism and research at least since the mid-nineteenth century.

The most pervasive of these norms is that there exists one culture, which operates as a cohesive force in a society plagued by social and political antagonisms. In Britain, a chief proponent of this view, Matthew Arnold (1822–88), developed his thoughts in *Culture and Anarchy* (1869), whose expressive title in itself is a clue to this norm. Another dominant norm within cultural criticism and the academic community relates more specifically to art. According to this norm, art is only real, "quality" art when it criticizes established power relations and challenges received moral and aesthetic ideas. Significantly, the German philosopher and cultural critic Theodor Adorno (1903–69) was among the most influential exponents of this view. His "aesthetics of negativity" (*Ästhetik der Negation*) is most thoroughly developed in *Aesthetic Theory*, written under the weight that the mass appeal of Nazism puts on the national German conscience and published posthumously in 1970. Although Adorno's avant-garde views on art seem directly opposite to Arnold's views on cultural unification, both approaches nevertheless share a normative view that regards culture as something that is made by the few for the many.

Questioning these prevalent views, cultural critics and researchers have again begun to ask: How is culture created by different people at different times? What is meant by aesthetic "quality"? Is reading a book different from reading a comic? If so, why? Questions such as these are as complex as the answers given. But the complexity of the questions at least prevents us from returning to simplified conclusions. Still, despite the fact that children and young people are among the most avid comic readers, music listeners, and film viewers, critics of juvenile culture have offered surprisingly few answers to such questions. Popular culture for the young, however, *is* discussed, and it is taken seriously: experts on juvenile culture are often in the forefront of public debate. But the discursive intensity is rarely matched by an equally intense exploration of new theories and methods of research. This contradiction is based on a common and widely shared assumption that children and, to a lesser degree, adolescents are not as developed as adults. Following this view, we acknowledge juvenile experiences and expressions as being different from our own; indeed, we often regard them as better or more "genuine." But this openness to difference means that we also tend to evaluate these experiences and expressions from an adult perspective in our research.

With regard to juvenile literature, this assumption implies that reading by children and adolescents is part of growing up and of growing into "real"—that is, adult—literature. And so adult literature becomes the stuff that serious research is made of. Moreover, juvenile literature is written, published, sold, and reviewed by adults. Thus, it is not surprising that literary and pedagogical research, while methodologically different, often share the same aims and interests in protecting the young by preserving "good" literature. These aims and interests, far from being inflexible facts, are variable historical constructs.

In the 1970s, for example, the dominant outlook on the young and their reading was influenced by politicized students and researchers as well as by librarians and teachers, who revealed much sexual, social, and ethnic bias in juvenile literature. Their efforts have spurred vigorous attempts to promote nonbiased reading materials, following the traditions in mainstream criticism to promote "high" culture and hinder the proliferation of "low" culture. But at the same time these efforts have been among the few to go against the grain of the critical tradition by enhancing our awareness of how literature in general operates in the lives of the young. The works of Fox and Hammond (1980), Bratton (1981), Proterough (1983), and Musgrave (1985) indicate that this awareness is growing also with researchers of juvenile literature. Their wide-ranging topics and their explicit references to current cultural and literary debate demonstrate that the difference between "adult" and "juvenile" may become an increasingly obsolete distinction of research.

However, none of these scholars takes up publications such as juvenile story-papers, comics, or serial books for specific treatment. This type of reading matter is still largely measured against the unflagging quality norms of the literary heritage. Such a comparison makes most researchers and critics conclude that popular literature is bad: its clipped language, flat characters, and repetitive plots are deplored, and new proposals are offered to improve the literary and moral outlook of the young. One of the most forceful accusations against "cheap" literature (referring not only to its price) was made by the American psychiatrist Fredric Wertham in his significantly titled book *The Seduction of the Innocent*. First published in 1954, it was instrumental in establishing the Comic Code, the guidelines for the American comic book industry's self-imposed censorship. Though by no means the first to challenge the wisdom of juvenile weeklies, Wertham spurred heated debate in European countries as diverse as Italy, Sweden, and Britain. All the same, children continued to read their "trash." Some have even continued to do so as adults. These are often the ones who found this literary fare, if perhaps inferior to "real" literature, nevertheless harmless: innocent entertainment. These two reactions to popular literature for the young continue to dominate research, hence they have also influenced my own investigation of the juvenile periodicals.

The history of British juvenile magazines has not been told in full before. And it is, indeed, a formidable task. With a total output of more than 450 titles, many of which appeared as sixteen-page weeklies and one of which ran for 108 years (the *Child's Companion; or, Sunday Scholar's Reward,* 1824–1932), it is impossible to cover all details of the voluminous magazine story. The first who have tried to patch together its checkered past are the avid adult readers. Boys' papers are now highly priced collectors' items, and in Britain, Australia, and North America, clubs exist in which members can share their bibliophile interest in famous characters, rare copies, and the dark spots in authors' biographies. Invaluable information on publication dates, writers of specific series, and the exact appearances of heroes and heroines can be culled from their groundwork. This information has been expanded on by Sheila Egoff (1951), by Brian Doyle (1964), and most extensively by William Lofts and Derek Adley (1969, 1970), who remain the most prolific connoisseurs in the field. Together with Kevin Carpenter's excellent updated survey (1981), these investigations comprise the only bibliographical indexes to the primary sources.

The earliest study of juvenile magazines is *A Brief History of Boys' Journals, with Interesting Facts about the Writers of Boys' Stories* (1913), written by Ralph Rollington (himself a writer and publisher of boys' papers), now available only at the British Library in London. The best-known history of the magazines, however, is Ernest S. Turner's fascinating *Boys Will be Boys: The Story of Sweeney Todd, Deadwood Dick, Sexton Blake, Billy Bunter, Dick Barton, et al.* (1948, 1976). As may be seen from its title, the book follows a biographical approach, and juvenile magazines are weighed on the scales of literary distinction. Turner's work remains the most complete study, but it deals solely with boys' papers of a commercial kind. Mary Cadogan and Patricia Craig have made a pioneering attempt to balance the picture in *You're a Brick, Angela! A New Look at Girls' Fiction from 1839 to 1975* (1976), which includes an examination of some of the most-favored girls' periodicals. All these works have offered valuable guidelines for this book, not least by delineating the literary contours of juvenile magazine development.

The social contours of this development are far more opaque. Literary sociologists have often shared the pedagogical zeal characterising many literary critics of juvenile fiction. No literary sociologist, for the period under consideration, has selected magazines for particular scrutiny, even if popular fiction has often fired his or her professional interest. Thus, as early as 1888, the young journalist Edward Salmon (he later became a distinguished biographer) published an investigation carried out among two thousand schoolchildren who were asked to state their literary preferences. Their answers, in Salmon's view, often revealed "a moral and material ruin . . . in the centre of the English working population" (Salmon 1888, p. 192). With a similar aim, in 1906 Florence B. Low undertook a smaller survey of adolescent girls' reading. Focusing upon the middle and lower-middle classes, she concluded that "good literature" was being ousted by "second-rate" fiction "upon which our girls feed greedily, with the very natural result that they cannot digest food of a superior nature" (Low 1906, p. 278). During the interwar years, the moral tone is subdued if still discernible, as can be gauged from J. H. Engledow and William Farr's *The Reading and Other Interests of School Children in St. Pancras* (1933), as well as from Augustus Jenkinson's *What Do Boys and Girls Read?* (1940, 1946).

These surveys are of much assistance in the history of juvenile magazines since they clarify the stated reading habits of the young and their conscious attitudes toward fiction. But, partly because the research material is scanty, partly because of its methodology, which registers only observable facts (often silver-lined ones as well), literary sociology remains only a guide to my initial questions, sharing with literary criticism in general the view that juveniles are adults in the making. Whether deploring popular literature for shortchanging the young with simplistic moral menus or extolling the mental fare offered by the "best" of the juvenile magazines, the majority of literary and sociological analyses of the juvenile magazines remains one-sided.

One of the major problems facing the researcher who wants to overcome this one-sidedness is that literary and sociological or psychological studies approach popular reading from opposite perspectives without sharing a common focus. While the literary expert analyzes the text and from this analysis perhaps tries to infer its possible impact or effect upon the reader, the sociologist or psychologist investigates the readers' habits or reactions without paying particular attention to the substance and style of what is being read. Each approach sees the other as mere context to the main concern. I began research on this book not only to enlarge the empirical context of my earlier work (Drotner 1977), but also to get beyond the impasse I found in my own approach to literature. I was lucky in that the Scandinavian research milieus of juvenile culture were particularly open and innovative during the 1970s, stimulating explorations of new vistas.

The resurgent interest in adult popular culture has produced a third perspective on literature, combining text-intrinsic and text-extrinsic theories. By focusing on the process of reading as a meeting ground between textual and social or historical realities, it becomes possible to analyze both perspectives as interacting aspects of one process. This interaction is essential to an understanding of why juveniles read popular literature when quality literature is available and why one form of popular literature, the juvenile magazine, changes.

The study of the reading process began in classical times, and a theoretical interest in literary change has persisted since art as a social institution separated itself from economic processes during the nineteenth century. Both these interests, however, have assumed a new relevance with recent cultural developments. Reader-response theories in the United States, irrespective of their theoretical and methodological differences, have been innovative in two main respects: they regard the text as a multifaceted conglomerate of meanings, and the reader is seen as an active participant in the constitution of meaning through the reading process (Suleiman and Crosman 1980; Tompkins 1980). Reading is therefore a coming-to-life of new meanings, new realities. Such theories are markedly different from the prevailing literary theories, in which literature is regarded as either a self-contained entity or a reflection of existing ideas or ideologies.

Reader-response theories have played a pivotal role in questioning simple notions of textual meaning, but they are less explicit about the variability of the readers' experiences. An acknowledgment of these experiences is crucial if we want to understand not only why juveniles read the magazines but also why the magazines changed. The so-called reception theory, which has been influential both in West Germany, where it originated, and in literary circles on the European continent, focuses on the question of literary change.[2] Inspired by hermeneutical philosophy, Hans Robert Jauss, the key figure of reception theory, has proposed the term "horizon of expectations" (*Erwartungshorizont*) to denote the readers' immediate response to the text based on shared assumptions of genre, tone, and style. When a text shatters existing expectations, a new horizon is established that in turn propels new changes (Jauss 1970).

Despite Jauss' criticisms of avant-garde theories of art (Jauss 1974), such an explanation of literary change accords perfectly with the development of modernist literature, with the breaking of conventions, aesthetic or otherwise, as a driving force. Reception theory, however, is far less adequate for analyses of popular literature. The theory is grounded on an unacknowledged notion of the text as existing within a dynamic market economy (hence the modernist possibility of breaking with convention), yet with an author unhampered by economic restrictions: his noble literary message never seems to be polluted by mean financial considerations, and hack writers are beyond the pale of theoretical reflection. Equally, the reader is an ideal adult male with ample time for contemplative immersion in the intricacies of the text. Clearly, one who shares such covert assumptions cannot fully explain the sudden absorption felt by a

---

2. For an illuminating critical introduction to reception theory, see Holub 1984.

newly literate ten-year-old girl reading the latest installment of a comic or a magazine between her lessons or home chores.

Reception theorists have prompted a new awareness of the historical change-ability of the reading process. But they do not specify the needs and experiences met or rejected through reading. It is therefore difficult within reception theory to explain all but the most consciously created literary changes. However, in trying to make such a social specification of needs and experiences, the researcher is faced with an old problem at a new level, as Robert Holub cogently notes in his criticism of German reception theory: "why should we be able to read the reading subject or this subject's reading more easily or accurately than what the subject was reading? . . . We admit that the text is multiple while simultaneously denying the plurality of readers and their writing" (Holub 1984, p. 156).

One solution to this basic problem of interpretation is to dispense with any distinction between social or historical reality and textual reality. We can, as many poststructuralists do, decenter the reader by textualizing history. Another solution (the one adopted in this book) is to retain a notion of "the plurality of readers" while at the same time acknowledging that we can never know *the* truth about juveniles' or any other readers' understanding and interpretation of a text. But this insight does not necessarily imply that one "truth" is as valid as another. Although our sources, literary as well as social or historical, are open to interpretation, to the reading of the present into the past, the sources remain. Our analysis need not be an arbitrary judgment of taste if we retain a self-critical openness toward these sources and toward the contradictions within and between them.

By specifying the multiplicity of textual as well as social and historical realities, we can analyze the interface between them as a dynamic process. More importantly perhaps, by correlating the literary and social processes we can discover not only the neat correspondences but also the incongruences between expression in the magazines and the experiences of the various readers at different times. Thus, we are given the possibility of evaluating literary quality for the young without embracing either the moral normativity of mainstream cultural criticism or the moral relativity of many poststructuralists.

Given these theoretical considerations, this book is structured so that changes in the juvenile magazines are correlated with changes facing the young. As already noted, the main argument of this book is that the development of modern childhood and youth rests on a structural paradox. This paradox creates contradictory experiences for the young into which the magazine intervenes as an aesthetic organiser. For each period, then, we attend to certain key questions: What are the focal concerns of children and adolescents, both working class and middle class, girls and boys? How do these concerns relate to prevalent character types, themes, and genres of the magazines? From this relation, the use value of the periodicals can be gauged: Why do the young read the magazines, and what are the possible implications of this reading? Comparing the periods under investigation, we consider: How and why do text-reader relations change? Why do new groups of juveniles enter the realm of magazine reading? How does their entry affect the output, substance, and style of periodicals?

Any author faces problems of interpretation. In this book, the theoretical problems are pertinent and have already been touched upon. As for the methodological problems, some are of a practical character, others of a more substantial nature. The main obstacle facing a book that involves the history of the young is that there is so little of it, although the last ten years have seen a widening professional interest in charting the lives of children and adolescents along with other forgotten groups of society. Philippe Ariès, through his classic study *Centuries of Childhood* (1960), has been a catalyst of this interest. My own view of childhood and youth as historical rather than biological phases of life is informed fundamentally by Ariès. Ariès, however, bases his conclusions upon artistic and institutional sources, underrating the continuities in growing up and neglecting the complexities of concrete experience. This neglect is balanced by John Gillis in *Youth and History: Tradition and Change in European Age Relations, 1700–Present* (1974), which remains a basic reference despite its concentration on male youth. Gillis' emphasis is shared by John Springhall, whose *Coming of Age: Adolescence in Britain, 1860–1960* (1986) came to my attention after my own research had finished.

The differences between Ivy Pinchbeck and Margaret Hewitt's pioneering institutional study *Children in English Society* (1969, 1973) and James Walvin's *A Child's World: A Social History of English Childhood, 1800–1914* (1982) are an indication of the shifting emphasis in historiography within the last decade. But we still need a history of English childhood and youth taking social as well as sexual differences into account and charting both continuities and changes over time, and a history in which "ordinary" youngsters emerge on the social and cultural scene displaying their overt and covert conflicts and the ingenuities of their resistance. Stephen Humphries' *Hooligans or Rebels? An Oral History of Working-Class Childhood and Youth, 1889–1939* (1981) is an attempt to uncover the more explicit of these resistances. Its limited coverage points toward a central reason for the absence of a dialectical history of childhood and youth.

Not only are juveniles in our society without any direct economic, social, or political significance, making them poor objects of serious analysis or academically influential investigation, but they have also left few permanent traces of their lives and thoughts. Children and adolescents have been either illiterate and too busy working for sheer survival to care about posterity or, if they have not been laborers, they have lived individual existences in economic dependence and social subjugation to their parents and to society in general. Beyond the period that can be covered by "oral histories," the personal accounts that we do possess about childhood and youth in the past are written either by well-to-do children or, chiefly, by adults, most of them middle class, some working-class men, and very few working-class women. Thus, the historical evidence left by children and adolescents contains either a class, an age, or a gender bias or various mixtures of them all. As Linda Pollock concludes in her extensive survey of British and American parent-child relations: "We still know little about how *parents actually reared* their children" (Pollock 1983, p. 67). Nor do we know how children experienced this upbringing. While far from surmounting these obstacles, I overcome some of them by relying on a variety of sources, both institutional and autobiographical, in my analysis of the prospective readers' social lives. Still, it has not been possible for me to let these authors come to life as historical persons in their own right. Their accounts merely yield examples of how juveniles experienced their social conditions and literary choices. The accounts remain guidelines of general tendencies.

Today we think of childhood and youth in terms of age, while two or three hundred years ago they were defined in relation to economic status and social role. This crucial transformation is a result of changes both in the lives of the young and in adults' perceptions of these changes. For want of a better solution, the terms "childhood," "youth," and "adolescence" will be used throughout this book, even if this use blurs the shifting boundaries of the terms during the two centuries under investigation.

The peripheral status that juvenile ephemera occupy in professional circles places severe obstacles to literary analysis in this book. Is it difficult to survey the bulk of primary material since the most complete holdings are available only at the British Library, which began systematically collecting copyrighted material only in the mid-nineteenth century (Esdaile 1946, p. 105). The circumstances of periodical production are equally veiled by the obliteration of time. There simply is no historical survey giving details about the technical changes in the printing methods employed in juvenile periodicals or describing the publishers' methods of distribution, their editorial policies, and their divisions of work. Equally, there is no index answering elementary but essential questions about circulation figures of the juvenile magazines.[3]

Lacking a stable statistical framework to corroborate my findings, I analyze two types of magazine: first, those that, in my own and other researchers' opinion, epitomize trends within their own period (often but not always the most popular ones); second, magazines that are portents of technical and fictional change (the two types of magazine sometimes coincide). Indications of such

---

3. Since the inception in 1846 of the *Newspaper Press Directory and Advertiser's Guide* (also termed *Mitchell's* after its publisher), professional trade guides have listed juvenile periodicals only when the publisher saw fit or needed to boost a flagging circulation. Figures were included only when acting as commercial assets.

changes have also guided the division of this book, but neither social nor fictional developments observe neat divisions of time. Bound volumes of magazines, the so-called annuals, and reprints of popular serials, often called libraries, are not included. My literary analysis is not quantitatively exhaustive but qualitatively selective in that I trace central themes in specific papers, and I investigate gradual transformations in the magazines and the possible reasons why such alterations took place.

This book follows the rise and fall of the juvenile magazine in Britain, guided by the question of why this journey took specific routes. Literary specialists may find that I put an undue emphasis on social history in favor of a fuller treatment of more magazines. Social historians, on the other hand, may find that by investigating only the juvenile magazines I narrow my view on juvenile reading, excluding adult newspapers, journals, and comics, not to mention the relation between reading and other forms of popular culture such as radio, film, and television. Both claims are valid: they reveal that we are still in the infancy of understanding popular culture, juveniles in the past, and how both relate to people's own cultural expressions. To elucidate such relations would form a natural continuation of my own endeavors. It is hoped that the journey traversed in the following can contribute to further explorations in still uncharted fields.

PART TWO

THE
CHILD'S COMPANION;
OR,
Sunday Scholar's Reward.

No. I.]   JANUARY, 1824.   [VOL. 1.

THE FIRST SABBATH OF THE YEAR.
" A HAPPY New Year to you," said James
Brown, to his shool-fellow, Thomas Jones, as
they met in their way to the Sunday School.
" The same to you," said Thomas, as he took
James by the hand, and gave it a hearty shake.
As they jogged on their way they talked about
VOL. I.   (Fouth Edition)   B

Reason and
Religion in the
First Juvenile
Magazines,
1751–1850

2

Virtue and Good Nature: The Early Development of Juvenile Magazines

In 1751, the enterprising printer-publisher John Newbery (1713–67) advertised a new venture, a monthly miscellany for children called the *Lilliputian Magazine: or the Young Gentleman & Lady's Golden Library, being An Attempt to Mend the World, to render the Society of Man More Amiable, & to establish the Plainness, Simplicity, Virtue & Wisdom of the Golden Age, so much Celebrated by the Poets and Historians . . . Printed for the Society, and Published by T. Carnan at Mr. Newbery's, the Bible & Sun in St. Paul's Church Yard.* The title, as was customary, served as a sales device by indicating the general aim and outline of this novel but shortlived undertaking. Two separate issues at threepence each were published in 1751 and bound with a third issue, which appeared in 1752.[1] With the *Lilliputian Magazine* the first real juvenile periodical had been born.

Interspersed with rhymes and riddles, scores for a new "country dance," and "A Receipt to make Mince-Pies, of such Materials as are cheap, agreeable to every Palate, and will not offend the Stomach," this 144-page duodecimo volume offered lively little stories such as "An Adventure of Master Tommy Trusty; and his delivering Miss Biddy Johnson, from the Thieves who were going to murder her." The tale recounts how the vain Miss Biddy, disobeying her parents, loses her way in the woods and is rescued by the resolute young Tommy at the very moment when two robbers, who had been attracted by the girl's finery, had "stripped her of her cloaths and was going to kill her" with a

1. Title quoted from the front page of this bound volume, of which a single copy exists at the British Library. The intended circulation of the magazine seems to have been 4,000 copies per issue (Grey 1970, p. 110). The article yields final proof that the magazine was indeed published serially. Before 1751, French publications for children had been called *"magasins"* without being issued periodically. Like Mme. le Prince de Beaumont's *Magasin des Enfans* (published in London in 1756 and translated into English in 1761), they adhered to the old meaning of the word, "a repository or storehouse of a rather general kind" (Darton 1982, pp. 353, 266).

large knife. A humble and "exceeding dutiful" Miss Biddy is returned to her parents. "She now despises fine cloaths, and says, *that* virtue and good nature are the best *ornaments a young lady can wear*" ([1751], pp. 18, 20). "The Adventures of Little Tommy Trip. And his Dog Jouler" features an equally vigorous youth. When the boy and his pet meet Woglog, "the great giant [who] attempted to seize little *Trip* between his finger and thumb, and thought to have cracked him as one does a walnut," Jouler frees his master by biting off the giant's thumb. Trip then lashes Woglog "till he lay down, and roared like a town bull, and promised never to meddle with any little boys and girls again" ([1751], pp. 52–53).[2]

Riddles and music, violence, giants, and a tagged-on moral—this was the mixture offered by the new magazine. John Newbery was a pioneer in seriously promoting juvenile reading matter, and his selection for the *Lilliputian Magazine* was in keeping with the contemporary trend to refashion traditional folktales, romances, and ballads into vehicles of edification. France and Britain were centers in the eighteenth-century bourgeois movement to rationalize society by cultivating forethought and good manners in its members. Reading played a pivotal role in this process of self-realization. While Britain can be said to have fostered the modern novel for an adult bourgeois public, contemporary literature for the young bore a heavy French influence.

Toward the end of the seventeenth century, two compilations of fairy tales were published in Paris, both with moral endings added to the story in an obvious effort to make this old folklore genre more palatable to a young readership. The collections, translated into English, became known as tales of Mother Bunch and tales of Mother Goose, respectively, the latter being translated in 1729 by Robert Samber as *Histories, or Tales of Past Times. Told by Mother Goose*. This adaptation of stories such as "Red Riding Hood," "Blue Beard," and "Goldylocks" was followed in 1744, the year Newbery set up business, by *Tommy Thumb's Pretty Songbook*, which made available in print old-time favorites like "London Bridge is broken down," "Oranges and Lemons," and other songs that were now increasingly thought of as children's verse or "nursery rhymes" (Darton 1982, pp. 85–89; Opie and Opie 1951, pp. 1–45).

John Newbery was not only in the forefront of publishing such children's books but the *Lilliputian Magazine* also made him an innovator of form. Between 1752 and 1800, a total of eleven juvenile periodicals were published, among them three by Newbery's rival, John Marshall—namely the *Juvenile Magazine; or, an Instructive and Entertaining Miscellany for Youth of Both Sexes* (1788), the *Children's Magazine; or, Monthly Repository of Instruction & Delight* (1798–99), and the *Picture Magazine; or, Monthly Exhibition for Young People*

2. Woglog the Great Giant is a recurring figure in Newbery's publications. He appears not only as a story character but also as a mock author (Darton 1982, p. 20).

The *Lilliputian Magazine* (1751), front cover. In the first juvenile magazine in the world, the printed word, not pictures, is of primary importance.

(1800–01).[3] The first of Marshall's magazines, setting the tone for his later ventures, essentially followed Newbery's score. The sixty pages of each monthly issue consisted mainly of fiction of various kinds: instructive tales, dialogues between parents and children, plays, parables, and some poetry. Titles such as "The Whimsical Child," "The Passionate Child Reclaimed," and "The Indigent, Industrious Child" indicate the simple story lines: the impetuous child—a boy—is guided toward prudence and perseverance (often learning through his own misdemeanors), while the good child sets an example to be followed more or less willingly by others. As in Thomas Day's contemporary moral tale *Sandford and Merton* (1783–89), the model child is often middle class and is set against passionate but malleable upper-class brats. Girls regularly received special attention in these late eighteenth-century magazines, which indicated that they must cultivate their minds and their manners just as intensely as their brothers (Kleinbaum 1977). "A young lady's best ornament is silence," declared the anonymous woman editor of the *Juvenile Magazine,* and in order to achieve this ideal, constant training in self-control was needed.[4] The reward was not beauty, fame, or praise, but an inner balance of mind. The young girl as she was described in the magazines clearly resembled the heroines found in the first English girls' book, which is also the first school story, Sarah Fielding's *The Governess* (1749).

Readers in general would find little difference between the new magazines and contemporary books for the young. Like *Evenings at Home* (1792–96), a six-volume work published by Mrs. Anna Barbauld and her brother, John Aikin, and frequently reprinted throughout the nineteenth century, the magazines sprinkled an assortment of uplifting fiction with equally educative samples of botany, metallurgy, astronomy, and geography and with an "instructive puzzle" thrown in for good measure. Thus, readers of the geography entries in the *Juvenile Magazine,* having acquainted themselves with the definitions of "peninsula," "promontory," "meridian," and "eclipse," were rewarded by articles describing the various peoples of Europe. In this continent, it is attested, "we find the greatest diversity of character, government, and manners" ([April 1788], pp. 183–84). The author starts with the Scandinavians and proceeds

3. In addition to these periodicals proper, serialization was also used for collections of stories. Perhaps the most popular of these was Arnaud Berquin's *L'Ami des Enfans* (1782–83), a huge collection of stories that was issued in monthly parts. It was brought to England in 1783 and translated in the same year (two numbers a month). In 1786, 1787, and 1787–88, respectively, three competing and heavily edited translations came to light (Darton 1982, p. 148). By 1800, the most popular of these, called the *Looking-Glass for the Mind; or, Intellectual Mirror* (1787), had sold more than 20,000 copies (Summerfield 1984, p. 103).

4. The anonymous editor of the *Juvenile Magazine* may well have been Lady Eleanor Fenn, Marshall's most popular author at the time and the editor of his *Juvenile Tatler* (1789) and *Fairy Spectator* (1789) (Darton 1982, pp. 163–64).

southward. "The *Norwegians*," we are told, "are in general strong, robust and brave; but very quick in resenting real or supposed injuries." Still, a note of consolation is added: "The *Norwegian* bears are remarkable for not hurting children." By contrast, Danes, living further to the south, are "generally indolent, timid, dull of apprehension, fond of parade, and much given to intemperance in drinking" ([May 1788], pp. 244, 245, 246). Unfortunately, the periodical ceased publication before the author had come to a description of the British.

The magazines were clearly in keeping with the contemporary trend in juvenile fiction to improve and instruct the young. In her opening address, the editor of the *Juvenile Magazine* captured general aims in expressing the hope that the new periodical would be "productive not only of your *present* amusement, but of your *future* welfare." The object was to "endear you to your friends, and render you, at maturer years, valuable members of society" ([January 1788], p. iii). Even so, it should be noted that this adult perspective was occasionally reversed. In Marshall's *Children's Magazine*, for example, the story of "Maria and William" described how Mr. Mason wrongly accuses his daughter Maria of picking "a very rare and curious flower" that he has cultivated. William puts him right, and in the authorial conclusion of the story the symbolic overtones are clear also to young minds: "The flower which Mr. Mason had lost, would probably have given him some pleasure; but he received infinitely more in viewing the fraternal tenderness, the candour and the discretion which florished in his children" ([December 1799], pp. 342, 345). Similarly, the *Juvenile Magazine* featured a correspondence column, in which a "Female Adviser" printed the answers to readers' inquiries. A modicum of two-way communication seemed feasible in the monthly, even if the object of the communication was clear: "Should you, my young friends, at any time perceive an *unruly passion* or *habit* intruding, or a *situation* in which you are at a loss to conduct yourselves," then the Female Adviser will "enable you to *overcome* the one, and accomodate yourselves to the other" ([January 1788], p. iv). Correspondence columns were to become stable ingredients in juvenile magazines from the mid-nineteenth century onward, a time when serial reading matter had entered the lives of a good portion of British youth.

Who, then, were the readers of the pioneering periodicals in the late eighteenth century? Judging from their contents and the editorials, the magazines were intended for both sexes and a wide-ranging age group. The editor of the *Juvenile Magazine*, for example, states that "young people from SEVEN to FOURTEEN" are her intended readers. Thus, "tales of GALLANTRY, LOVE, COURTSHIP, or MARRIAGE cannot be admitted" ([January 1788], p. ii). Moreover, the monthlies were all clearly aimed at children of the gentry and of the affluent merchant bourgeoisie. The Society of Man mentioned in the title of the *Lilliputian Magazine* is a good indication of this. The society,

allegedly "little Master Meanwell's" scheme of pledging mutual juvenile obedience to parents and all "elders and betters," was revealed to be a group of
subscribers pledging their financial assistance to the publisher. Among them
were "several of the young nobility, and a great many little gentlemen and
ladies" whose names (letters A to H) ran to over nine pages in the little periodical. Other magazine publishers adopted Newbery's and from the outset
secured themselves a group of prosperous subscribers whose parents were sufficiently affluent to take on the new ventures and sufficiently well known to have
their names make good advertisements. Most importantly, these parents agreed
with the publishers' maxims of juvenile prudence and good manners since the
"proper" upbringing of their offspring was an essential preoccupation.

The first juvenile magazines did not last very long: none of them seemed to
have "a serial soul" (Darton 1982, p. 267), and their well-to-do readership
made up a minority of British youngsters. The majority of children got acquainted with "Tommy Trip and his Dog Jouler" along with older favorites, not
through moral modernizations but through chapbooks and broadsides sold for
the enjoyment of the general household by itinerant peddlers. Children across a
wide social spectrum would share the enthusiasm, if not the actual experience,
expressed by the shepherd and poet John Clare (1793–1864): "I saved all the
pence I got to buy [chapbook tales] for they were the whole world of literature to
me and I knew of no other. . . . Nay, I cannot help fancying now that Cock
Robin, Babes in the Wood, Mother Hubbard and her Cat, etc., etc., are real
poetry in all its naive simplicity and as it should be" (Summerfield 1984, p. 60).

A growing segment of society fiercely disagreed with Clare's conclusions.
Indeed, from the 1790s a zealous campaign was launched to counteract this
popular fare and to control what was regarded as its depraving influence. The
onslaught took as its literary inspiration not the moral tale but the very first
children's books to be distinguished from primers and ABCs. These had been
published by the Puritans in the seventeenth century on the model of what has
been called the first children's book, James Janeway's *A Token for Children, an
exact account of the Conversion, Holy, and Exemplary Lives and Joyful Deaths of
several Young Children* (1671–72). An outcome of the early nineteenth-century
moral crusade was the first wave of juvenile periodicals. Like Newbery's and
Marshall's pioneering publications, it developed in the tension between the two
literary sources shaping the history of the juvenile magazine: the folktale and the
children's book. But the result was different from the eighteenth-century concoctions, and the reasons for this difference were not merely literary.

RELIGIOUS REVIVAL

Toward the end of the eighteenth century, an industrial bourgeoisie was beginning to establish itself as a social segment against the opposition of landed capital
and the "lower orders," many of whom were now being dislocated by a dawning

industrialization that forced them into the sprawling new towns and cities. The French Revolution fired democratic sentiments especially among artisans and self-employed craftsmen, while to the aspirant and the already established orders of society, its popular appeal brought fears of political radicalism and rampant promiscuity. In the wake of the political upheavals an evangelical revivalism followed. It affected old Nonconformist denominations such as the Presbyterians, the Independents, the Baptists, and the Quakers, and it found its clearest expression in the growing influence among the poor of John Wesley's (1703–91) Methodism, with its equivocal connection to the Church of England, and in the emergence of the Evangelical movement within the Anglican Church itself. The introvert Christianity of evangelism, whether in its established or Dissenting versions, with its emphasis upon obedience, orderliness, spiritual purity, and bodily cleanliness was to reverberate as the dominant ethic of Victorian society.

The first to gain a literary influence were the Anglican Evangelicals, whose rallying points became the abolition of slavery overseas and the reformation of national manners and morals. Like the Methodists, they had a strong belief in original sin, whose sole remedies were constant personal struggle and a firm regulation of family life—the only area that now seemed safe from social strife and economic anarchy. Their reforming zeal was channeled into philanthropic work at home and missionary work abroad. Philanthropic concern with morality was in itself nothing new, it had already resulted in the establishment of the Society for the Propagation of Christian Knowledge by 1699. But with the Evangelicals, a deep anxiety concerning the morality of the nation was combined with an acute fear of radicalism that made mass education seem a political necessity. The crucial instigators of juvenile betterment became a new generation of domesticated middle-class women.

Foremost among them was Hannah More (1745–1833), friend of Samuel Johnson and closely connected to William Wilberforce and the Evangelical Clapham Sect. The popular ballads and chapbook tales were suffused with death, sexual innuendo, and clear political overtones in their descriptions of dashing highwaymen, audacious murderers, and pretty maidens. Miss More, intent upon defying demoralizing influences when she saw them, set about writing so-called cheap repository tracts. These were deliberately designed as a series of sheep in wolf's clothing. Pious tales urging the poor to stay in their place and to see to their spiritual salvation were decked out as genuine chapbooks with their pennyworth of crude woodcuts, coarse paper, and bad print. The tracts were issued between 1795 and 1798, and in the first year alone more than two million copies were sold. Of the first 114 titles, More wrote forty-nine (Spinney 1939, p. 296).

This was no proof of a popular demand, however. Most of the tracts were bought by church dignitaries and distributed in workhouses and prisons or given away, perhaps as prizes, in the growing number of Sunday schools, a system of education which was popularized from 1780 by Robert Raikes, a newspaper proprietor and active philanthropist. Hannah More's invention sparked a host of tract societies, among them the Religious Tract Society (1799), which was to be the most prolific institutional publisher of juvenile fiction in the nineteenth century (Bratton 1981, p. 32).[5] But the tracts did not create a genuine mass market. Their pious coercion was often resented, especially by the urban poor, and they were not a commercial success (Altick 1967, pp. 102–08; James 1963, pp. 114–23; Neuburg 1977, pp. 259–64; Webb 1955, pp. 27–28).[6] Their chief literary importance for the young lay in charting an unknown territory that a wave of religious children's magazines was to explore.

As multitudes were plunged into urbanized distress by the advance of the first Industrial Revolution, religious philanthropy expanded its activities into new areas such as tract and temperance societies, missionary associations, and Sunday school organizations. Their members all agreed that reading was of central importance in the moral edification of the young. Reading for the eighteenth-century gentry and the enlightened merchant bourgeoisie had been consciously limited to the personal attainments and the cultural refinement of these genteel groups and their offspring. For the religious propagators, moral zeal made them focus not only on the Heavens above but also on the social orders below them. In their efforts, they did not limit themselves to disseminating Bibles, tracts, and spelling books. Except for a few dilatory attempts to create Sunday school pamphlets, the early Evangelicals had published no magazines for the young (Bratton 1981, pp. 39–40).[7] But in 1805 the first religious juvenile periodical, the *Youth's Magazine; or, Evangelical Miscellany*, was begun by the eighteen-year-old William Lloyd of the interdenominational Sunday School Union, which had been established two years previously.

An editorial address immediately cast the fictional mold for future issues. Adult "friends" were invited to furnish the new monthly publication "with biographical communications, essays, obituaries of young people, extracts from scripture history, remarks on passages of scripture, anecdotes, poetry, or with instances of the beneficial effects of schools for religious instruction, &c" (No. 1 [September 1805], p. 2). Joyful deaths and didactic stories in the Janeway tradition are offset in subsequent volumes by extracts from travel books describing exotic countries such as China, Ceylon, and Greenland and the even more exotic customs of their peoples. The alleged cruelty of the Japanese emperor toward his subjects is given the following justification: "This extreme rigour, though contrary to every sentiment of humanity and justice, is founded in the

5. Chaps. 2 and 3 in Bratton (1981) give an excellent account of publishers, both philanthropic and commercial, and their religious reward books.

6. For a contrary opinion of the appeal of tracts, see Quinlan 1941, pp. 191–92.

7. On material in adult magazines directed to the young, see Sangster 1963, pp. 66–69.

most barbarous policy, to check the licentiousness of the common people, and to preserve internal tranquility." For the benefit of readers who might still feel a contradiction here between ethics and politics, or who might even find some unholy parallels to their domestic situation, a consoling explanation is added: "The religion of the Japanese is the extreme of idolatry" (1 [October 1805], pp. 56–57). The British could count their blessings.

Its association with the Sunday School Union won the little *Youth's Magazine* a solid following and its ideas caught on. By 1867, (when the periodical was incorporated with the *Bible Class Magazine*), it had a plethora of imitators in similar inexpensive periodicals issued by denominational or church organizations, by private publishers and Sunday school associations. Like their secular precursors, the religious magazines were aimed at a wide age group of both sexes. But a far larger audience could now be reached owing partly to the organizational facilities offered by the religious bodies and partly to a decrease in the price of paper after the Napoleonic wars. This decrease was to speed up both the introduction of the paper-making machine, used in England since 1803, and the cylinder steam press, patented by Frederich König in 1811. Thus, the religious magazines pioneered halfpenny papers, the first of which was the *Children's Missionary Record* (1839–48), a monthly issued by the Presbyterian Free Church in Scotland. Judged on its social importance and personal impact, the high tide of the religious trend was from the 1820s to the 1840s, and during that period two pious perennials got underway.

The first of these monthlies, the *Child's Companion; or, Sunday Scholar's Reward*, was launched by the Religious Tract Society in 1824, the year of the society's silver jubilee. The magazine was set up by George Stokes, who had joined the society's general committee in 1818 and had already established himself as a prolific writer with a historical interest (Bratton 1981, pp. 38ff.). This secular interest is reflected in the new magazine, in which stories of dedicated missionaries, "scriptural beacons," or poor but pious children mingle with entries on natural history and geography—all recounted in the voice of a concerned father or a conscientious minister and firmly lodged within the perspective of human frailty in permanent need of spiritual improvement. Four years after its inception, the earnest periodical had a circulation of 20,000 copies a month (Cutt 1979, p. 31). As its subtitle indicates, the *Child's Companion*, like other religious magazines, was intended not only for private circulation but equally for distribution, often through individual subscriptions, within the outbranching educational market. Thus, a history of the Religious Tract Society published in 1850 to commemorate its jubilee said that the *Child's Companion* was "invaluable as a reward book for schools, and also very acceptable in private families" (Bratton 1981, p. 40). Under the society's auspices, the magazine became the longest lived of all juvenile periodicals, lingering on in different forms and under various titles (the last was *Every Girl's Paper*) until 1932.

THE

CHILD'S COMPANION;

OR,

Sunday Scholar's Reward.

No. 1.]　　JANUARY, 1824.　　[VOL. 1.

THE FIRST SABBATH OF THE YEAR.

" A ʜᴀᴘᴘʏ New Year to you," said James
Brown, to his shool-fellow, Thomas Jones, as
they met in their way to the Sunday School.
"The same to you," said Thomas, as he took
James by the hand, and gave it a hearty shake.
As they jogged on their way they talked about

VOL. I.　　(Fourth Edition)　　ᴮ

The *Child's Companion; or, Sunday Scholar's Reward* 1, no. 1 (January
1824), front cover. The religious magazines, aimed at both sexes and
all classes, flourished from the 1820s.

Also in 1824, the *Children's Friend* was started by the Reverend W. Carus Wilson, better known, perhaps, from Charlotte Brontë's portrait of him in *Jane Eyre* as the harsh Mr. Brocklebank from Lowood Institution. A stern, religious tone certainly pervades his periodical, which ceased publication only in 1930. Together with two other magazines from Wilson's hand, the *Friendly Visitor* and the *Visitor's Friend*, the *Children's Friend* had a monthly circulation of about 50,000 in 1850 (Laqueur 1976, p. 117).[8] This figure was easily rivaled by later missionary magazines such as the *Juvenile Missionary Herald*, published by the Baptist Missionary Society, which sold 45,000 copies per month in 1846, the second year of its existence. The output of religious periodicals remained high throughout the nineteenth century (Prochaska 1978, p. 112). In chapter 3, the *Child's Companion* and the *Children's Friend* are analyzed as joint examples of this first wave of magazine development.

As with the secular pioneers, the success of the religious ventures was clearly dependent on adult attitudes. Conscientious parents subscribed to the magazines or had their children buy copies at Sunday school and missionary meetings. Diligent teachers might use the papers as prizes donated to attentive or deserving pupils, as was the case with the Repository Tracts. Practical circumstances equally influenced the children's reading. In general, parents secured the money and nurtured the motivation necessary to purchase the periodicals. Children themselves needed at least a little leisure time to peruse the magazines, whose contents in turn demanded some literacy, and at rather a good level too. These general preconditions of magazine success—money, motivation, leisure and literacy—varied enormously for different groups of children. Though the monthly magazines were initially aimed at the poor, the religious zeal suffusing them had a deeper influence on juveniles from artisan or middle-class homes. That poverty-stricken little angels were extolled in fiction was no certain indication of the readership's poverty, but it might well be that their profusion proved that real children had difficulties in being sufficiently angelical.

8. Wilson also issued a companion to the *Children's Friend* for a younger audience, called the *Infant's Magazine* (1866–1931).

Labor and Learning:
Childhood and Youth, 1800–50

AT NO OTHER time in history were the lives of British children so disparate as during the first half of the nineteenth century. The Industrial Revolution meant a qualitative transformation of capitalism whereby machines progressively set the pace of production. With the separation of industrial capital and labor, middle-class manufacturers and the urban working class spearheaded new class alignments and new sexual relations, whose repercussions are still with us today.[1] The old family economy was being disrupted and traditional skills were gradually rendered obsolete. All this was to have a profound influence on the daily existence of children and the methods employed in their upbringing. And there were more children to be affected.

The combined effects of a fall in the death rate and a rise in the birth rate meant that Britain's population increased from 8.9 million in 1801 (the year of the first census) to 22.7 million by 1871. In no decade was the rate of increase less than 11.9 percent (Census 1950, p. 22). This growing population retained the youthfulness of preindustrial times. Children under fifteen years of age still comprised more than a third of all Britons, and the young formed a constant, but vulnerable, physical presence (Altick 1967, p. 81). In 1800, death was a reality for all classes, and in the 1840s "about one-quarter of all deaths recorded in England and Wales were of infants under one year, and almost half of all deaths were infants under five" (Smith 1979, p. 65). The chances for survival displayed stark social contrasts until the early 1900s. In 1839, one of every two children born into artisan or servant families died before reaching the age of five. The comparable rate in professional circles, which benefited the most from improvements in sanitation, hygiene, and medical knowledge, was one in eleven (Smith 1979, p. 68; Thompson 1975, pp. 356–66). The uneven distribution of

---

1. The term "middle class" originated between 1810 and 1820 when it was used by self-assertive new industrialists in favor of the former "middle rank" or "middling order." The term "working classes" was applied by others before it was taken over by the working class itself in the 1820s and 1830s (Briggs 1967, pp. 43–73).

these improvements highlighted the effects of social inequality on the lives of children and adolescents.

"STUNNED WITH THE ROAR OF REVOLVING WHEELS"

Whether living in the countryside or carving out a precarious existence in urban slum dwellings, poor children in the nineteenth century worked in terrible conditions. The images of the Industrial Revolution that first spring to mind are those of child exploitation: ragged little "trappers" huddled in narrow mining passages to operate the ventilation doors; or young "piecers" being beaten up in the textile mills for falling asleep, hands bleeding from joining together broken threads at the spinning machines. Indeed, it was children like these who were most directly affected by the introduction of machines that changed not only the intensity of work but also its quality.

In preindustrial times, hard work was intermittent and geared to the age and abilities of the child. But "in the mill," says E. P. Thompson, "the machinery dictated environment, discipline, speed and regularity of work and working hours, for the delicate and the strong alike" (Thompson 1975, p. 370). As nimble speed and extreme endurance became sought-after qualities in the new industries, even young children were employed, with linguistic precision, as "hands" in large numbers. Many parents resisted sending their offspring to the mills, so initially pauper children and orphans under the care of parish authorities were simply shipped north to fill the increasing demand. Being completely dependent for their own survival on the whims of the masters or, in larger mills, on the often meticulous overseers, these six- or eight-year-old "apprentices" (who later became "free labourers") make up the earliest, and perhaps the most extreme, victims of a general industrial exploitation.

The evidence of this is as massive as it is moving. By the early 1830s, between one-third and one-half of all laborers in cotton mills were under twenty-one (Thompson 1975, p. 341).[2] When sustained pressure from concerned individuals and groups finally forced Parliamentary committees to seriously investigate the problem of child labor in the 1830s and 1840s, immense suffering and inhumanity were revealed. According to the Tory M. P. Michael Sadler (1780–1835), one of the early factory reformers, children in the mills were "confined in heated rooms, bathed in perspiration, stunned with the roar of revolving wheels, poisoned with the noxious effluvia of grease and gas" until, utterly exhausted, they would be replaced by a new relay of children (Pike 1978, p. 120).[3] It was claimed that their beds never got cold.

2. By 1836, there were 30,000 children working in the Lancashire mills alone (Walvin 1982, p. 62).
3. Sadler chaired a select committee on whose report the Factory Act of 1833 was based. (The previous two factory acts, the Health and Morals of Apprentices Act of 1802 and the

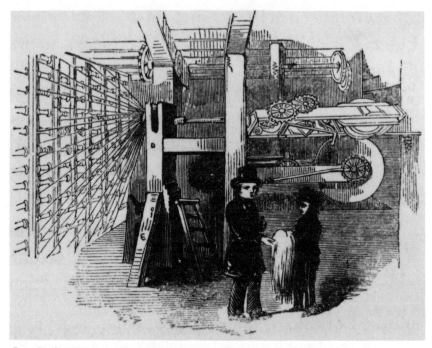

Peter Parley's Magazine (August 1849), p. 247. Illustration for the serial "True Heroism; or, Perseverance." In the juvenile periodicals, working in a silk mill, and elsewhere, is a somewhat more orderly and well-conducted experience than in reality.

Stunted growth, crippled backs, and broken limbs were the physical proofs of inhuman treatment. Mining and manufacturing were only the most documented and controlled areas of juvenile employment. Many more children and young people worked without legal protection in a variety of trades producing everything from pins, nails, pots, glass, and matches to lace, baskets, gloves, and wheels.[4] The small domestic industries and workshops of rural areas added to the traditional tasks performed by children in the field, the kitchen, and the

---

Factory Act of 1819, had proved largely ineffective.) The act prohibited employment in the textile industry (except silk mills) of children under nine years of age and obliged employers to secure two hours' daily schooling for nine- to thirteen-year-old employees (on top of their 48 hours' work per week). Four factory inspectors were appointed to secure the enforcement of the law. Registration of births only began in 1837.

4. An English sense of humor has preserved it as one of the better-known facts of nineteenth-century childhood that the Royal Society for the Prevention of Cruelty to Animals was founded in 1824, the National Society for the Prevention of Cruelty to Children in 1884. For descriptions of early nineteenth-century child labor and the legislation against it, see Pinchbeck and Hewitt 1973, pp. 387–413; Walvin 1982, pp. 61–78; Henriques 1971.

barn. The effect of the changes brought on by the Industrial Revolution varied enormously according to region, trade, actual work conditions, and, of course, personal relations, but for the majority of peasant and working-class children and adolescents, work restricted the time left for other pursuits. Moreover, the monotony of most work, irrespective of its contents, set a new standard for leisurely pursuits, including leisure reading.

Illiteracy was not a primary obstacle to the success of the religious magazines. As noted, chapbooks abounded in poor households of the eighteenth century, and investigations carried out in the 1830s revealed that about three-quarters of working-class homes possessed books, chiefly of a religious nature (Vincent 1983, pp. 210–11). If the contents mattered, even illiterate people could get to know the books from a friendly grandfather, a "learned" neighbor, or perhaps an older brother who had attended one of the parish schools or, more likely, the local "dame" or "gaffer" school. Here an old woman or man from within the community earned a meager living by offering at least a perfunctory tuition in the three Rs—reading, writing, and arithmetic—although not all pupils were as fortunate, or as gifted, as Thomas Cooper (1805–92), "the Chartist poet" and prototype of Charles Kingsley's *Alton Locke* (1850), who at the age of three was set "on a stool, in Dame Brown's school, to teach one Master Bodley, who was seven years old, his letters" (Stickland 1973, p. 106), or Charles Shaw, born in 1832, who could read his Bible "with remarkable ease" at the age of seven when he started work as a "mould runner" in a Cheshire pottery (Shaw 1903, p. 2).[5]

The pious tone that suffused the *Children's Friend* and similar publications was not foreign to poor children's ears. Religion was not only a crucial point of identification for budding manufacturers during this period, but it also found resonance, especially in the Primitive and Bible Christian forms of Methodism, among small tradespeople and artisans, textile workers and miners. The Sunday school movement made hymn singing and praying essential cultural embellishments on spelling and writing exercises. While it is debated whether the Sunday schools were integral to or opposed to the formation of working-class consciousness in the first half of the nineteenth century, their success in recruitment is undisputed.[6] In 1801, 13.8 percent of all working-class children between the

---

5. Shaw's exceptional abilities made him ideal for the portrayal of Darius Clayhanger's early life in Arnold Bennett's *Clayhanger* (1910). While the dame schools were fee-charging private establishments, the charity schools, like the so-called endowed grammar schools that were to form the backbone of middle-class education, were founded for philanthropic purposes (the first before the Reformation), and charity tuition was free (Lawson and Silver 1973, pp. 181–95).

6. The social composition of Methodism is given in Gilbert 1976, pp. 60, 67. For an analysis of the Sunday school movement as a basis for class expression see Laqueur 1976. By contrast, Thompson 1975, pp. 412–16, describes the Sunday schools as a powerful agent of social control.

ages of five and fifteen attended Sunday schools. Fifty years later it was 75.4 percent, an attendance rate that did not drop until the 1880s (Laqueur 1976, p. 44). The Sunday school movement was undoubtedly the strongest educational force for working people during the nineteenth century, and, at a time when there was no other national system of cheap or free schooling, it was instrumental in raising the literacy of poor children and adolescents.

Throughout the nineteenth century, education was defined in class and gender terms, and it was not dependent upon the level of instruction. Poor children were offered no full public provision of education until 1870. But early in the century, a charitable option was added to existing schools. In 1811, Andrew Bell established the National Society for Promoting the Education of the Poor in the Principles of the Established Church of England. This was followed three years later by the foundation of a smaller rival, the nonsectarian British and Foreign School Society based on the educational work of Joseph Lancaster (1778–1838). Both societies created a network of day schools, the so-called monitorial or mutual schools, whose course of instruction, the three Rs and needlework for girls, was based on Jeremy Bentham's utilitarian principles of education.[7] Whether large or small, the school consisted of one room in which older scholars, or monitors, of perhaps ten or eleven years of age would drill their own knowledge into groups of younger pupils. Flash cards were used for spelling exercises, silent reading was not encouraged, and discipline was kept up by an intricate system of rewards and punishments.[8]

With pride, Andrew Bell called this educational method "the steam engine of the moral world"; its combination of religious morality and secular efficiency decisively influenced elementary—that is, working-class—education as evangelical fervor merged with utilitarian rationalism in the Victorian middle class. The monitorial system was adopted in many charity schools, in the education of factory and pauper children, and even in some endowed grammar schools,

---

7. The philosophy of utilitarianism, which was to form the ideological basis of mid-Victorian free enterprise, was based on Adam Smith's economic theories as developed in *The Wealth of Nations* (1776) combined with Bentham's social philosophy, whose central tenets were expressed in his *Introduction to Principles of Morals and Legislation* (1780): "It is the greatest happiness of the greatest number that is the measure of right and wrong." This was the quantifiable doctrine on which society should be organized. An equally mechanistic idealism pervades Bentham's educational principles as expressed in *Chrestomathia* (1816). Though these principles can be traced back to the Bishop John Earle's (1601?–65) and later John Locke's theories of the child as a tabula rasa, a clean slate, they were more directly influenced by the associationist psychology advanced in England by David Hartley (1705–57) in his *Observations on Man* (1749): simple sensory impressions merge through repetition into increasingly complex ideas, ideas which in turn are ordered or "associated" in the mind. Hartley's theory, by basing knowledge mechanically on external stimuli, "is the key to a grasp of the educational optimism so characteristic of this time," as noted by Simon 1974a, p. 45.

8. In the British and Foreign Society's schools, the Bible was the only textbook used until the 1840s (See Altick 1967, p. 152).

frequented by older pupils from more secure backgrounds.[9] In 1833, the House of Commons made its first educational grant. Twenty thousand pounds was distributed through the National and British societies, which formed the most powerful educational agencies until greater state control was inaugurated by the establishment in 1839 of the Committee of the Privy Council on Education. In 1840, the first educational inspectors were appointed.

The expansion of educational opportunities for working people at the close of the eighteenth century had a positive effect on the literacy of the poor, except for those in large urban centers. Estimates made from people's abilities to sign the marriage registers range from a literacy rate in the 1840s of about two-thirds of all adult men and half of adult women to around two-thirds of all adult workers, men and women.[10] While more men than women could read (boys often stayed longer at school), any general assessment covers vast regional and social differences. For some, the ability to read meant the ability to sign one's own name and to know a few letters. Others could read the Bible without understanding much of its meaning but often enjoying the sound and rhythm of its poetry. With persistent interest, these semiliterate people might spell their way through the text of a handbill or an advertising poster, while the dedication of a few led them to *Pilgrim's Progress, Paradise Lost*—and then, perhaps, to secular graduation through William Cobbett's *Political Register* and later the *Poor Man's Guardian*. Not surprisingly, it is primarily the last, radicalizing effect of literacy that has been preserved for posterity through the autobiographies of politicized working men.[11] If by necessity more speculatively, the impact of the religious magazines should be assessed not only on children's and adolescents' formal options of reading but also on the function of reading within their daily lives.

RELIGION AND RECREATION

The utter monotony of tasks performed for upwards of twelve hours a day from a tender age left many working-class and peasant children with a pittance in earnings and very little time and incentive left for fictional flights even of a

9. Compulsory education of young factory employees, initiated by the Factory Act of 1833, developed into the so-called half-time system with the Factory Act of 1844. It obliged children between eight and thirteen, now working a maximum of six-and-a-half hours per day, to attend school three whole days or six half days. The last vestiges of this system were abandoned only in 1918. For an account of education in workhouses, see Walvin 1982, pp. 116–20.

10. For the lower estimate, see Stone 1969, p. 119. The higher estimate is given in Webb 1955, p. 22.

11. These authors did not necessarily belong to what a later age termed the labor aristocracy. According to Vincent 1982, pp. 7, 9, there is only a slight bias toward nonindustrial skilled trades among the 142 recorded autobiographies covering the period 1790–1850. But all the authors, except 6, were men and of these more than a quarter held official or unofficial posts of leadership in the community.

religious nature. For them, sleep would often constitute a mainstay of leisure. Having been hedged in for days on end (or nights as production and the foreman deemed fit), they would naturally spend what little time was left with their friends. "James Taylor, alias Lump Lad'," said one witness to a parliamentary commission in 1842, "has only one shirt, one pair of stockings, and the ragged and dirty coat, waistcoat, and trousers he has on. When he has had something to eat, runs into the street and plays; always finds someone to play wi', and can play at aught as they can: plays at 'trinnill' and 'th'hammer and block'—these oftener than aught else" (Pike 1978, pp. 174–75).

Like other poor children, this ten-year-old colliery boy had to stay at home when his only clothes needed washing. Family relations, especially among unskilled laborers, often fluctuated as people sought to combine their pre-industrial kinship networks with the exigencies caused by an insecure economy. Parents, older sisters, or grandmothers in charge of children would not, or could not because of their own labor, keep them from roaming around the countryside or the streets enjoying games and pranks. Especially early in the century, when Methodism had a genuine stronghold in many poor communities, children would often be sent to Sunday school by their adult relatives. But religion and recreation need not be opposed, as attested by Thomas Cooper, whose widowed mother would take him to the fields to pick flowers on sunny Sundays while reading to him from the Bible on Sundays when it rained. Charles Shaw would enjoy a rare outing to the fair at Trentham Park "with its shows, flying boats, hobby horses, board and canvas theatres" (Shaw 1903, p. 197). Yet he, who at the age of seven worked between thirteen and fifteen hours six days a week, would also remember Sunday school as "a life within my life." He loved it not only because he learned "words up to five syllables," but equally because the Sabbath ceremonial included having his hair "brushed and combed and oiled (with scented oil)" (Shaw 1903, p. 7).

The majority of overworked children were not such model students. Seen from the vantage point of a Sunday school rostrum or the parish church pulpit, football, fishing, bird's-nesting, and the other pursuits that working children enjoyed clearly needed a spiritual substitute. For the many children whose religious sentiments were thus coerced into them from above like yet another work task, religion and repression could have merged in their minds, resulting in stubborn, if covert, resistance—or perhaps merely inattention and in-comprehension. In 1842, one little girl told the Children's Employment Commission (Mines): "If I died a good girl I should go to Heaven—if I were bad I should have to be burned in brimstone and fire: they told me that at school yesterday, I did not know it before" (Thompson 1975, p. 415).

Concerned middle-class reformers might have taken this as an example of the fatal ignorance, even depravity, of the poor. With hindsight, we can see this girl as a child whose center of life lay not in organized religion but in work, paid or unpaid, in family relations, in the collective vitality and ingenuity of child lore, urban or rural. Even if by 1842 some weekday schooling had been prescribed for children working in industry, this girl and juveniles living under similar conditions would hardly make use of what modicum of written knowledge came their way. To them, the earnest messages of the religious magazines would most likely fall on stony ground. Other working children, though, were more deeply imbued with the early nineteenth-century advances of education and religious faith.

THE PURSUIT OF KNOWLEDGE

Many small shopkeepers, artisans, and members of the laboring poor were spurred by dissenting Bible reading to follow a path of educational self-help, which was full of obstacles as simple and yet insuperable as fatigue, noise, and lack of candles. These groups were often at the forefront in the battle over knowledge, which became a seminal element in the class struggle during the first half of the nineteenth century. While evangelical philanthropists such as Hannah More sought to limit literacy to Bible reading and moral indoctrination, many working people found literacy a stepping stone to their personal aspirations and hence an indirect means to gain political power. The difference in goals highlights the contradictory aims of education, which all types of formal training variously seek to resolve. Schools must teach specific skills, necessary to secure the continuity of production, and they must also inculcate social skills, essential for the ideological acceptance (or rejection) of that continuity.

In the early part of the nineteenth century, a host of informal study groups promoted adult workingmen's self-organized education. Although middle-class philanthropy encroached more upon the organization of poor children's schooling, the educational optimism permeating many artisan cottages and laborers' dwellings deeply influenced children's upbringing. Boys, especially, in such families would almost certainly spend some years at school. Education was added to their daily work load and often had to be suspended in harvest time, when a parent fell ill, or when a baby was born. Children from this growing segment of the population became the lower-middle-class core of the Victorian reading public and reaped the benefits of the spread of elementary education. Together with middle-class children "proper," they constituted the readership most influenced by the religious periodicals.

Until the 1830s, private day schools provided more than half of all elementary education, and many parents went to considerable trouble in choosing a school for their offspring over which they might exercise some control rather than send their children to a British or a National school (Vincent 1982, p. 101 ff.).[12] The monitorial system spread to other types of schools during this

12. According to the 1851 Census Document on Education, there was an attendance rate of 91 percent in private day schools on census day, while in other elementary schools, such as

period, but discipline tended to be less strict in a smaller day school. The methodical precision of the monitorial system, under which boys and girls were segregated, would hardly make it possible for a schoolboy to combine his spelling exercises with the knitting of socks as was allowed Charles Shaw at a dame school (Shaw 1903, p. 3). Elementary education might be rudimentary, but an enthusiastic Sunday or day school teacher and parents with a love of books might develop a child's reading interests. Children could also avail themselves of the "improving" books, mostly religious, that were available from an increasing number of small lending libraries attached to day and Sunday schools.[13] Since religious periodicals abounded, and no book could rival their price of a penny or even a halfpenny, parents would be likely to buy them and the children to read them. With juvenile fiction still hard to come by, it would hold an immediate attraction just to have a magazine of one's own, a possession to be shared with friends or read alone, with pictures to be shown to younger siblings.

Education was important, but, as noted, it was still short and might be interrupted by busy spells of work, deaths in the family, or a sudden lack of money. During this turbulent period, the division of labor and increased mechanization made constant inroads upon the local economy and upon established traditions; the shopkeeper had to move from village to town, the shoemaker was forced on the roads in search of a job. Work, however, still bounded the daily existences of the carpenter's son and the watchmaker's daughter. It was an area of personal identification even when such worth was created only by the knowledge of contributing to the family's survival. Leisure reading, even of an "educational" nature, was not regarded as a necessary part of the preparation for adult life as literacy and numeracy often were, at least for boys. It took time away from the tasks that simply had to be performed; thus, it often had to be fought for. Mary Anne Hearne's experiences were typical for a girl of her class. Born in 1834, she grew up in a small Kentish village where her father was a tradesman and village postmaster. "The cheery voice of my mother," she remembers, "would call me into the house to amuse my brothers and sisters, or do some work. Dear Mother! she did not like my always having a book in my hand or pocket, and would have been better pleased if I had been equally fond of the brush or needle" (Gorham 1982, p. 144).[14] To Mary Anne and the majority of

---

charity, British, and National schools, the attendance was 79 percent (See West 1975, p. 34). For an additional account of parental preference of working-class-controlled schools, despite the greater costs, see McCann 1977, pp. 1–40.

13. By 1840, libraries were found in between half and three-quarters of urban Sunday schools and in about a quarter of the rural schools (See Laqueur 1976, pp. 117–18).

14. Hearne grew up in a Particular Baptist household, defied her father's concepts of femininity, and lived to become a teacher and writer. Gorham 1982, chap. 7, provides interesting examples of the variations in middle-class girls' upbringing during the first part of the nineteenth century.

children in her position, boys as well as girls, the reading of fiction was not thought of as integral to their upbringing. It was different with middle-class children.

MIDDLE-CLASS EDUCATIONAL IDEALS

Middle-class children were as deeply affected by the Industrial Revolution as were their poorer contemporaries, but the influence was indirectly felt, although perhaps more profound in nature. The debate over education at the beginning of the nineteenth century was not confined to discussions about who should rescue the morality of the poor. Middle-class parents were as concerned with the upbringing of their own offspring, and the number of child-care manuals and educational treatises proliferated. Counsel on the physical care of children was being given by virtuous clergymen and dutiful mothers with the express aim of securing the spiritual salvation of the young. The mounting popularity of professional advice testified to a growing interest in upbringing among the book-reading public, also indicating that upbringing was no longer left as a matter of tradition but had become an object of intense debate. The differences of pedagogical opinion voiced in writings on child-care and education followed the intellectual divide early in the century between utilitarian philosophy and evangelical religion.

In the late eighteenth century, Jean-Jacques Rousseau's educational ideas, as expressed in *La Nouvelle Héloïse* (1761) and *Emile* (1762), were transplanted to British soil by intellectuals such as Richard Lovell Edgeworth (1744–1817), Thomas Day (1748–89) and Erasmus Darwin (1731–1802), the grandfather of Charles Darwin. Following Rousseau, they regarded the child as inherently good, but unlike him they stressed the need for adult reasoning to guide the process of juvenile maturation (Simon 1974a, pp. 17–71; Summerfield 1984, pp. 114–73). While Rousseau had decried children's literature (except Defoe's survival kit, *Robinson Crusoe*), his British proponents found reading an admirable medium for such reasoning. Day's *Sandford and Merton* and other moral tales that emanated from his circle illustrate the secular ideals of education. Domestic seclusion and close proximity to nature were infallible aids in bringing out the best even in the richest and most spoiled of fictional and, it was understood, real characters. While girls apparently needed mental training to perfect their natural propensities to marriage and motherhood, boys' physical constitutions must be hardened along Rousseauvian lines by their lying on damp grass or sleeping on hard beds. This secular outlook was fortified into Spartan efficiency early in the nineteenth century by Jeremy Bentham and James Mill, whose radical utilitarianism clashed with the reformatory zeal of the evangelicals.

To the evangelicals, mental hardening strengthened children against worldly temptations. From their Puritan forbears they received a view of the child as inherently evil, a bearer of original sin whose manifestations, irrespective of sex, had to be not only curbed but completely eradicated in order to secure salvation. "Spare the rod and spoil the child" was the maxim parents most often intoned and acted upon, Bible in hand. [15] It was also the sentiment prevailing in the well-intentioned admonitions found in evangelical literature, including the religious children's magazines. These contrasting views of the child as either good or evil resonated in Victorian educational debate. While the differences between utilitarians and evangelicals stand out clearly, their similarities are less discernible, though they are equally important.

First, both approaches stressed social differences of upbringing. While they regarded the education of the poor as a collective and indeed a social problem, the education of their own offspring was seen as a possibility for developing the entire personality, even if some traits were to be nurtured more intensely than others. The child was unanimously perceived as an individual who could be and should be raised under parental protection. Second, whether obeying natural or divine laws, both movements promulgated a sex-specific upbringing aimed at separate adult functions. The benefits of this ideal socialization would be secured through methodical habits, orderly conduct, and a simple life-style spiced only by the occasional hardening of the body or the soul. These shared assumptions concerning the subservience of children to adults and the natural differences between rich and poor, men and women, formed a common ground in which Victorian standards of upbringing were formed, regardless of the contradictions undercutting the lofty ideals of education.

MIDDLE-CLASS CHILDREARING PRACTICES

In the early decades of the nineteenth century, Rousseauvian ideals of education were put into practice chiefly by upper- and upper-middle-class families, which, through "a vigorous, widespread and self-conscious movement," were becoming more child-centered and more domesticated (Musgrove 1965, p. 37). [16] Thus, when the seven-year-old Frances Power Cobbe (1822–1904), exasperated by her governess's lessons, drew on the gravel walk of her parents' spacious garden: "Lessons! Thou tyrant of the mind!" her mother reacted with hilarity, not horror (Cobbe 1904, p. 39). [17] But she did not change Frances' daily

15. While Victorians almost universally attributed this maxim to Solomon and thus saw their actions justified through the Bible, it was in fact created by Samuel Butler in his satirical poem *Hudibras* (1664) (See Gibson 1978, p. 49).

16. Stone 1979, pp. 217–99, traces back even further the rise of what he calls the "companionate marriage" among the upper classes and the merchant bourgeoisie.

17. Despite (or perhaps because of) her misgivings over lessons, Cobbe in adult life became a writer, philanthropist, and advocate of woman's suffrage.

schedule. Children were to respect their parents and accept their decrees, but they were generally cajoled rather than coerced into doing so.

In middle-class and lower-middle-class families, the more Puritan brands of dissent were stronger. The majority of children in such households were raised to an unquestioned obedience of parental demands and religious dogma. At a time when personal relations and not educational or work institutions took center stage in the lives of middle-class juveniles, the variability of experiences naturally defies neat generalizations. We have no way of assessing the extent to which parents heeded the precepts for a strict domestic regimen offered them in child-care manuals, educational treatises, and in the advice columns of the new family magazines. But bearing in mind the central importance of the printed word in bourgeois culture, we should not be surprised to find that many diaries and autobiographies from this period, and more than in the centuries before, dwell on the punishments to be endured in childhood (Pollock 1983, p. 184).

With the imminence of death an all too vivid reality in most middle-class families, working on children's salvation could not start early and earnestly enough. Since parents, and more particularly fathers, were regarded as God's representatives on earth, juvenile disobedience became a direct violation of divine power. Augustus Hare (1834–1903) was not raised by aspirant middle-class parents. However, his early upbringing in an Anglican rectory at Alton Barnes highlights the punishments that could be justified by fervent piety. Raised by his widowed aunt, Maria, whom he called mother and who was "just a little High Church," Augustus lived under her rigorous daily routine. Days were meticulously divided and his behavior was carefully supervised. "I never recollect the moment of (indoor) childhood in which I was not undergoing education of some kind, and generally of an unwelcome kind." At the age of five his home lessons apart from the three Rs included history, geography, German reading and writing, and "a little Latin." His dutiful grandmother or his other aunt would drill him in writing and arithmetic, "sitting over me with a ruler, and by a succession of hearty bangs on the knuckles, forced my fingers to go the right way" (Hare 1952, p. 24).

Any sign of curiosity or spontaneity was regarded as a prime sign of sinfulness, which only went to prove Hannah More's doctrine that children were of "a corrupt nature and evil dispositions" (Thompson 1975, p. 441). Toys, playmates, and juvenile fiction were strictly prohibited, and the prohibition was only transgressed because inventiveness or boredom conquered Augustus' fears of yet another whipping: he would retrieve discarded fragments of *The Pickwick Papers* from his aunt's wastepaper basket (she read the installments in her dressing room behind closed doors) or he would snatch bits of used paper to draw on. That his two favorite drawing subjects were the Day of Judgement and Adam and Eve being turned out of Paradise should not surprise us when we get a glimpse of his adoptive mother's pedagogical ideals: "Augustus would, I believe, always do a thing if *reasoned* with about it, but the necessity of obedience without reasoning is specially necessary in such a disposition as his. The will is the thing that needs being brought into subjection" (Hare 1952, p. 27). Although Methodism was at the opposite end of Aunt Maria's religious scale, her ideas were strikingly similar to John Wesley's notorious maxim: "Whatever pains it costs, break the will if you would not damn the child. Let a child from a year old be taught to fear the rod and to cry softly. . . . Break his will now, and his sould shall live, and he will probably bless you to all eternity" (Thompson 1975, p. 412).

Wesley's predictions seemed uncannily accurate in Augustus Hare's case. In adult life, Hare would complain of "the want of self-confidence engendered by reproaches and taunts which never ceased" (Hare 1952, p. 41). Still, as a boy he loved his Aunt Maria "most passionately, and many fearful fits, for which I was severely punished as fits of naughtiness, were really caused by anguish at the thought that I had displeased her or been a trouble to her" (Hare 1952, p. 26).

The extreme rigidity of Hare's early childhood is offset by the comparative lenience with which Marjory Fleming was raised. Born in 1803 in Kirkcaldy, Scotland, as the daughter of an accountant, she grew up in the security of a middle-class home, yet in relative freedom from adult restrictions. Apart from her daily lessons, she was at liberty to roam the house and garden. Browsing in her father's study led her at the age of seven to literature as diverse as Thomas Gray's *Ode on the Death of a Favourite Cat* (c. 1747), James Thomson's *Seasons* (1726–30), and *The Arabian Nights* (extracts in a chapbook version), as well as some cheap repository tracts, the *Newgate Calendar* (c. 1774), and Mrs. Radcliffe's *Mysteries of Udolpho* (1794). The last book was read together with her seventeen-year-old cousin Isabella who also tutored Marjory's home lessons and made her seven-year-old pupil keep a diary as a writing exercise. At the age of eight, Marjory Fleming caught measles and then died of meningitis.

That a child of Marjory's age should write about her daily life was not in itself exceptional at a time when many middle-class girls were brought up to value introspection and self-reflection. But the fact that the diary has been preserved offers us a unique insight into a little girl's experiences put in her own words (and her own spelling, which was duly corrected by Isabella). Disobedience and its possible punishments is the central theme of Marjory's journals. Sulkiness, inattention, and a general lack of comprehension are recurring reactions brought on by her three-hour lessons when Isabella teaches her the three Rs "and many other things and religion into the bargan." Multiplication is the most "horrible and wretched *plaege*" to her. "The most Devilish thing is 8 times 8 & 7 times 7 it is what nature itself cant endure" (Fleming 1934, pp. 54, 46–47).[18] She is not

18. While some diaries have survived written by upper- and middle-class adolescents in

The *Child's Companion; or, Sunday Scholar's Reward,* 3rd series, no. 45 (September 1841), p. 265. According to the evangelicals, prayer and unquestioned obedience were the child's chief remedies against its evil nature.

beaten for being "dreadfuly passionate," but she fears Isabella's punishments and praises herself for escaping what she thinks she deserves: "the Devil got the better of me but she never never whip[s] me so that I think I would be the better of it and the next time that I behave ill I think she should do it for she never does it but she is very indulgent to me but I am very ungratefll to . . . hir" (Fleming 1934, p. 42).

Although Marjory's diary was an indirect conversation with her older cousin, who corrected it so that it may display more penitence than the little girl actually felt, her writings show with clarity how incomprehension of why she had to learn multiplication, for instance, led to equivocal reactions: guilt and shame for her

the first part of the nineteenth century, only a few journals that were written by younger children have been preserved. Among these are Pocock 1980, whose author was eleven years old at the inception of his diary in 1826; and Shore 1898, a diary that Emily Shore kept from the age of eleven until her death at nineteen in 1839. For a discussion of Shore's life, see Gorham 1982, pp. 129–35.

resistance are coupled with a stubborn defiance that shows through her repeated acts of recalcitrance and through her writings. Religious sayings intersperse Marjory's childish account, cropping up as clever explanations of her own reactions that she probably did not fully understand but nevertheless internalized as faults.

Marjory Fleming was brought up differently from Augustus Hare. While he was being beaten into subjection, she was admonished and encouraged to behave. Thus, she received regular pocket money, part of which was withheld as a fine if she was disobedient. The contrasts could be explained by sexual differences of upbringing, but we should be cautious about applying standards of a later age to what seems to have been personal variation rather than distinctions of gender. Through most of the nineteenth century, many middle-class children were physically punished, at least until they reached the age of puberty when bodily development forced parental recognition of at least a potential for procreation in their offspring if not, in the early decades, any acknowledgement of sexual activity.

In theory, child sexuality was defined as abnormal, and although the relationship between sexual excitement and physical punishment was noted in England by Dr. Michael Ryan in 1839, his warnings went unheeded until late in the century (Gibson 1978, pp. 29 ff.). In religious households, spontaneity, sensuality, or any other kind of bodily and mental curiosity characterizing the young child's sexuality were interpreted in religious terms as obstinate acts of self-will and signs of original sin. Since the hereafter was for both sexes, girls as well as boys had to submit in this world to God's earthly representatives. Even the novelist Mrs. Gaskell, an unusually sensitive and observant parent, felt "obliged" in 1837, when her beloved daughter Marianne was three years old, to give her "a slight whipping, sorrowfully and gently" (Robertson 1974, p. 416). Rather than displaying sexual differences of upbringing during this period, then, Marjory's and Augustus' childhoods probably make up the poles of personal experience within which the young were brought up in middle-class homes.

Once a common religious foundation had been laid, the sexes were certainly raised for different social functions, and the older the children became, the more separate were their daily lives. While mothers, aunts, or older sisters would teach the younger children, fathers often took over as spiritual guides and mental tutors for their older sons and occasionally for their daughters. Maria Edgeworth and John Stuart Mill are among the best-known examples of children who were brought up at home in close proximity to their fathers. And while James Mill's and Richard Edgeworth's intellectual pursuits allowed an unusual domestic flexibility to prompt their educational interests, diarists and autobiographers who grew up in evangelical households often testify to similar ideals if not equal practical facilities. In further preparation for their commercial or professional careers, sons might be sent to a private day school offering a broader spectrum of subjects than did the classical curricula of the old grammar schools. Conversely, until the 1830s the local grammar schools and the few national public schools saw a steady decline in attendance and standards of tuition.

The education of girls was still chiefly a domestic affair. As the aspirant middle class increasingly separated their work place from their living quarters and women and children were tugged away to a rural idyll in the new suburbs of the great cities, the home attained a renewed ideological status as a sanctuary in an otherwise turbulent world. Public and private spheres not only underwent a social and physical division, they were equally transformed through a strict segregation according to age and sex, which was regarded as enjoined by God (Hall 1979). As future wives and mothers, daughters should be trained as earnestly as sons. But since the adult woman's role was seen as a direct extension of her natural feminine instincts toward moral rectitude and self-denial, the moral preparation of daughters was often perfected at home by the mother along with the inculcation of more domestic duties.

Thus, Emily and Ellen Hall, who were born in 1819 and 1822, respectively, as the youngest children in a large evangelical family (the father being a retired captain of the Sixteenth Light Dragoons), were tutored in their home as adolescents in singing, harp playing, and French. They spent a fair amount of their time copying musical scores, just as they always devoted part of their day to reading, chiefly memoirs, poetry, and sermons, which were deemed more appropriate than novels. They equally took their share in more mundane tasks such as making jam and "washing manchettes" (Sherrard 1966, pp. 3–5). Had there been younger siblings in the family, Ellen and Emily would probably have acted as their tutors, perhaps after a brief spell at a "female academy"—small eighteenth-century boarding schools frequented by middle- and upper-class girls to learn what Frances Cobbe called "the great Art of Society." As a stepping stone to their most decisive phase of life, the period of courting, the students learned to write letters of compliment, how to pay and receive visits, and similar social graces. Lessons were conducted in an intimate home atmosphere, and violaters of the dull and orderly routine were punished like little girls: "I have seen (after a week in which a sort of feminine barring-out had taken place) no less than nine young ladies obliged to sit for hours in the angles of the three rooms, like naughty babies, with their faces to the wall; half of them being quite of marriageable age, and all dressed, as was *de rigueur* with us every day, in full evening attire of silk or muslin, with gloves and kid slippers" (Cobbe 1904, p. 62). The boarding schools for girls were united in their social aims, although standards of tuition varied considerably: few parents could, like Frances Cobbe's, foot a bill of one thousand pounds for two years' educational polishing at a Brighton establishment in the late 1830s.

THE PARADOX OF CHILDHOOD AND YOUTH

While the education of adolescent boys and girls differed as widely as their adult functions, their upbringing had important common characteristics. For both sexes, the family formed the locus of the child's earliest experiences, and it remained a central framework of learning, not least for the girl, who might spend her entire life in her parents' home if she was not married off. With the domestication of family life, parents became the child's nodal points of identification, and whether lenient or strict in childrearing they would kindle contradictory feelings in their offspring. Despite Augustus Hare's and Marjory Fleming's different treatment, they both displayed moments of rebellion and resistance followed by periods of deep-felt anguish and remorse. The wrath generated by parental punishments, physical as well as mental, was suppressed by both children. They came to accept parental maxims by internalizing them as their own.

Injustice was certainly felt, just as social and sexual discrimination was keenly perceived and sometimes resisted. Whatever their reactions, middle- and upper-class children had no means of comprehending the social roots of such discrimination. Thus, for the gifted Florence Nightingale and other privileged girls who struggled against the restrictions of domestic femininity, their battle was as much an internal as an external one (Gorham 1982, pp. 125–51). The younger the child, the more would social contradictions be experienced as personal conflicts, as clashes between the child and his or her relatives or within himself or herself.

Having a domesticated family and sometimes school as their bases of upbringing—that is, experiencing what we today understand as an ordinary childhood and adolescence—the offspring of the well-to-do grew up in apparent freedom, yet constantly preparing for the seriousness of adult life and its gender roles. Compared with their poor contemporaries who depended directly on paid work, middle- and upper-class juveniles were liberated from strenuous toil and severe abuse. But the mental and sometimes physical strain may have been augmented because its causes were hidden to the young. Both sexes underwent an education whose practical applications seemed abstract and obscure, perhaps even irrelevant. John Thomas Pocock's parents may have thought their efforts well rewarded had they peeped into the diary of their twelve-year-old son recording his daily trials with the accepting resignation of a well-behaved student: "To school in the morning where the usual routine of Spelling, Writing, Cyphering, Burching and Caneing took place" (Pocock 1980, p. 9).[19] One wonders whether the boy was as happy as his parents.

19. The entry is from 1827 before John Thomas' (1814–76) thirteenth birthday. The son of a banker, he lived in a spacious new house in Kilburn, then a London suburb. After his

Peasant and working-class juveniles worked and hence learned by doing. "Real" children and adolescents of the upper and middle classes learned by learning. Their experiences were being shaped by what we might call a *structural paradox of childhood and youth,* namely a discontinuity between the juveniles' present situation and their future station, a separation of personal learning and social use, of the process and result of socialization. As is evident in the early nineteenth century, this paradox was by no means felt to the same extent by all. The realms of childhood and youth were slowly being built since the seventeenth century when women and children were beginning to be secluded, first behind the walls of the manor and later behind the tall hedges of suburban gardens. Working-class and peasant juveniles had yet to be included among "real" children and adolescents, and even within the sanctuary of childhood its paradox was experienced differently by the sexes at this time. The girl tended to feel fewer contradictions in her daily life than would her brother, since her upbringing within the home was less competitive and more congenial to her adult role—that is, as long as she accepted and succeeded in fulfilling that role.

These differences of experience indicate the contradictory possibilities that were engendered through the historical development of childhood and youth as distinct age categories and as a social space of subordination. As childrearing became domesticated and personalized, social contradictions would be perceived by the young as individual conflicts.[20] Thus, the closer family ties that this form of socialization facilitated offered new means of parental supervision and adult repression, but the strengthening of personal bonds equally enhanced the possibilities of intimate emotional attachments, as attested in Marjory Fleming's humorous declaration of love for her cousin:

> I love in Isas bed to lie
> O such a joy & luxury
> The bottom of the bed I sleep
> And with great care I myself keep
> Oft I embrace her feet of lillys
> But she has *gotton* all the pillies
> Her neck I never can embrace
> But I do hug her feet in place.
> (Fleming 1934, p. 23)

The ballad verse not only displays a little girl's imaginative use of literary convention, its humor also reveals that the situation described is familiar enough

---

father's bankruptcy, John Thomas emigrated at the age of fourteen and became an apothecary in Cape Town, South Africa.

20. Conversely, the entry into the world of work or education often impregnated into working-class children an acute sense of social injustice, shaping their subsequent experiences and being remembered even in old age (See Vincent 1982, pp. 90–94).

to allow for a covert (perhaps unconscious) criticism of Isabella's power, under-cutting the love theme. If all parents are objects of both love and hate, a closer proximity to adults would deeply ingrain these contradictory emotions into the individual. Thus, the historical development of childhood and youth at once fostered a gendered individualism and jeopardized its means of autonomous expression. It should therefore come as no surprise that the adult concern with the young had as its inevitable corollary a wish to control juvenile sexuality. Whatever their moral guises, child-care manuals and educational treatises were essentially discussions about bodily control and sexual expression, as is still the case.

Why then was this discussion couched in religious terms early in the nine-teenth century? Why were the strict evangelical childrearing ideals—whether in their Anglican or Dissenting forms—so favored by the middle and lower-middle classes? Answers to such questions are necessarily speculative: most parents did not consciously adopt certain pedagogical strategies but would choose (often unconsciously) those means of upbringing that felt right.

Many of these parents found themselves in a vulnerable social position since the end of the eighteenth century. Like the Puritans, the up-and-coming middle class carved out its precarious status in a tension between the gentry and the destitute "masses." Without land or peerage as social safety nets, its members possessed only their own marketable skills and perhaps some accumulated cap-ital. Their hopes for the future would naturally be placed on their children, giving them a new importance. Parents in general have always been interested in the survival and well-being of their offspring. But to this basic interest was now increasingly added a parental concern with developing the individual child morally, mentally, and intellectually. Proper training, especially of boys, in general skills that could be adapted to changing demands became vital conditions of social survival within a dynamic capitalist economy. Precisely this unpredict-ability helps explain why an educational interest and optimism, if not the goals of schooling, were shared by social segments as different as artisans, self-employed craftsmen, manufacturers, and bankers.

In such a dynamic society certain personal attitudes, including the right morality, facilitated social survival necessitating the careful rearing also of girls, who were to remain outside the turbulence of financial necessity. Evangelical ethics found particular resonance with people whose daily experiences if not their conscious reflections taught them that shifting social demands could best be met by those whose personal inclinations enhanced foresight and self-control—and not simply in the sphere of production. The budding industrialist and his aspirant wife, as well as the hard-working artisan family, were still only a few steps removed from the cyclical life rhythm of the masses with their "uncouth" manners and their fighting, drunkenness, and unbridled festivities. As a mental protection against this popular culture, both sexes were urged to repress their own spontaneity and sexuality. This repression was all the more rigid and methodical because it was a historical development of comparative novelty not yet firmly lodged as a "natural" ingredient of the personality.

For middle-class people, the French Revolution quickened their fears of backsliding and boosted their desire for a mental stronghold. For many artisans, the ideological impasse following the failings of the Revolution fostered religious revivalism. The ability to serve the equivocal mental needs of both middle-class and working-class people gave evangelism, and especially Methodism, its strength in the early part of the nineteenth century (Thompson 1975, pp. 411–40).[21] Evangelism embraced a forceful protection of the young against physical, social, and mental "pollution."

For middle-class juveniles, parental protection created new problems, but it also suggested new solutions. The emphasis on individualism and the separation of childrearing from work reshaped the role of the imagination. No longer bound by practical applications, the imagination became a channel for mental transgression. By anticipating alternatives, the imagination became a means to acknowledge and possibly heal the disparities of childhood. But precisely because of its free-wheeling status, individual imagination often remained, as it can today, a mental process with no practical consequences. It is within this historical perspective that the function of juvenile leisure reading can be understood. It offers a direct line to the reader's conscious mind and even his or her unconscious mind. The Puritans found fiction an admirable means of moral instruction, and, indeed, books as well as magazines, and later comics, have been used as such.

The morality of fiction, however, is indirect even when it is didactic. Morality is inculcated through a physical and mental reading process that offers readers a communal area of feeling if the text is read aloud. Experienced individually, the reading process shapes a mental space within which the young can create a totality of experience and a coherence of understanding that they lack in real life. What they get out of reading is thus at once dependent on their previous experiences and on how these correspond to the imaginary experiences created through fiction.

What is this reading process and how does it work? To answer this, we must look for what is being described in the juvenile magazines, concentrating on social relations (gender, class, age, and race) and social structures (family,

21. The success of evangelism early in the nineteenth century spurred its demise in later decades. "Its ethos had always been particularly suited to the ethic of self-help and self-improvement: it did not satisfy to the same extent those who had achieved their social ambitions" (Thompson 1972, p. 15).

school, leisure, and the adult world). These are all areas that seem incoherent to "real" children. Equally, we must explore how these areas are described in the magazines and how that description operates within the lives of the young. We can surmise that the religious magazines would be perceived differently by an Augustus Hare who was allowed few self-defined activities; by a Marjory Fleming who might read a selection of printed matter as one of her childish pursuits; and by a Mary Anne Hearne or a Charles Shaw who found fiction an often unattainable luxury.

4

Better to Be Pious than Rich:
The *Child's Companion* and
the *Children's Friend*

WHEN THE Religious Tract Society set out to compose a magazine for children in 1824, it already had ten years' experience in publishing tracts for juveniles. To this traditional evangelical fare, the society had recently added books of fiction for younger children, an innovation which was probably inspired by Mrs. Sherwood's recent success with *The History of the Fairchild Family* whose first and most popular part was published in 1818 (parts 2 and 3 followed in 1842 and 1847 respectively). Mrs. Sherwood's narrative of a happy and close family life in which the three children's quarrels and occasional mishaps lend apt occasions for parental homilies was to remain a mainstay of Victorian children's Sunday reading (Avery 1975, pp. 92–99).[1] George Stokes, the editor of the new *Child's Companion; or, Sunday Scholar's Reward,* had lately tried his hand at such fiction for younger children. Although the society's version was leavened by a more pious tone and fewer examples of happy families, Stokes carried this broadened perspective into his new magazine venture. The Anglican counterpart to the *Child's Companion* was the *Children's Friend,* edited by the assiduous W. Carus Wilson, "rector of Whittington and vicar of Tunstall" as the first issue proclaimed, and also a friend of William Wilberforce and himself one of the leading spokesmen of the Evangelical movement within the Church of England. The Reverend, leaning toward bombastic pedagogical strategies, pitched the moral tone of his periodical higher than his companion. But from their inception, both magazines had a similar style, containing a mixture of uplifting fiction and almost as uplifting articles on geography, history, and botany.

The small print of the thirty-two (or twenty-four) page duodecimos was

---

1. Darton 1982, pp. 170–71 quotes the famous episode at the gibbet, which, when taken out of its historical and literary contexts, lends support to critics' frequent denunciations of evangelical literature and its macabre means of moral teaching. For an alternative reading of the story and the "gibbet episode," see Bratton 1981, pp. 55–57.

enlivened by four or six engravings per issue, which either depicted children reading, children praying, and children in their deathbeds, or—in a more exotic vein—showed an elephant or a giraffe. The illustrations acted as comments to the written text as a whole rather than to specific details of the accounts. Characters remained as static as the situation they were part of, and the background was generally unadorned by details that might detract the readers' attention from the importance of the words. Material was universally selected for its religious weight rather than for its virtues of narrative. Stories often bore subtitles such as "A True Story" or "From the *Gloucestershire Chronicle*," thus not only indicating the editors' want of appropriate fictional supplies, but equally revealing an earnest endeavor to promulgate the truth value of the tales. Although the early evangelical ban on fiction was gradually being lifted, flights of fantasy were firmly discouraged and, especially in the earlier volumes, the moral strictures conveyed by the magazines enveloped clear social and racial messages.

"Poor and Pious" is the emblematic title of one such story whose moral could stand as a common denominator for the social outlook characterizing the religious monthlies: "Perhaps you are poor; but this need be no hindrance to your being religious. You, my young friends, may be pious without being rich; and it is far better to be pious than rich, for man, when he dieth, can carry nothing away with him" (*Child's Companion*, new ser., 3, no. 28 [April 1834], p. 127). For the benefit of ill-clad and undernourished Sunday scholars, this consoling message was often stressed by exemplifying juvenile characters whose lives were even more wretched than the intended readers'. Crippled, deaf, and mute children recur as the patient bearers of the their inflictions, just as the chimney sweepers' lot is a favorite theme: "We ought to be very much obliged to the chimney sweepers for the great trouble they take to be useful to us . . . Be kind to the little sweeps, and to all that are poorer than yourself, for it is by the grace of God, and not on account of your own goodness, that you are any better off than they."[2] If a streak of self-assertion can still be left in the young readers' minds, the stark symbolism offered by the dejected sweeper is rubbed in to secure their humble submission: "If the chimney sweeper looks black *outside*, remember that you are black *inside*" (*Child's Companion* 4, no. 29 [May 1826], pp. 131, 130).

Social division apparently was so close to the everyday experiences of the readers (and the author) that its acceptance needed a certain measure of divine justification. Less reasoning, however, was brought in to account for human differences existing beyond the purview of English evangelism. The missionary

2. The lot of the chimney sweeps was, indeed, deplorable and perhaps the saddest result of the early industrial exploitation of human labor in favor of more capital-intensive machines. Although Jonas Hanway (inventor of the umbrella) in 1773 pointed toward the possible substitution of the sweeps by "machinery," their numbers actually increased (Lynd 1942, pp. 38–39).

path, entered by the *Youth's Magazine* in 1805, was followed even more zeal-ously by subsequent magazine editors. Compared to their efforts, the rationalist prejudice of the eighteenth-century periodicals pales completely. Foreign customs and rituals were described with fascinated incredulity, and an iota of Christian forbearance is left only for the converted such as the Indian boy who by his prayers shows "more power of mind and understanding than is usual among the Natives of [his] class" or the African juvenile whose devoutness could shame domestic readers' own lack of deference and perseverance. "I often go to bed with an empty stomach, but I pray to our Saviour, to make me satisfied, and feel no inclination to complain," he says in the anecdote "Faith and Patience of Christian Hottentots" (*Child's Companion* 2, no. 9 [September 1824], pp. 90, 87–88). In the *Children's Friend*, the stern religious manner is combined with an added ferocity in the accounts of "heathen" religion. In an article on "Mex-ican Worship," the rituals of human sacrifice are described with such gory minuteness that it easily rivals the secular "trash" that the arbiters of religious feeling did everything to combat:

> The victim was laid on his back on a large stone. Two priests held down his legs, two of them his arms, and another his head and neck. When the head priest, with a sharp flint, cut open his body and tore out the yet beating heart of the poor wretch, and holding it up towards the sun, offered the fume of it as an acceptable sacrifice!
> Think, dear children, that it is from such horrid rites as these, that we wish to free our fellow-creatures by means of our missionaries and our Bibles! (*Children's Friend* 3, no. 33 [September 1826], p. 209)

The self-righteous tone is entirely typical of the contemporary religious maga-zines for children who, as adults at both ends of the social spectrum, were to sanction and approve the gradual expansion of the British Empire. The ideology of imperialism, it can be seen, took root in the 1820s and 1830s and not only, as it is often assumed from analyses of children's books, in the mid- or late nine-teenth century.

While missionary tales by definition were removed geographically from the readers' everyday experiences, other narratives achieved a similar distance by being set in the past. In the late 1820s, for instance, the *Children's Friend* exulted in the persecution of Huguenots in sixteenth-century France. Again dramatic detail—here the particulars of Catholic cruelties—creates antirevolutionary and antipapist sentiments: a perfect framework for highlighting evangelical hu-maneness and political status quo at a time when Irish immigration and petitions to grant civil liberties to all denominations frightened most rightminded cler-gymen. Thus, in 1828, the year when the Test and Corporation Acts were repealed and one year before the passing of the Catholic Emancipation Act, the *Children's Friend* carried a vivid account of "St. Bartholomew's Day," the

The *Children's Friend* 9, no. 105 (September 1832), p. 213. This is a common illustration for the periodical's missionary tales describing the alleged barbarities of foreign peoples. In this case, the picture, probably taken from the publisher's stock of woodcuts, accompanies an article, "New Zealand."

Catholic eradication of Huguenots in 1572: "Neither the aged nor the tender infants were spared, nor women great with child; some were stabbed, others were hewn in pieces with halberts, or shot with muskets or pistols, some thrown headlong out of the windows, many dragged to the rivers, and divers had their brains beaten out with mallets, clubs and such like instruments" (*Children's Friend* 5, no. 49 [January 1828], pp. 8–9).

Most children, certainly, would miss the political associations and the moral justification propelling the account. Adult expositions, possibly accompanying the children's reading, would undoubtedly be overshadowed by the powerful fictional images of personal agony. Such mental impressions were sharpened by focusing on the fate of an individual—for example, the fate befalling the young Brissonet whose uncle was the Protestant Bishop of Meaux: "she was stabbed with iron rods, and thrown half alive into the river; where floating on the surface, the watermen pursued her as their prey, and put her to a slow and lingering death" (*Children's Friend* 5, no. 49 [January 1828], p. 6).

Missionary and historical narratives were common in both the *Child's Companion* and the *Children's Friend*. Descriptions of exotic death rites and past religious strife contain a mixture of vagueness about time and place and precision of detail, opening for the reader a distant and malleable universe populated by lifelike characters and realistic actions. This type of fiction would facilitate the children's projection of their own fears and anxieties ("it could be me") while allowing them to control those fears because of the thematic distance ("it is not me after all"). But there was another type of fiction, treating death closer to the readership's personal experiences, that operated on a different psychological level.

Accounts of pious or sinful children's deaths were a marked feature of the religious magazines. These accounts have often been denounced by latter-day critics entertaining no strong religious beliefs and living closer to the facts of birth than to the reality of death. The preoccupation with death and dying in the periodicals is indeed striking and often seems macabre. Prayers, poems, and occasional obituaries continued the tradition initiated by James Janeway and the Puritans almost a century and a half earlier. The didacticism, which is as stark as it is direct, is typified in titles such as "You Are Not too Young to Die," "The Dying Sunday Scholar," and "Happy Death of a Little Boy." Thus, under the heading "The Frailty of Children," no effort is spared to admonish the young and vigorous:

> Though now you may be blessed with health and strength and youth, yet soon you may be stretched lifeless and breathless within the silent tomb . . . Many a lovely blossom has perished in the spring; many a fragrant flower has been nipped in the bud; many a little bird has just lived to sing, to flutter and to die; and many a little child has just opened its eyes in life, to close them in death forever. It may be thus with you. A few days more, and your earthly existence may close;—a few days more, and the blast of death may pass over you, and you will feel the stroke and die. (*Child's Companion* 5, no. 37 [January 1827], pp. 21–2.)

Often such eloquent exhortations are accompanied by narrative demonstrations of the moral message, as if the editor wants to make sure that even the selective reader, skipping the prayers and the homilies, will grasp the essence of universal sinfulness. One tale, for instance, published in the *Child's Companion* in October 1830, recounts how, "on Thursday, the 15th of August," a fourteen-year-old boy goes for a swim and narrowly escapes drowning, twice. Defying his mother's prohibition, he "declared with an oath he would immediately go again; he did so, but he had not been in many minutes, when he sunk to rise no more" (*Child's Companion* 8, no. 82 [October 1830], pp. 309–10). While this narrative details the death of a sinful child, other stories recount the joyful deaths of pious juveniles. In one of these tales, Ellen, the eldest of three poor, fatherless

THE

CHILD'S COMPANION;

OR,

Sunday Scholar's Reward.

No. 42.]   JUNE, 1827.   VOL. 5.

THE PIOUS GIRL AND HER SWEAR-ING FATHER.

A LADY addressed the following letter to the Secretary of the Blackburn Religious Tract Society, the fact it contains will no doubt be interesting to our young readers. "We do

VOL. V.

The *Child's Companion; or, Sunday Scholar's Reward* 5, no. 42 (June 1827), front cover.

children, is dying from tuberculosis: "On recovering from a convulsive attack, she said, with a heavenly smile, 'I thought it had been over; come, Lord Jesus, come quickly.'" With perfect ease, Ellen says goodbye to her siblings and then "she took her mother's hand and put it to her heart, saying, 'I hope you will be able to give me up. O do not grieve for me.' Her mother remarked, 'I shall miss you; I shall want your advice.' She replied: 'Ah, never mind; you have a God to go to; you have always found deliverance at hand in extremity; God is good to the widow and the fatherless—we have found it so' . . . The happy spirit took its flight from sin and sorrow, to endless bliss and glory" (*Children's Friend* 13, no. 150 [June 1836], pp. 124, 125, 126). In the stories of pious children, their heroic stoicism and patient anticipation of a happy afterlife serve as a spiritual tonic, strengthening their mourning parents as in Ellen's case. Or the young act as a personal example, causing the conversion of irreligious relatives.

When assessing how the accounts of dying children would be received, we should remember that through much of the nineteenth century children were close to death. Although infant mortality decreased in middle-class families, even juveniles who were raised in secure circumstances were likely to experience the death of at least one brother or sister. To many young readers, the prospect of death was not particularly frightening. Few, however, were as fortunate as Frances Power Cobbe who as a little girl never doubted her salvation because she heard it pronounced every Sunday in church: "The Heavens and *all the Powers* therein" (Cobbe 1904, p. 42). The seven-year-old Marjory Fleming found the *Newgate Calendar* with its many dying speeches "very instructive, Amusing, & shews us the ne*se*sity of doing good and not evil" (Fleming 1934, p. 107).

Older children and adolescents, who would be more impressed by the prospect of their own dying, would mourn the bereavement of a beloved sibling, but such feelings were invoked by a known reality, not a mental lacuna causing vague and hence pervasive fears. For most of the century, it was common for children to have a "last look" at the deceased and also to attend funerals. Writing her diary in the mid-Victorian era, the thirteen-year-old Ellen Buxton recorded how she went to see her younger brother, Leo, two days after he died:

> He was lying in the large bed, and he looked so beautiful and so perfectly at rest; but he did not look at all like himself when he was alive, he was so changed I should not have known him I am sure and so exactly like Papa he looked much older than he really was, and so very handsome, his lips were very dark purple nearly black, and he had a sort of yellowish hue all over his face; his hands were under the sheets so we did not see them, there was a handkerchief tied round his face because Mama said that it wanted support. (Creighton 1967, p. 20)[3]

3. This entry can be compared with one for 5 December 1861 where Ellen describes in general terms the news of her sister Effie's birth. Personal illness would often prompt more anguished considerations of death; see, for instance, Emily Shore's diary as quoted in Gorham 1982, pp. 133–34.

A touching but not a harrowing memory. Conversely, for children who were brought up under the constant shadow of sin, the dread of eternal damnation and parental punishment, not death itself, caused them profound feelings of horror and guilt.[4] Thus, Mary Anne Hearne, raised by Baptist parents, felt that "hell was a very real thing to me" (Burnett 1984, p. 142). To John James Bezer, (born 1816), whose father was a Spitalfields hairdresser and who himself became a cobbler and a Chartist radical, the brimstone preaching of his Dissenting Sunday school teacher made him do "as the '*ancients*' did." Of being eight years old and alone in the house, Bezer wrote: "I actually undressed myself to the skin, got out of the cupboard father's sawdust bag, wrapped myself in it, poured some ashes over my head, and stretched myself on the ground, imploring for mercy, with such mental agony and such loud cries that the people in the house heard me, and told my parents about it, though nobody even then knew the truth" (Vincent 1982, pp. 88–89). Bezer's act of penitent purification was a heroic attempt to master fears threatening to overpower him. That he dared not tell anyone of his agonies reveals an inseparable connection in the child's mind between religious faith and unquestioning obedience toward his parents. The direct admonishings, suffusing the numerous deathbed scenes of the religious monthlies, chiefly impressed children whose everyday experiences, like John Bezer's, were leavened with the mixed fears of divine and mundane punishment. Such children, when reading of joyful deaths, could well equate the reward of redemption with the parental praise granted them for their obedience. Moreover, stories in which the dying child acted as a strong spiritual guide to skeptical adults would likely be favorites because they made a last, almost diabolical, turning of the tables of power. The activity of reading offered children a mental space where they could negotiate their daily defeats. Reading anticipated the perfect and unsanctioned love that the child longed for, but the price paid for this love was daily submission and self-denial.

Stories of dying sinners had an equally equivocal impact upon these readers. Disobedient, and hence impious, fictional characters invariably met their fatal ends in the magazines. Playing with fireworks, swimming, climbing, going to the circus or a country fair, and, of course, drinking and swearing were all direct signs of sin bearing the direst of consequences. In the face of such fascinating temptations one would have to be an unusually submissive and sedate child not to feel a certain satisfaction when seeing that one's own hard-won obedience paid

4. According to the psychoanalytical survey, made by Taylor 1958, the evangelical child's often intense preoccupation with death and dying was caused by its introjection of aggression originally felt toward the strict father but then turned towards itself—as death wishes—for fear of reprisal, real or imagined (see especially chaps. 7, 13 and 15). Taylor, while initially linking a stern religious zeal to "the trading middle class" (p. 11), does not pursue historically the social and sexual variations of this link and thus turns his study into an unfortunate psychological generalization.

off: one was still alive. Children living in strict households could vent their hate and aggression upon the defenseless narrative personae, thus gaining a certain feeling of independence and power to ameliorate their suppression.

But the reverse side of such momentary victories was the fear of personal relapse, the sudden and irrevocable digression from the mental straight and narrow—a path that was seldom traversed in full consciousness of its possible pitfalls. The dual purpose of liberation and repression served by homiletic fiction in the religious magazines chiefly spoke to the converted. The overt didacticism suffusing the deathbed stories and the obituaries as well as the poems and the sermons made hellfire morality conscious and almost tangible. Didacticism thus facilitated a mental dismissal of this morality, or at least a disregard, by readers raised with more lenience, liberty, and personal love. Conversely, to such readers the other dominant type of fiction in the magazines, the historical and the missionary tales with their psychological distancing mechanisms and their indirect moral, would be a far more effective medium of personal conversion.

This difference of aesthetic function, unnoticed by critics, was crucial in determining the wide, and varying, reception of the magazines and other forms of religious fiction for the young. While the social range of religious reading matter is commonly acknowledged, the variability of its reception is often overridden by proclamations decrying its menacing indoctrination of children at all social levels. Certainly, both Stokes and Wilson applied forceful methods to convey their earnest messages, and we do not know whether they consciously selected different types of fiction to secure the broadest possible influence of these messages. We do know, however, that from their inception both periodicals combined forceful stories with nonfictional entries on natural and historical phenomena, which took up more than half of the space in the magazines. Some critics think that the inclusion of factual articles was prompted by the evangelicals' fear of competition from the utilitarians (Bratton 1981, p. 40; Laqueur 1976, p. 208). But, comparing the insignificant output and the short life of secular periodicals up until the 1840s with the long-running religious monthlies, utilitarianism posed no serious challenge to the clerical leadership of juvenile magazine publishing.

Stokes' and Wilson's concoction of periodical reading matter seems rather to have been guided by moral considerations. If a selective reader skipped the homilies and went straight to accounts of the Egyptian pyramids or the lava flow of Mount Etna, he or she would still encounter some invigorating spiritual counsel. In an article in the *Child's Companion*, "The India Rubber Tree," a detailed description of how sap is used for making wellingtons and waterproof clothing concludes: "May the youthful reader, while reading the wonders of nature, admire the wisdom and glory of the Creator who made nothing in vain" (*Child's Companion*, new ser., 3, no. 28 [April 1834], pp. 110–11). Similarly, an account of the magnetism generated by the Niagara Falls makes the author think "of the feebleness of man to resist it, and of His almighty power who stems at his pleasure the most impetuous torrent" (*Child's Companion*, new ser., 4, no. 45 [September 1835], pp. 267–68).

Factual snippets would often "balance" the fantasy elements that cropped up in the religious magazines from midcentury. Thus, in a story from 1850 bearing the captivating title "French Fishermen and the Magician Fish," the underwater monster turns out to be an electric eel; this discovery provides the occasion for explaining that "electricity is a fluid existing in all bodies, and transmitting itself from one to another with more or less rapidity, and more or less sensible results, according to the nature of these bodies" (*Child's Companion*, new ser., no. 70 [October 1850], p. 309). By this time, the religious monthlies had come of age, and they vied for the readers' attention with secular magazines. That the religious periodicals, however, sought to move with the times is indicated not only by their inclusion of fantasy (their own specific brand), but also by a new social awareness, which characterized mid-Victorian Britain in general and found its particular expression in the second evangelical revival of the 1860s.

For the *Children's Friend*, the limit of innovation was to adopt an intimate rather than a condescending tone. In one of the last issues of the first series, the "dear reader" was advised to conquer "the storm of passion" by going into a corner and reciting the letters of the alphabet (*Children's Friend* 36, no. 425 [May 1859], p. 117).[5] This clever formula of combining moral restriction with educational instruction was transcended by the *Child's Companion*. In the early 1850s, for example, the magazine ran several stories of ragged schools, which were set up in the 1840s on Lord Shaftesbury's initiative to benefit the poorest of urban children, the "street arabs." In one of these tales, Arthur and Jane accompany their parents to one of the new schools. Their father tells them that the school is not only for "the very poorest class of children, [but also] for those who are familiar with something far worse than poverty—with idleness, and bad companions, and sin." When Jane expresses her apprehension of encountering such specimens, her mother, bolstering the girl's philanthropic spirit, explains that "tickets of admission will be given tonight to such children only as have attended before, and have become accustomed to order and obedience." The experience so moves the two children that "Arthur longed to be a man that he might help to teach them, and Jane whispered to her mother that they could easily make some frocks and pinafores for the poor ragged girls" (*Child's Companion*, new ser., no. 78 [June 1851], pp. 170–72). The theme of the street

5. From 1850 to 1860 the editor was C. Carus Wilson. Editorial policies, however, remained much the same. In the last volume of the original series (1860), one can still find obituaries and stories of happy or unhappy deaths.

arab settled into a popular pattern in juvenile fiction with the bestselling books of Hesba Stretton [Sara Smith] in the 1860s (Bratton 1981, pp. 81–98). The early appearance of this theme in the religious monthlies testifies to the topical sensitivity of the editors and demonstrates that by midcentury the magazine as a literary form had become a fictional trendsetter testing out themes and plots that were subsequently taken up in children's books.

Since the purchase of both books and periodicals was firmly guided by adults, the output of religious monthlies is no true measure of their influence on the juvenile readership. To get a qualitative understanding of their appeal, we must assess the magazine contents against the everyday experiences of the young. As already indicated, the result shows a variation that, although rooted in social and sexual differences, was determined by the readers' religious affiliation. The strong presence of poor characters does not imply that the magazines were read solely by the poor. The *Child's Companion* was read in Florence Nightingale's upper-class home, and the religious message of inner faith and of reflection on one's inherent sinfulness applied to rich and poor alike (with different effects, as noted).

Literature was widely recognized as a means of moral introspection. In poor religious households, the magazines, together with the Bible, some tracts, and possibly the odd reward book gleaned from the Sunday school library, would offer the range of approved mental nourishment for the young. The religious periodicals began at a time when the enormous expansion of the radical press could have easily rendered any periodical publication morally suspect, especially to people who could afford to be selective, but there are no examples of well-heeled parents professing any misgivings in that respect. The estimable names of publishers and editors in conjunction with the vigorous promotion efforts in the Sunday schools seem to have offset what heretical doubts the purchasers may have entertained.

To children raised under strict adult supervision and given few outlets to experience independence or self-worth, the activity of reading must have offered a welcome opportunity of retreat, a moment of relief from overwhelming demands, mundane as well as divine. Reading would form an essential space for the negotiation of these demands and the anxieties they created. In curious ways, religious literature could even invigorate a budding mental resistance. Mary Anne Hearne recalled "a series of descriptive articles on men who had been poor boys, and risen to be rich and great. Every month I hoped to find the story of some poor, ignorant *girl*, who beginning life as handicapped as I, had yet been able by her own efforts and the blessing of God upon them to live a life of usefulness, if not of greatness. But I believe there was not a woman in the whole series" (Gorham 1982, pp. 145–46).

Especially in devout families, such as Hearne's, the tales of joyful deaths, as noted, could enhance a child's feelings of personal power, however brief. The reverse, however, was the fear of a fall from grace—a painful experience when external reality reappeared in force on closing the magazine. The pain would be exacerbated for those middle-class children whose daily hardships left them few other possibilities for creating that sense of freedom than reading. Lower-middle-class and working-class childrearing was equally severe, but paid work tasks and the responsibilities to younger siblings or to grandparents yielded alternative areas of identification, self-respect, and social contact for children— no matter how onerous these duties were. The variety of their daily lives equally facilitated unobserved play and opportunities to subvert adult admonition: Mary Anne Hearne and her play fellows, for example, invented a sacrilegious game at a nearby river. Climbing the branch of a tree overhanging the water, she would baptize some "candidates" in the river "while the other children on the bank sang Hallelujah" (Gorham 1982, 144–45).

Middle-class children, growing up with few restrictions, lacked work as an area of identification but had options similar to those of poorer children in acting out in play problems facing them in their domestic relations with adults. While geographical and botanical articles in the magazines might satisfy a yearning for knowledge about the outside world, a child would probably remember the narrative rather than the moral aspects of magazine fiction. In a similar fashion, the vivid imagery to be found in the missionary and the historical tales stirred strong emotions of aggression and fear while the fictional distancing mechanisms of time and place made these emotions more manageable, but also less understandable. As stories, they did not help negotiate the reader's real-life anxieties—let alone help unravel the origins of these anxieties—which included questions on the fallibilities of parents created by an infallible God, on why God had singled out running and swimming as particularly wicked pursuits, and on whether it was indeed better to be pious than rich.

The periodicals provided no answers to the contradictions facing the young, and they gave no reasons for the pervasive influence of religion in their lives. The magazines, on the other hand, stimulated the imagination so that it might subsequently be used in the negotiation of pertinent problems through play. The religious magazines, then, were neither a monolithic medium of indoctrination, nor did they offer juveniles universal, spiritual consolation. They operated on several psychological levels and their influence varied decisively according to the readers' class and gender experiences. To generalize about the reception of the periodicals would not only prove futile, but would also miss an important reason for their continued acceptance by parents and children alike. The pious fictional surface that adults perceived and commended as morally beneficial hid a narrative structure that the young were probably equally unaware of. It nevertheless gripped their imaginations with a forceful hold, which the readers had different means of releasing and reformulating for their own ends.

PART THREE

Moral
Entertainment
in Mid-Victorian
Boys' Magazines

5

Too High, Too Solid, Too Good: The Upsurge of Boys' Magazines

T H E E M E R G E N C E of the religious magazines had pointed to a young reading public that had hitherto gone unnoticed. The middle of the nineteenth century saw that not only spiritual but also commercial benefits could be reaped from the children's field. Although the importance of Newbery's secular commercialism had dwindled under the weight of religious monthlies, whose circulation figures remained high, there had been a steady stream of intent if short-lived secular ventures in the first three decades of the century. One of these was the *Youth's Monthly Visitor* (1822–23), whose bound volumes were termed the *Youth's Miscellany of Knowledge and Entertainment*. According to the editorial address printed in the first issue, the purpose of the magazine was to "strew flowers over the thorny path of science" (*Youth's Monthly Visitor* 1, no. 1, [February 1822], p. 1). Judging from its brief run (a year was about average for secular magazines at that time), the neat print of the periodical, its occasional color plates, and Miss Macaulay's adaptations of famous dramas failed to overcome the preponderance of articles about chemistry, arithmetic, "optics," and "natural and experimental philosophy." The reader was asked to guess the number of pores in the human body (2,016 million), and the coal supply—apparently a vexed question already in 1822—was estimated after considerable calculation to be enough for about five hundred years. Despite its lack of success, the *Youth's Monthly Visitor* nevertheless exemplified the direction that secular periodicals were taking.

The "pursuit of useful knowledge," which tenuously united many working-class and middle-class radicals, found expression during the 1820s and 1830s in the formation of numerous formal and informal educational agencies. The best known of these were the Mechanics' Institutes and Henry Brougham's Society for the Diffusion of Useful Knowledge (founded in 1826). Together with the monitorial National and British schools, these agencies paved the way for a wider acceptance of utilitarian ideas. By the 1840s, when many young radicals had themselves become parents, publishers, or politicians, secular periodicals for children flourished. The literary impetus came, not unnaturally, from North

America. In New England, Samuel Griswold Goodrich (1793–1860) had established a phenomenal popularity among juvenile readers with his "Peter Parley" books on various countries (the first was *Tales of Peter Parley about America* [1827]) as well as with his "Peter Parley" magazines, launched in 1833. Since no copyright agreement was made between England and the United States until 1891, any author's work was left open to foreign appropriation. British publishers were quick off the mark. They imported genuine Parleys (more than seven million issues in thirty years), and they copied the name: six different "pseudo-Peter Parleys" have been identified and at least two rival firms issued a *Peter Parley's Magazine* (1839–63) and a *Peter Parley's Annual* (1840–92) (Darton 1982, pp. 221–28).[1]

Genuine or not, the Peter Parley magazines put facts into focus. The magazines featured articles on every aspect of natural history, geology, and astronomy, detailing height, duration, or dates of origin with a diligence that surpassed all former efforts. In 1844, for example, the first of a regular series, "Natural Wonders," dealt with the "Falls of Niagara." First the "principle of the gravitation of fluids" is defined: "From the natural property which water has to seek the lowest level, by the force of gravity, the most stupendous effects arise as well as the most important." Then follows a detailed description of the falls and their surroundings. "The Horse-Shoe Fall," the reader is informed, "measures about 700 yards, following the curvature from the Canadian bank to Goat Island. The end of the island, between the falls, is about 330 yards across, and the breadth of the American Fall is above 350 yards." So it goes on with enumeration of the length of the wooden bridge across the American Fall, the width of the river above and below the falls, and the depth of Lake Erie. Yet, the author's numeric ingenuity is at a loss when it comes to the thunder issuing from the falls: "It is said to resemble the distant cannonading between two engaging fleets; others more correctly admit that there are no familiar sounds to which it can be compared" (*Peter Parley's Magazine* [April 1844], pp. 117, 121, 120). In the tales, "the dark ages" was a favorite theme, offsetting the progress and mechanical rationale of the readers' own time. The British career of the Peter Parleys after 1840 indicates that secular rationalism was encroaching upon religious sentiment in the world of magazine publishing at a time when pious tales still dominated books for the young.[2] The ensuing competition between religious and rationalist magazines resulted in the creation of a new fictional meeting ground, the secular "quality" paper for boys.

1. The annuals were adaptations for a middle-class readership of the so-called keepsakes, elaborate and expensive gift books that had enjoyed a brief vogue with the aristocracy earlier in the century (Renier 1964). The success of the annuals proved Christmas to be a prime publishing season, and they were to become a stable complement to many juvenile periodicals, either as reprints of popular series or as bound yearly volumes of regular magazines.

2. Compare Bratton 1981, p. 63, who, judging by the output of children's books, assesses the heyday of religious publishing to be the 1850s–1860s.

As the political and social unrest of the 1830s and the 1840s gave way to the temporary equilibrium of the mid-nineteenth century, Britain stood unrivaled as the most powerful industrial nation, "the workshop of the world." The enfranchisement of the male industrial middle class in 1832 and the inaugura- tion of Free Trade with the repeal of the Corn Laws in 1846 established the financial and political leadership of the middle class. It is estimated that during the first half of the nineteenth century the middle class, ranging from clerks to bank managers, was the single most expanding social group. Initially, the expansion was largest among the lower reaches of the group, while in the third quarter of the century the number of families at the upper end of the scale more than tripled; and the middle class in general spent progressively more money on luxury consumption.[3] The sense of material security unified evangelical piety, which was essential in buttressing the middle-class family, and utilitarian prag- matism, which was central to the capitalist economy. In the form of "decorum," this union dominated the moral outlook of the Victorian era.

The new morality soon found its way into juvenile publishing. In 1855, twenty-four-year-old Samuel Orchard Beeton (1831–77) set out to create "a periodical literature for the young folk of our country, such as exists in no other land, sail you East or West" (Hyde 1951, pp. 49–50; Spain 1956). The young publisher-editor's pioneering spirit had already been tested in 1852 when he had struck a lead by being the first in Britain to import Harriet Beecher Stowe's *Uncle Tom's Cabin.*[4] The runaway bestseller helped to sustain Beeton's first periodical venture, the monthly *Englishwoman's Domestic Magazine,* launched in the same month as Stowe's novel. The periodical was the first to cater to middle-class women, and its immediate success demonstrated the commercial potential of this growing market.[5] The entry into this untapped market, gradu- ally linked by a national network of railways, was greatly facilitated in the 1850s by the disappearance of the various "taxes on knowledge." The tax on advertise-

3. According to Branca 1975, p. 2, the rate of increase for the middle class was 223 percent between 1803 and 1867 against an average increase in the population of 206 percent. Altick 1967, p. 306, records that in 1850–51 there were 83,300 families with an income of £150–£400, while in 1879–80 the number had risen to 285,100. The average income of a lower-middle-class family rose from £90 in 1851 to £110 in 1881. For the rise in the power of consumption, see Banks 1954, p. 101. Problems of definition and measurement of Victorian classes are discussed in Laslett 1965, pp. 216–18.

4. Within a year, forty British editions had been issued with a total sale of 1.5 million copies, "probably the greatest short-term sale of any book published in nineteenth-century England," according to Altick 1967, p. 384 (See also Cruse 1935, pp. 250–55).

5. On the development of the *Englishwoman's Domestic Magazine,* see White 1970, pp. 44–57. Highly conductive to the early success of the periodical was its publication in 24 monthly parts (November 1859–October 1861) of the *Book of Household Management,* written by the equally enterprising Mrs. Beeton. When appearing in book form (1861), the manual sold more than 60,000 copies within a year, and it has remained in print ever since (Hyde 1951, p. 109).

ments was abolished in 1853, and the newspaper tax was removed two years later. Production methods were also being transformed. In the 1840s, the steam press was put into wide use, and in 1855 *Lloyd's Weekly Newspaper* had the first American Hoe rotary press installed. In 1854, Esparto grass began to replace wood pulp, bringing down the price of paper, and better illustration techniques enhanced the use of steel engravings and color. Red, blue, and green embossed with gold graced the covers of children's books and also brightened, if less flamboyantly, juvenile periodicals.

In 1855, the versatile Beeton turned his interest from the middle-class woman to the middle-class boy with the publication of the *Boy's Own Magazine; An Illustrated Journal of Fact, Fiction, History and Adventure* (1855–74). With its thirty-two pages, this small octavo-sized paper with the orange-colored cover was the first juvenile periodical to promote "boy" as part of its title. As for the subtitle, said Beeton, it covered his express aim "to help to form the taste and influence the mind of a youth; whose glorious heritage it is to possess the Empire that their fathers have founded and preserved and whose duty it will be to hold that Empire, handing it down greater, more prosperous, to future generations" (Hyde 1951, p. 50).

The future wielders of world power were offered a wordy mixture of historical romances, biographies of "Poor Boys Who have become Great Men," as well as exotic adventures of snake charmers and kangaroos, buffalo and boaconstrictors, wolves and eagles (later volumes would run a few school stories). In addition, there were regular entries on nature study, "sports, and pastimes," scientific experiments ("the combustible thread," "the elastic egg") as well as riddles, puzzles, and charades. Early contributors included Captain Mayne Reid (*The Scalp Hunters* was serialized in the *Boy's Own Magazine*), the Reverend J. G. Wood (1827–89) whose books on natural history were already well known, and the itinerant W. B. Rands, a press gallery reporter in the House of Commons who also tried his hand at more youthful topics such as cricket for Beeton's journals. In volume two, Edgar Allan Poe's "Gold Bug" (1843) made its first British appearance. Later volumes featured historical serials by J. G. Edgar, (d. 1864) and W. H. G. Kingston (1814–80) and James Greenwood contributed a number of adventure stories.

The *Boy's Own Magazine* was a monthly for the (pre)adolescent boy. It was created at a time when the teenager had to wait another hundred years to be invented. The periodical initiated a trend that was to grow into a norm—namely, the grading of potential readers by age and sex.[6] By the same token, the

6. The *Girls' and Boys' Penny Magazine; Consisting of Light, Moral and Amusing Tales, calculated to Improve and Instruct the Rising Generation* (1832–33) and the *Boys' and Girls' Penny Magazine* (1832–33) were the first juvenile periodicals distinguishing between the sexes in their titles although still catering to the general reader in their contents. The former

magazine marked the beginning of a change in juvenile papers from religious didacticism or secular rationalism toward moral entertainment where an extrovert, imperial manliness mattered more than introspective piety or dry memorizing. The *Boy's Own Magazine* was, as Sheila Egoff remarks, "a turning point both in the social and the literary sphere, and formed one of the most important parts of that transition of the fifties, although more in what it foretold than in what it contributed" (Egoff 1951, p. 15).

Beeton as a publisher-editor personified a new, professional endeavor to balance moral obligation with commercial remuneration. From the *Englishwoman's Domestic Magazine* the idea of prize competitions was successfully introduced into the *Boy's Own Magazine*. The winning contributors on subjects like "True Courage," "The Use and Abuse of Animals," and "The Buccaneers and their Exploits" received a silver pencil-case ("value one guinea"). The maximum age of entry was sixteen, later twenty. A more direct promotional feature was a ballot, drawn among purchasers of each issue, for prizes such as gold chains, "silver lever watches," chemical chests, and pocket knives.

As the magazine established itself, cheap advertising gained ground and the number of advertisements grew. The ever-present "Holloway's Ointment, a Sovereign Remedy for the Afflicted," curing diseases as diverse as "ringworm, scald heads, recent tumors or old ulcers," and "Mr. Bennet's Model Watch" (the gentleman who also supplied the coveted prizes) found their places next to "Slack's Nickel Silver: tablespoons and forks per dozen 12*s*. 15*d*." and various notices from upholsterers, lithographers, and "the London Stereoscopic Company." Entrepreneurial salesmanship was balanced by editorial praise of the paper's qualities: "It is too *high*, too *solid*, too *good*" was Beeton's initial verdict, expressed in the preface of the first, bound volume, which was sold, as was customary, by a special offer at the end of the year's run to unload excess stock. "We then pitched the tone of the Magazine a little higher; and more Boys— more thousands of Boys—rushed to buy. The experiment succeeded" (1, p. ii). And so it did.

In 1862, at the end of its first series, and two years after the repeal of the paper duty, the *Boy's Own Magazine* could boast of having forty thousand readers (Hyde 1951, p. 53). This popularity caused the price of the paper to rise from

---

was a penny weekly, issued by G. Cowie, perhaps in an attempt to popularize the utilitarian monthlies that it emulated. The latter, also an eight-page weekly, was unusual in issuing imaginative narratives in the chapbook vein. "Ali Baba, or the Forty Thieves" (from the *Arabian Nights*) was featured along with Richard Johnson's "The Seven Champions of Christendom" (the old story about the deeds of St. George is first known to be in print in 1608) and a shortened version of *Goody Two Shoes* (1765). Only three issues have been preserved in the British Library. Before 1832, the titles of periodicals for the young would include *juvenile*, *youth*, *young persons*, *minor*, *child*, or *children*—names that remained popular in the religious monthlies throughout the century.

twopence to sixpence and sparked off the short-lived *Boy's Penny Magazine* (1862), the *Boy's Monthly Magazine* (1863–66), and numerous "Beeton's Books" on travel, chemistry, games, pets, and poetry. Behind the scenes, the success of the *Boy's Own Magazine* was demonstrated by its incorporation of the *Boy's Own Journal and Youth's Miscellany* in 1857, the *Youth's Instructor* one year later, and finally *Kingston's Magazine for Boys* in 1863. After Beeton's business failed in 1866, the magazine was bought by Messrs. Ward, Lock, and Company, and the fictional emphasis shifted toward adventure series. A "new second series" (1870–74) issued mainly reprints from 1863 to 1870. Finally, in 1889 the periodical was briefly and unsuccessfully resuscitated by George Alfred Henty (1832–1902) as *Beeton's Boy's Own Magazine* (Jay 9 October 1920, p. 164). Its time had come and passed.

The *Boy's Own Magazine* was created at a time when English children's books entered a golden era in which new genres were being adopted for different age groups. Thus, the adventure story was introduced by Captain Marryat's *Mr. Midshipman Easy* (1836); Charles Kingsley's *Westward Ho!* (1855) popularized the historical romance; Thomas Hughes inaugurated the school story with *Tom Brown's Schooldays* (1856), and, to crown them all, Lewis Caroll's (Charles L. Dodgson's) *Alice's Adventures in Wonderland* (1865) gave fantasy preeminence in the nursery. With their well-balanced commercial morality, Beeton's magazines conveyed this proliferation of genres in a periodical version catering to middle- and lower-middle-class boys, who could afford a monthly sixpence or twopence or who might persuade their fathers to do so. Other publishers followed Beeton's attempt to concoct a wholesome mixture of juvenile entertainment.

New quality magazines for older boys included Hodder and Stoughton's *Merry and Wise: a Magazine for Young People* (1865–71) and Routledge's *Every Boy's Magazine* (1862–88, title varies), both sixpenny monthlies featuring renowned authors and illustrators. Thus, in the first volume of *Every Boy's Magazine* the reader would find "The Wild Man of the West: A Tale of the Rocky Mountains," a serial written by R. M. Ballantyne, and short stories by J. G. Edgar (the first is "The True Story of the Man in the Iron Mask"). Regular entries included articles on football, cricket, and athletics, on "Our Domestic Pets," and on the use of a microscope and the preservation of shells and seaweeds.

In 1871, Cassell and Company addressed a new reading public by issuing the monthly *Little Folks* (1871–1933), catering to younger children but otherwise resembling the other periodicals with its attractive illustrations and well-known contributors. The traditional type of magazine for both sexes of various ages also saw important newcomers. Alexander Strahan's sixpenny monthly, *Good Words for the Young* (1868–77, title changes), edited by Norman Macleod from 1868 to 1870 and by George MacDonald from 1870 to 1872, blended a broad Christian outlook with a keen interest in fairy tales. Thus, in its opening issue began Charles Kingsley's "Madam How and Lady Why" (published as a book

Routledge's Magazine for Boys, no. 45 (September 1868), facing p. 576. The
mid-Victorian boys' periodicals introduced colored pages carrying advertisements. This stable feature denotes publishers' commercial interests, just as it
highlights the sex-specific ideal of useful recreation.

in 1870) and also George MacDonald's "At the Back of the North Wind," which, when issued in book form in 1871, became one of the best-known children's tales of the period. While Kingsley replaces the factual approach of Peter Parley with two little fairies who explain the wonders of nature, Mac-Donald works his parable of death and eternal life into an account of poor Diamond's strange journey toward the back of the North Wind. The story line clearly resembles Hans Christian Andersen's "Ice Maiden," translated in 1863, and other Andersen stories were serialized in later issues of the periodical.

The famous Danish storyteller found an even stronger promotion in *Aunt Judy's Magazine* (1866–85). This sixpenny monthly undoubtedly won the highest critical acclaim among the quality periodicals for its fervent defense of the fabulous and its unflagging standards of literary merit: "We have everywhere sought for excellence, both in art and literature," it was explained in the opening issue. *Aunt Judy* was the brainchild of Mrs. Alfred Gatty, its editor until her death at the age of sixty-four in 1873, and the monthly remained a family effort. Mrs. Gatty's daughter, Julia Horatia Ewing, was a main contributor. Her quiet domestic stories such as "Mrs. Overtheway's Remembrances" and "Six to Sixteen" appeared among tales by Andersen and Lewis Carroll. Such fictional quality, however, seemed incompatible with the proprietors' financial prosperity. "The absence of 'sensational' tales—the endeavour to instruct in virtue, without drawing loathsome pictures of vice—. . . restricts [*Aunt Judy's*] circulation to the judicious and the domestic," its hardworking editor wrote in 1867 when trying to "open a little campaign" to make the periodical "more generally known" ("Editor's Address," *Aunt Judy's Magazine* 4, no. 19 [November 1867], pp. 1–2).[7] But the appeal of *Aunt Judy* was restricted to the vicarage and the university lodge.

The "sensational" tales that Mrs. Gatty and others laboriously struggled against were a group of juvenile magazines whose enormous output rapidly ousted all that had gone before, including the more or less subsidized religious periodicals. The *Boy's Own Magazine* had not only inaugurated a grading of readers according to age and sex, but also a literary separation according to class. While the religious monthlies, for obvious moral reasons, tried to reach a wide range of children, the Beeton-type publishers, combining morals and profits, had a narrower aim. Hence, a whole group of lower-middle-class and working-class juveniles was excluded, both for financial reasons and because they were nurtured on a completely different type of fictional fare.

With the advancement of capitalist production, the small freeholders and manufacturers, the shopkeepers and the domestic craftsmen—the social core groups of evangelism—were gradually replaced with new lower-middle-class

---

7. Only in one year did the magazine actually yield its proprietors a profit (Lang 1980, p. 23; see also Hazeltine 1940).

and working-class occupations in towns and cities. Vacancies in banks, in the transport and publishing industries, for instance, were peopled by clerks, technicians, and supervisors—all men with social aspirations removed from their cultural and religious backgrounds. Similarly, mechanization and the capital-intensive production of steel and iron increasingly pushed rural artisans and laborers toward urban factories and industrial workshops and made women and children more marginal elements of the paid labor force.

The urban working class, which had been most deeply affected by the upheavals of the Industrial Revolution, was least affected by evangelical religion, and working people in the cities had been especially hostile to the sugar-coated sermonizings of the religious tracts. By the 1830s, the swelling numbers and increasing purchasing power of the urban working and lower middle classes were catered to by a handful of publishers, the so-called Salisbury Square group, providing this market with entertainment as cheap as the old chapbooks and somewhat more alluring. A cascade of domestic romances, pirated and plagiarized serials of the solid, three-decker novels, as well as sensational stories or "penny bloods" issued in weekly parts, flooded the literary market. [8]

The penny bloods were especially popular among urban adolescents. These stories were a spine-tingling medley of crime and vice, feeding on at least two literary traditions: the chapbook editions of the *Newgate Calendar, or Malefactors' Bloody Register* (1774), which had chronicled the vivacious lives and vicious endings of robbers, rogues, and other renowned criminals, and the Gothic vogue, typified by Ann Radcliffe's *Mysteries of Udolpho* (1794): pitch-dark dungeons, creaking doors and howling wolves created the stirring settings for the rescue by a disinherited young nobleman of virtuous maidens hopelessly trapped by perverted counts or deranged nuns. To this literary heritage was sometimes added a dose of slapstick humor in the music-hall vein.

The longest of these weekly eight-page serials written by a single author was undoubtedly Edward Viles' *Black Bess, or the Knight of the Road*. For 254 weeks, it recounted the hazardous adventures of the notorious highwayman Dick Turpin and his three cronies, bringing the story to a total of 2.5 million words, or 2,028 pages (Turner 1976, p. 54). But perhaps the most popular, and certainly the most macabre, penny hero was Sweeney Todd, the "demon barber" of Fleet Street. When seated to be shaved, Sweeney's unfortunate customers mysteriously disappear only to reemerge as main ingredients in the delicious meat pies manufactured by his neighbor and accomplice who is, in most series, a woman. Edward Lloyd of Salisbury Square is best known, perhaps, as the proprietor of *Lloyd's Weekly Newspaper* (founded in 1842), but he was also the first to publish,

---

8. The development of popular literature for adults has been well documented (See especially James 1963, chaps. 3, 4, 6; Neuburg 1977, pp. 144–70; Turner 1976, chap. 1). Women's popular reading-matter is explored in Mitchell 1981.

and to profit on, the excitements of this cannibalistic couple (in *A String of Pearls*, 1840). Sweeney Todd was later revived in numerous stories, plays, films, and even ballet. Lloyd's manager described how Sweeney Todd and similar series had their popular appeal tried out: "Our publications circulate among a class so different in education and social position from the readers of three-volume novels that we sometimes distrust our own judgement and place the manuscript in the hands of an illiterate person—a servant, or machine boy, for instance. If they pronounce favourably upon it, we think it will do."[9]

Even if apocryphal, the explanation demonstrates that the sensational penny blood, though originally aimed at an adult audience, was equally entertaining to an adolescent readership. By the 1860s, fierce competition made the penny-part publishers increase the lurid details of their narratives (according to Turner [1976], especially sexual innuendo), while they consciously sought to captivate younger customers by introducing as heroes adolescent pirates, soldiers, apprentices, and errand boys. This combination was particularly effective in the so-called Wild Boys series. Public outcries, echoing Hannah More, persistently deplored the sensational excrescences as the cause of working people's alleged immorality. Not only the Beeton-style publications, but also new religious periodicals were unsuccessfully launched as counterattacks on what the Reverend J. Erskine Clarke called the "blood and thunder." In an attempt to undercut this "trash" (at least in price), he brought out the *Children's Prize* (1863–1931, title changes) and the halfpenny weekly, the *Chatterbox* (1866–1948).

Entirely true to tradition and quite contrary to its alluring title, the *Chatterbox* in its opening issue promised to "whisper a few words about the solemn lessons we must learn from our Bibles . . . if we would be happy here, and happy in the great For-Ever!" (1, no. 1 [December 1866], p. 2).[10] Happiness was not exactly John Ruskin's response after reading the *Children's Prize*, which was singled out for severe criticism in *Fors Clavigera* (1875) because of its lack of beauty and its sanctimonious preponderance which would bring its readers to "ruin—inevitable and terrible, such as no nation has yet suffered" (Ruskin 1907, p. 263). But where well-meaning publishers and poets failed to direct the morality of the young, the police succeeded, at least for a while. They suppressed publication of one of the Wild Boys series, *The Wild Boys of London*, thus

9. Recorded by Thomas Frost, a compositor-turned-publisher, in *Forty Years Recollections, Literary and Political* (London, 1880), and quoted in Turner 1976, pp. 20–1. Frost's career is briefly described in Vincent 1982, pp. 152–53.

10. From January 1867, the magazine was also issued as a 3 *d.* monthly. In "The Youth of a Children's Magazine" (1931), reprinted in Darton 1982, pp. 339–48, Darton casts interesting sidelights on Clarke's autocratic editorship and his own difficulties in updating the contents of the periodical when succeeding Clarke as editor of the *Chatterbox* and the *Children's Prize* in 1901, a post he retained until 1930.

indirectly bringing about the creation of a "new and original style" of boys' magazines (Rollington 1913, p. 28; Turner 1976, p. 66).

Most publishers, after this onslaught by middle-class morality, continued by well-trodden, if somewhat narrower, paths milling out so-called penny dreadfuls for youngsters with few coppers to spare.[11] Edwin J. Brett (1828–95), however, staked out a completely new narrative domain for this growing readership at a safer distance from social pressure. As the founder of the Newsagents Publishing Company, which specialized in sensational fiction, Brett possessed a lucrative sense of timing. In November 1866, he launched a penny weekly, the *Boys of England; A Magazine of Sport, Sensation, Fun, and Instruction* (1866–99). Charles Stevens, the editor of the first nine issues until Brett himself took over the editorship, promised in his initial reader address "to enthral you by wild and wonderful, but healthy fiction" (*Boys of England* 1, no. 1 [24 November 1866], p. 16).[12] This token attack on the penny dreadful was nicely balanced by a prize competition of unrivaled dimensions: Fourteen hundred trophies were advertised, the first prize being two Shetland ponies. One may only speculate how impecunious winners would accommodate their gifts.

The *Boys of England* became an instant success. For his weekly penny, the reader got not just part of a single story as in the penny dreadful, but an exciting sixteen pages of historical romance, a sea adventure, along with the occasional school serial, all laced with large illustrations, usually in black and white. Apart from Charles Stevens, early contributors included John Cecil Stagg, Captain Mayne Reid and Percy B. St. John. From 1871, when the renowned Jack Harkaway first made his bow, the school hero became institutionalized as a stable ingredient in this and other popular boys' papers.

As in the narratives, the clipped style of the penny dreadful dominated entries in the magazine on sports, jokes ("Quips and cranks"), as well as the infrequent correspondence column. Detailed descriptions of scientific experiments and articles on nature study as found in the Beeton publications were the obvious losers in trying to keep up such a breezy pace. Brett's rewarding publishing formula created a new equilibrium between morals and profits. Within the first

---

11. This transition from the adult periodical, the "blood and thunder," or "penny blood," of the 1830s–1850s on to the more subdued, juvenile "penny dreadful," which became popular in the 1860s, has often been remarked on (See e.g. Dunae 1979, pp. 133–34; Haining 1975, pp. 17, 302; James 1963, p. 44, and James 1970, pp. 127–28; Turner 1976, pp. 73–75; Wilson 1932). Some of these critics note the building up of a moral pressure from a concerned middle class, but no one links this with equally harsh economic pressure as a reason for change.

12. In later recollections, Brett maintained that a moral responsibility to lead a "crusade against pernicious literature" was his main inducement in launching the *Boys of England* (Jay 29 March 1919, p. 89).

The *Boys of England; A Magazine of Sport, Sensation, Fun, and Instruction* 1, no. 1 (24 November 1866), front cover. The most successful of the mid-Victorian boys' periodicals, striking a new balance between moralism and commercialism.

few weeks, the circulation of the *Boys of England* steadied itself around "the then meritorious figure of 150,000," an opinion which Brett the editor confirmed in the early 1870s (Hopperton 1962, p. 34; *Boys of England*, 13, no. 332 [22 March 1873], p. 352). Thanks to Jack Harkaway's popular escapades, the weekly circulation by 1879 had reached 250,000 copies, an unprecedented popularity which indeed "changed the pattern of Victorian juvenile fiction" (James 1970, p. 128).[13] The paper held sway until 1899 when halfpenny ventures were rapidly undercutting former successes.

Stevens in his first "Editor's Address" had imagined his readers "returning from school, from the office, the workroom, or the shop, and taking up our weekly number of the 'Boys' to soothe and enliven your 'caretired thoughts'" (*Boys of England* 1, no. 1 [24 November 1866], p. 16). The paper, indeed, did have the greatest following among lower-middle-class and working-class adolescents.[14] The boast below the title in later issues that the paper was "subscribed to by H. R. H. Prince Arthur, the Prince Imperial of France and Count William Bernstorff" certainly did not encompass a general acceptance of the periodical across the social board (even if the boast was true). Thus, G. L. Beresford, Rudyard Kipling's friend and the prototype of "McTurk" in *Stalky & Co.*, stated in his memoirs that Kipling was very angry at the popularity that the *Boys of England* and similar publications enjoyed with their fellow boarders: "It really got on his nerves that they should keep on reading *Jack Harkaway* and the cheap paper-backed novels that were to be had in such plenty in those days, and which Gigger [Kipling] seemed to take as an infliction aimed especially at himself" (Musgrave 1985, p. 114).

But perhaps precisely because the *Boys of England* was nerve-racking and because it was almost invariably banned by conscientious parents, a good many middle-class boys were spellbound by its contents. H. G. Wells and Havelock Ellis were among the more aspiring readers devouring, as Ellis said, the "wild and extravagant action" of the paper for a brief period in their boyhood. "It is doubtless in its appeal to the latent motor energies of developing youth that its fascination lies," Ellis ruminated in his autobiography (Turner 1976, p. 76). Motor energies or not, the action-packed stories in the *Boys of England* put the more sedate quality papers completely in the shade, while its large format and neat style, its competitions, and the broader range of contents compared favorably with the penny dreadful to the lower reaches of the readership.

The success of the *Boys of England* inaugurated one of the fiercest periods of

13. Authors were paid fifty shillings for each installment that was typeset for fifty shillings and printed for five shillings per thousand. Sale price to the trade was fifty shillings a thousand, leaving Brett a nice margin of profit. (Jay 18 January 1919, p. 49).

14. James 1973, p. 90, notes that "the main readership" was the "upwardly mobile lower middle classes." But it seems evident, not only from the editorial address but also from the correspondence pages, that the paper reached many older working-class boys.

competition in the history of juvenile magazines. Charles Fox, Ralph Rolling-ton, and James Henderson were among the notorious contestants, but Brett's closest rival was William L. Emmett, another old hand in the penny-part business. According to the account of the publishing feud between the two firms by Ralph Rollington (H. J. Allingham), Emmett launched the *Young Gen-tleman's Journal* in 1867 as an answer to the *Boys of England*. The following year, Brett started the *Young Men of Great Britain*, while Emmett followed suit with the *Young Gentlemen of Britain*. In 1869, Emmett started out with the *Young Briton*, closely followed by Brett's *Sons of Britannia* in 1870. But the grand finale came in 1872 when Brett brought out the *Rovers of the Sea* and Emmett issued the *Rover's Log*—both on the same day! (Rollington 1913, pp. 28–9, 65–70). [15] Though founded on personal antagonism bordering on the ludicrous, the Brett-Emmett feud symbolizes the jungle laws governing the new periodical market at this time. Their nearly identical publications were portents of future trends in this market.

By the 1870s, it was clear that the religious monthly, though still energetically backed by well-intentioned adults, was not going to carry the day in periodical publishing for the young. The secular magazine, so drastically transformed since Newbery's bold beginnings, had come to stay. The main innovation of the mid-nineteenth century was the emergence of periodicals for older boys and what we would now call adolescents. This was where the money lay. These readers were not only the ones with pennies to spare: they also, to varying degrees, possessed some literacy and a little leisure for literary pursuits. The expansion of the boys' magazines and their more selective social appeal indicate how the trade was going to develop under the weight of commercial competition. Publishers had to be increasingly attuned to the needs and preferences of their intended readership.

15. Brett's publications seem to have been the more popular. According to an answer to a correspondent in the *Boys of England* 3, no. 78 (15 May 1868), its new companion paper, the *Young Men of Great Britain*, had a weekly circulation of 150,000–160,000 copies, a likely figure compared to the fate of its precursor. Both publishers made a fortune, though. Brett subsidized the maintenance of a salvage vessel at Southend and various cricket and football clubs, undertakings that were all well-publicized in his papers. By the 1870s, Brett and Emmett each earned about £8,000 a year (Hopperton 1962, p. 32). People occupied in highly skilled manual work would make £50–£73 a year in 1867 (Branca 1975, p. 45).

6

Secular Moralities:
Mid-Victorian Childhood and Youth

CHILDREN WHO grew up in the middle decades of the nineteenth century experienced the Victorian golden age with its increased prosperity, its social doubt, and its scientific acumen. But as earlier in the century, juvenile life experiences differed widely. Kate Greenaway's delicate illustrations in contemporary children's books epitomize received notions of the young: little girls, all violet eyes, golden ringlets, and frilly white muslin frocks, peacefully watching their carefree brothers playing with hoops in a spacious garden or earnestly preoccupied with their miniature trains or toy theatres. The innocence of childhood truly came of age for grown-ups in the Victorian era, precisely at a time when the harsher realities of the adult world could no longer be written off as unfortunate, but temporary, inconveniences.

The image of perfect childhood hid stark contrasts. In 1851, 35.4 percent of Britain's nearly eighteen million inhabitants were below fifteen years of age, while thirty years later the percentage had increased to 36.5, taken out of a population of nearly twenty-six million. More than four-fifths of those children were working class. But since infant mortality remained high, and even increased in working-class families, it was mostly middle-class children who came to feel the joys and the exasperations of a large and self-contained family. The average of 5.5 or 6 live children in the mid-Victorian home concealed considerable differences in women's experience of childbirth and in the babies' chances of survival (Census 1951, p. 22; Census 1915, p. 127; Banks 1954, p. 3).

In the overcrowded and infested slum areas of the urban centers, improvements in sewage were especially slow, and the physical and mental deterioration resulting from bad housing and ill-health was felt by more and more people. The Industrial Revolution had propelled a migration from village to town and from town to city, so that by 1850 half of all Britons were town dwellers: by 1880 it was two-thirds. In 1801, only eight towns held more than fifty thousand people, but by 1851 that number had swelled to twenty-nine towns, nine of which had more than one hundred thousand inhabitants. Although London had become the largest city in the world, the population explosion was more keenly felt in the factory towns of the Midlands and the North. The middle-class move toward the countrified suburbs increased with prosperity, and the fumes, the rubbish yards, and the dungheaps of the inner cities were left to the destitute working class. Octavia Hill (d. 1912), one of the first campaigners for open spaces to urban children, described her entry into one of the slum courts created between the back-to-back houses: "The children are crawling or sitting on the hard hot stones till every corner of the place looks alive, and it seems as if I must step on them if I am to walk up the Court" (Walvin 1983, p. 235).

Like contemporary social reformers such as Mary Carpenter and Henry Mayhew, Hill was fired by an earnest Christian compassion channeled through her middle-class morality. This blend characterized not only the energetic voluntary endeavors of the period, but also it influenced the statutory reforms that were gradually gaining ground. The economic and political leadership of the wealthy middle class solidified, in modified form, the Evangelicals' family ideal as a social norm. Measured against its "natural" standards of behavior, the different personal relations of the poor not only compared infavorably, but also seemed to stem from individual defaults. While a growing body of feminist research has uncovered the origins and explored the effects upon women and men of the Victorians' pervasive domestic ideology, little is known about its implications for the young.

"PERFECT FREEDOM AND TOTAL IGNORANCE"

Toward mid-century, the debate on middle-class and lower-middle-class child-rearing turned secular and professional. The clearest indications of that develop-ment were the heated debates on juvenile masturbation—a recurring topic through the latter half of the century. While such debates are, of course, no safe measure of actual socialization practices, the shifting tone and emphasis of argumentation are nevertheless a good indication of the mental setting of child-rearing. Child-care manuals, which had formerly been written by clergymen or concerned mothers and which had often been directed toward both parents, were increasingly becoming the doctor's address to his conscientious female clientele. Religion still bounded the lives of the young, but professional interest shifted from inner faith and individual introspection toward "good works" and orderly conduct as the measurable signs of a pure soul.

Bodily cleanliness, too, became a powerful symbol, which was all the more complex because it took root at a time when housekeeping was still an arduous daily battle against smoke and dirt, making the starched pinafores of daughters and servants seem necessary inoculations against social and moral backsliding (Davidoff 1974, p. 413). Advice books became preoccupied with the physical care of children, making ventilation in the nursery and the proper clothing of boys and girls subjects for minute description. This interest in children's physical well-being was as equivocal as it was complex. White frills for daughters and immaculate collars for the sons were signs not only of spiritual and social elevation, but also of sexual innocence. In the battle waged early in the century between the Puritan belief in the inherent evil of children and the rationalist or romantic notions of natural goodness, the secular notions carried the day.

Although juvenile salvation remained a major adult concern, sinfulness was increasingly expressed in terms of sexual rather than spiritual transgression. Religion had acted as an unconscious means of sexual regulation for groups with social aspirations. By the mid-nineteenth century a more pragmatic outlook of the established middle class at once popularized an image of childish innocence and facilitated a more conscious regulation of juvenile sexuality. The late Michel Foucault's proposition that this sexual regulation should not be thought of merely as repression but as a concomitant to power and self-control has permanently dislodged simplified notions of Victorian prudery and censorship set against modern liberation and sexual permissiveness. But in exploring the nineteenth-century obsession with sexuality, we should not forget who discussed those matters and who had power over them. In Foucault's theory, the working class in general and women and children in particular are at the receiving end of the educated males' mutual fascination with sexuality as a unique means of self-expression and self-regulation. The actual resistance expressed by these objectified groups is difficult to perceive and analyze within Foucault's omnipresent power structure (Foucault 1979).[1]

The innocence of childhood should rather be regarded as a double-edged concept: its development marked a positive view of the young as individual beings adults might emulate, but this view was made possible only by obliterating from memory all sexual and aggressive impulses. As original sin was being refashioned into gendered biology, this obliteration took on sex-specific forms. The image of innocence landed parents and professionals with a curious, if unconscious, contradiction. Although the psychologist Henry Maudsley had alleged (in 1867) that "the purity and innocence of the child's mind, insofar as they exist, testify to the absence of mind; and the impulses which actually move it are the selfish impulses of passion," child sexuality was blocked out as mental anathema, or it was labeled as being pathological (Kern 1973, p. 135). Thus, Dr. William Acton in his popular *Functions and Disorders of the Reproductive Organs* (1857) confidently affirmed that "in healthy subjects, and especially in children brought up in the pure air, and amid the simple amusements of the country, perfect freedom from, and indeed total ignorance of any sexual affection is, as it should always be, the rule" (Gathorne-Hardy 1972, p. 266). At the

---

1. Foucault builds his argument mainly around official printed sources: religious treatises, legal documents and medical books, leaving the raped servant or the guilty masturbating child as (perhaps necessary) silent victims. For a review and criticism of Foucault's theory as seen in relation to other approaches to the study of sexuality, see Weeks 1981, pp. 1–18.

same time, the inevitable expressions of juvenile sexuality were shaped according to the Victorians' strict gender norms. The problem of maintaining a view of childish innocence while raising the young for different roles became acute in adolescence. This was not only a period when bodily changes in both boys and girls made sexuality an inescapable issue, it was also a period over which adults exercised an increasing control through the agencies of family and school.[2]

"A CALM AND HEALTHFUL ATMOSPHERE"

Servants were a hallmark of the Victorian middle-class home, but they influenced children's lives to different degrees. Our image of the Victorian family, luxuriating on cucumber sandwiches and croquet games while being surrounded by a plenitude of well-starched servants, is an ideal that was shaped by a wealthy, albeit rapidly growing, minority of the middle class, the people who most diligently put their thoughts on record (Branca 1974, p. 183). Prosperous merchants, manufacturers, and professionals, who were all men, spent most of their time in the city on business or in their clubs. Domestic life was equally segregated with wives being socially and economically dependent upon their husbands, children being subservient to parents, and a duplicate hierarchy of employees carrying out the lowly and most irksome daily tasks. The amply staffed households facilitated parental imitation of the physical and emotional distance from children that by midcentury had become the corollary of the ideal of childhood innocence, which could only be kept up by avoiding close contact with the young. Children "should be reared in a calm and healthful atmosphere as far aloof as possible from the restless world of their elders" insisted the *St. James Medley* in 1862 (Lang 1980, p. 21).

With paterfamilias receding into the background of his children's lives as an unquestioned but distant shadow of authority, the contours of maternal power were sharpened. In affluent homes, the mother was the day-to-day ruler for children and servants alike. But since the mother often busied herself with philanthropic or social activities a nursery-maid or nanny acted as a mother-substitute for young children in the nursery, now an obligatory room in large homes. For older children and adolescent girls a governess (preferably French) might be employed as their home tutor.[3]

2. The intense debate in the mid-nineteenth century over adolescents' masturbation (especially that of boys) highlights the contradictions inherent in the notion of innocence and it demonstrates the intensity with which adults sought to maintain their control. For surveys of the debate and its professional context, see Spitz 1952; Hare 1962; Neuman 1975; Comfort 1967, pp. 69–113; Kern 1974; and Fee 1978. An undercurrent in the spate of Victorian publications on sexuality did acknowledge as healthy both male and female sexual expressions (See Cominos 1963, esp. pp. 44–48; Pearsall 1971, pp. 241–53, 292–303; Smith 1977).

3. In 1871, there were merely 55,000 governesses in Britain, not nearly enough to serve

The many servants left upper-class and upper-middle-class children room to maneuver between different levels of authority. Thus, they learned an early lesson in class differences. Large households also made it easier for siblings to create closed childhood worlds within which they shaped and resolved conflicts themselves. Constance Maynard, for example, who was born in 1849 as the second youngest of six children in a wealthy family (her father was a successful businessman) and who herself became a pioneer of women's education, recalled that her home-life was "extremely smooth and cheerful and orderly on the surface, and sometimes it was rough and hard underneath" (Gorham 1982, p. 156).

The majority of middle- and lower-middle-class households, while often trying to emulate their betters, could not afford such elaborate childrearing arrangements. Their situation was dominated by the expansion in the 1840s and 1850s of trade and the transformation of industry, which created new urban occupations to be filled by men with social aspirations. A central and growing segment of families, comprising almost half of the middle class in 1867, lived on 100 to 300 pounds a year (Branca 1975, p. 45; Best 1971, pp. 82–83). This income allowed for the employment of only one "general servant" (also called a "maid-of-all-work" in a less genteel but more accurate expression) or perhaps a cook and a nursery-maid-cum-housemaid. Under these circumstances, mothers and their children were much closer in physical terms.

Motherhood was a demanding responsibility that became all the more taxing because of the acute need for social advancement through jobs or marriage, which often had to be furthered without the assistance of social connections or established cultural traditions. Thus, in H. G. Wells' small Bromley home (then on the outskirts of London), his mother had the sole responsibility for childrearing since the family employed only an occasional charwoman. Mrs. Wells made extreme efforts to keep up appearances under adverse circumstances. She prohibited her young son from taking off his coat when playing with other children "because my underclothing was never quite up to the promise of my exterior garments. It was never ragged but it abounded in compromises. This hindered my playing games" (Wells 1934, p. 73).[4]

---

middle-class needs. Average wages ranged between £20 and £45 per year, a cost that was prohibitive to most middle-class budgets, but still well below the salient £70–£130 demanded by the average boarding establishment (Branca 1975, p. 46; Pedersen 1975, p. 141).

4. The division of domestic functions in many families was in total agreement with the bourgeois distinction between mental and manual work. This distinction was fortified by pre-Freudian utilitarian beliefs whereby the training in orderly conduct as well as the daily routines of cleaning, cooking, feeding, and bathing were merely "technical" elements of upbringing that could be separated as inferior from spiritual and intellectual guidance. Such beliefs can help to explain why nusery-maids were often the youngest, least experienced, and certainly the worst paid group of domestic servants. In 1851, 46 percent of nursery-maids

Aunt Judy's Magazine, no. 3 (July 1866), facing p. 186. The ideal division of sex-roles in the Victorian nursery is physically demonstrated in F. Gilbert's illustration to "Eòineîn's" poem "Wooden Legs:" the girl, sitting at her brother's feet, deplores his wish to become a soldier facing injuries and death.

Most middle- and lower-middle-class children would experience neither unbridled lenience nor extreme severity, but a lot of adult anxiety and concern over their behavior. This "golden mean" of upbringing was, crucially, built on a thorough sexual regulation in early childhood.[5] The effects of this regulation, in both modest and wealthy homes, colored the experiences of boys and girls in different measure.

The mid-Victorian decades witnessed a burgeoning of mechanized toy industries providing the well-heeled young customer with everything from steam engines to talking dolls and books turning into miniature theatres when opened, while offering to less affluent children inexpensive tin soldiers, marbles, and penny dolls.[6] The commercial success of standardized toys and reading matter at once reflected the widespread application of childhood as a concept and reinforced the stricter gender separation emerging in middle-class childhood and adolescence. In typical mid-Victorian fashion, "useful recreation" was propagated for both sexes. But while boys were encouraged to do fretwork, to perform chemical experiments, and to play football or cricket, girls were relegated to more sedate indoor occupations such as sewing and the collecting of pressed flowers.[7]

Reading formed perhaps the most important useful recreation, and the evening reading circle has become almost a truism of Victorian domestic life. Both boys and girls had far more specially designed books and magazines to choose from than earlier generations. This wider selection became more sex-specific, and the contents were examined closely by discriminating parents who would ink

were under the age of twenty, in 1871 the percentage had risen to 51, 23 percent of whom were less than fourteen years old (McBride 1978, p. 49). Their earnings would be similar to those of a general servant, namely, £9–£14 a year (Branca 1975, p. 55).

5. This sexual regulation would generally include intense toilet-training from an early age, reprimands for bed-wetting and punishment of autoerotic practices or mere curiosity (Kern 1974; Robertson 1974; McBride 1978).

6. England seems to have invented the baby doll and some specialized manufacturers produced only eyes or wigs for these novelties. The equivocal function of toys exemplify the intrinsic paradox of childhood: while midget tin soldiers and miniature dolls highlight childish irresponsibility, their existence and their parody of adult occupations point toward their preparatory functions. For general descriptions of Victorian toys and children's play, see, for example, Walvin 1983, and 1982, pp. 79–100. Among contemporary accounts of toy manufacturing, Henry Mayhew offers a mine of useful information (See Thompson and Yeo 1973, pp. 337–59).

7. Thus, E. Landell, author of *The Girl's Own Toy-maker and Book of Recreation* (London, 1860), devoted only three pages to outdoor games (Walvin 1983, p. 230). Conversely, Mrs. Child, author of *The Girl's Own Book*, 14th ed. (London, 1848), included gymnastic exercises specifically selected for girls ("calisthenics") just as "skating, driving hoop, and other boyish sports" were recommended "provided they can be pursued within the inclosure of a garden, or court; in the street, they would, of course, be highly improper" (Temple 1970, p. 159).

out or paste over improper passages or who would plainly prohibit what they deemed unsuitable forms of reading matter. As the formative influence of secular literature was acknowledged and as reference to the right sort of fiction became an essential element of "good" conversation, girls' reading in particular was censored, encumbering such fictional surprises as were found by Marjory Fleming earlier in the century (Gorham 1982, pp. 163–64, 184–85). The copious articles on everything from skating and rabbit-feeding to angling and photography featured in the *Boy's Own Magazine* and similar papers testified to a widening of boys' activities. Since the boys' papers had no female equivalents, they indirectly highlighted the strict gender separation, whose expression the new magazines in turn helped to shape.

While it can be safely deduced that commercial as well as professional agencies sought to reinforce the gender differences of mid-Victorian children, it would be misguided to conclude that middle-class girls had no available options but passive docility while the boys were offered all the fun. Boys were indeed allowed a wider range of action than were their sisters, but during childhood both sexes still relied very much on their own resources: puzzles were cut out from colored magazines, matchboxes and tea chests were used to make doll's houses or Noah's Arks, and games such as dominoes, draughts, and bagatelle needed little fancy equipment. Alice Pollock (née Wykeham-Martin), born in 1868 as the eldest of three children in an upper-middle-class family of Broad Church outlook (her father was a magistrate in Swindon), was raised by a strict governess from Norfolk. She instructed her wards in a proper conduct according to their sex, whipping them when they misbehaved and rapping their knuckles with a long wooden ruler if they rested their hands on the dinner table. Still, as a girl Alice bowled hoops on her walks, went skating in wintertime, and did fretwork just like boys. Being sent to bed in the afternoon as a punishment prompted Alice's and her younger brother Robert's ingenuity at evading their elders and betters: "I had a basket for holding string, to which I attached a long string and let it down from my bedroom window to Robert, who was then small. He filled it with delicious ripe gooseberries, which I hauled up and devoured with great satisfaction. It was not such fun in the winter, when we had no light." Alice Pollock never remembered "being played with by grown-ups, except at Christmas when they organised and sometimes joined in musical chairs, Sir Roger de Coverley, and hunt-the-slipper" (Pollock 1971, pp. 40, 49).

The mid-Victorian conflict, noted earlier, between childish innocence and sexual divisions in childrearing thus emanated as contradictions in children's lives. Contrary to earlier nineteenth-century attitudes, the increasing and direct preoccupation with juvenile sexuality made these contradictions more tangible as personal conflicts. Just as Alice Pollock experienced an opposition between feminine decorum and girlish vitality, so her brothers would note a conflict between parental relishing in their boyish exuberance and the demands made to continence and a manly self-discipline. For young children, the collectivity and partial autonomy of a "juvenile republic" that existed even under modest circumstances might enhance their abilities to solve personal problems. For adolescents, however, sexual divisions were crucially reinforced. For while the mid-Victorian girl as a rule stayed at home, her brothers were now more likely to be sent away to school. Girls were taught sewing and cooking, even when the family's affluence rendered such female accomplishments obsolete. Boys were confronted in day, grammar, or public school with Latin prose, algebra, and "manly" games as indirect, but acknowledged, preparations for a future career.

New and reformed girls' schools were slowly encroaching upon the old female academies from midcentury onward and feminist stirrings might also reach susceptible ears. But the impact of these developments was still restricted to a select minority of adolescent girls, especially those from London. For most middle-class girls the contradictions of their upbringing were perhaps deeper than had been the case for their mothers. But although they were often engaged in philanthropic work or might experience a brief spell at a day or even boarding school, their personal problems revolved around the home, and they had to find their solutions within the domestic sphere.[8]

Charlotte Yonge's and other popular books for adolescent girls negotiated the contradictions of femininity within the purview of domesticity and personal relations (Bratton 1981, pp. 148–90; Cadogan and Craig 1976, pp. 15–43). For boys, books as well as magazines were beginning to chart other vistas in accordance with the new and optimistic prospects offered mid-Victorian men of the middle class. From an early age, the boy was informed that growing up meant some sort of break. School as an institution exemplified the contradictions between boy and man, release and responsibility. The reformed public schools, as they developed during the midcentury decades, at once highlighted those contradictions and mediated their effects. The preeminent social and literary influence of the public school ethos during the latter part of the century testifies to the success of this formula.

"MANLY, EARNEST, AND TRUE"

The mid-Victorian decades saw a close tailoring of education to perceived class and gender differences. To the growing number of well-off middle-class parents, public school training for their sons buttressed a newfound social status,

8. For children's, and especially girls', involvement from the age of twelve or thirteen in working parties, children's bazaars, and in the fund-raising activities of missionary societies, as tract distributors and collectors, see Prochaska, 1978, pp. 99–118, and 1977, p. 75. Despite these genuine outlets for female energies, contemporary death rates for girls and women exceeded the male death rate only between the ages of ten and thirty-four. Half of these girls and women died of tuberculosis. See Johansson 1977, pp. 166, 169, who offers anxiety, deficient diet, and poor occupational options (but not corseting as contemporaries suggested) as main dangers to female health.

while for the boys themselves this training secured their genteel introduction into a business or, more likely, a professional career. After their disrepute earlier in the century, the public schools began to forge a viable connection between the new middle-class demands and their traditional role as breeding grounds for the aristocracy.

Thomas Arnold's reforms as headmaster at Rugby (1828–42) have come to symbolize this mediation. To the classical curriculum of Latin and Greek parsing, glossing, and memorizing, he added a moral training whose earnestness and idealism had clear evangelical overtones. Arnold's ideal of the "Christian gentleman" was promoted through a firm and hierarchical self-government. The prefects, chosen among the senior pupils of the sixth form (grade), had their power and privileges widened along with an increase in their responsibilities. By their personal example they were to set the moral tone of the school, and they were to be the living proofs that juvenile submission to authority ultimately bred conscientious adults. The public school system simultaneously removed its pupils from the female influences of domestic life and reinforced the tenets of the boys' family upbringing. In both spheres, their deferential behavior was a prerequisite for love and for adult acceptance of individual predilections, and a strong fear of juvenile sexuality legitimated intricate measures of bodily and mental control.

When successfully internalized, this submission to adult power and sexual regulation was mitigated by the middle-class boy's knowledge that one day he would wield the power, he would be in control—a prospect that the public school system highlighted and that the economic stability of his class seemed to confirm. But victimization might be so degrading and so persistent that acceptance of the gentlemanly norm was rendered difficult or impossible. Thus, George Melly, who went to Rugby in the 1840s, recalls with dismay the ritualized proceedings of his monitor (whom schoolboy wit had named "Coarser" because of his habit of sleeping with white kid gloves in order to preserve the unique complexion of his hands). On Tuesdays and Fridays, the young George was flogged while on other nights he would be "pulled out of bed or smothered in the clothes . . . grand tossings in a blanket took place on Saturday" (Melly 1854, p. 113). The Achilles' heel of Arnold's reformatory ideals was clearly the "belief that older boys could bear the weight of excessive moral responsibility" (Newsome 1961, p. 41; Mack 1938, pp. 275–81). Certainly, some boys felt overburdened.

However, until midcentury pupils still had means of escape. They could roam over the countryside, go fishing, bathing, or bird's-nesting, and in the 1840s spinning tops was "a highly popular Eton game" (Lamb 1959, p. 223). But from the 1850s, staff supervision increased, days became more strictly regimented with organized and compulsory sports and games taking up more time and energy. Similarly, housemasters' and headmasters' regular flogging sessions, already a traditional ingredient in public school history, were endowed with the symbolism of a ritual. The writer James Brinsley-Richards, who was a pupil at Eton in the 1870s, "turned almost faint" when he witnessed his first flogging, "six cuts that sounded like the splashing of so many buckets of water." Later, James' own detachment enabled him to describe the rules of the ritual:

> After fumbling over several brace buttons you took your station on the block, while two acolyte "Tugs" held up your shirt, then you crammed a handkerchief into your mouth with one hand and held the other straight down, protected with starched cuff, to prevent the ends of the birch from curling round your body. This the old man always resented as a baulking him of his due. "He-he! very idle boy, take your hand away"; a command which, when disobeyed, resulted in ten or fourteen cuts, a matter ascertained by the knowing ones to be preferable to the usual six unprotected strokes. (Lamb 1959, pp. 150, 161)

Arnold's ideal of the compassionate Christian gentleman was gradually ousted by Charles Kingsley's more robust and virile "muscular Christian." Although the games cult, with its anti-intellectualism, its glory in physical prowess, and its latent jingoism, was an erratic development that fully bloomed only since the 1870s, when Brinsley-Richards went to Eton, the manly public school ethos was widely influential in the 1850s and 1860s. "The whole efforts of a school," wrote Edward Thring, headmaster at Uppingham, in 1864, "ought to be directed to making boys manly, earnest and true" (Newsome 1961, p. 195). The reformed public school ethos equated manliness with morals. This equation has survived in the numerous sports expressions denoting moral attitudes ("it's not cricket," "playing it straight," and so forth). A sense of responsibility, fairness, and esprit de corps, it was thought, was best developed through the formation of a masculine character. "Coarser" would never have survived this new regime.

The new grammar schools such as Marlborough, Malvern, and Cheltenham were often the fiercest proponents of manliness. Numerous grammar and private schools, in which the majority of middle- and lower-middle-class boys received their education, also sought to the best of their abilities to emulate the public school ethos of manliness, if under different material circumstances. Not unnaturally, this preoccupation with manliness, which first found its fictional expression in juvenile books through *Tom Brown's Schooldays*, is strongly reflected and reinforced in the reputable boys' magazines emerging in the 1850s and 1860s.[9]

Not all eulogized the public schools, however. Charles Darwin's *Origin of Species* (1859) and Herbert Spencer's *Education* (1861) were influential in

9. For the contemporary upsurge in adult public school novels and memoirs, see Mack 1941, pp. 134–52; Reed 1964; pp. 15–33. Musgrave 1985 emphasizes juvenile literature. All authors concentrate almost exclusively on books.

voicing the need for a more scientific and a more direct vocational training, a need which was deepened in the 1850s through the introduction of entrance examinations as passports to careers within the civil service, the armed forces, and the universities. After Parliamentary commissions in the 1860s had confirmed the necessity of reform, a Public Schools Act in 1868 and an Endowed Schools Act in 1869 mediated new needs and established traditions. These acts confirmed the social divisions of society. Curricular change was left largely in the hands of individual school authorities, while the old foundation scholarships were opened to competition, thus indirectly favoring boys from preparatory schools.

But with Britain unchallenged as an economic and military power, curricular changes seemed less pertinent than the moral formation of self-disciplined leaders. However, the reasons for the wide influence of the public school ethos went beyond conscious, or at least rational, arguments. The cultivation of manliness, according to David Newsome, had two separate roots—namely, Coleridge's distrust of childishness and Kingley's later disapproval of effeminacy. From those two roots emerged the Christian gentleman and the muscular Christian, respectively (Newsome 1961, pp. 196–99; see also Vance 1975). But despite important differences of expression, both ideas had a common mold that nurtured more than the minds of a few individuals. To most Victorian men, the child with its bodily spontaneity and the woman with her sexual and procreative potentials both posed forceful, if indirect, challenges to his power, and to male heterosexuality.

Behind the teaching of moral manliness lay acute fears of unbridled sexuality and bodily sensations. The intensity given to this teaching both at home and at school indicates that the proper masculine reserve and self-restraint was dearly bought through vigilant self-control. For the middle-class schoolboy, standing midway in this process of (self)regulation, its contradictions were acutely felt and all the more difficult to combat because partly unknown. Thus, Coventry Patmore, the author of perhaps the most famous eulogy of Victorian domesticity, *The Angel in the House*, implored in a letter sent to his son at public school that he should "be *pure*, (you know what I mean) . . . When the other boys say and do dirty things (as many boys at all great schools will) remember those words of Jesus Christ, "The pure in heart shall see God"—that is to say they will go to heaven" (Houghton 1957, p. 354).

Such oblique references to sexuality, here rendered all the more conspicuous by the father's religious explicitness, were bound to exacerbate the boy's conflicts. In general, the public school ethos both highlighted and modulated the domestic contradictions between exuberance and responsibility. Individual prowess and boyish gusto were allowed, even encouraged, and games might indeed invigorate intense pleasure and camaraderie. But physical exhilaration was allowed only within certain rules laid down from above. The psychological

The *Boy's Own Magazine; An Illustrated Journal of Fact, Fiction, History and Adventure*, new series, 1, no. 5 (May 1863), facing p. 401. Artist: W. L. Thomas. In this illustration for an article, "The Rugby Boys," the prowess of the young "muscular Christians" is offset by the majestic spirituality suggested by the gothic school building.

costs of negotiating these contradictions must have been often outbursts of anxiety and feelings of insufficiency in living up to the rules rather than open rebellion.

Because the concept of innocent childhood curiously allowed a more conscious regulation of juvenile sexuality, the acceptance in many secondary schools of the "boys will be boys" dictum offered new ways of imposing—and of opposing—responsibility and male reserve. For the adolescent boy from the middle and lower-middle class, wavering between moral obedience and the prospect of adult status and then severe doubts as to the price to be paid for this coveted future, the new boys' magazines offered useful testing grounds for these experiences. Not only their literacy, their leisure time, and their relative affluence but also their life experiences made these boys likely magazine fans.

BANDS OF HOPE AND MINSTREL SHOWS

Among working-class juveniles, the ones with interest, time, and coppers enough to spare for fictional entertainment were primarily the sons of urban artisans and skilled laborers—the groups of working people who profited the most from the general rise in prosperity during the third quarter of the century when real wages rose by about a third. Allowing for regional variations, temporary slumps, and periods of unemployment, it was men in the traditional, small-scale crafts—the plumbers, masons, and wheelwrights—who commanded the highest wages and who, together with some new skilled laborers such as boiler-makers, lithographers, and engineers, formed what was now called the aristocracy of labor, a group comprising about ten or fifteen percent of the working class (Cole and Postgate 1976, p. 351; Hobsbawm 1964, pp. 272, 279; Burnett 1977, p. 252).[10]

These were the men who formed new and strong unions, who fought for Parliamentary representation, who in "honourable" firms worked an unprecedented low of nine hours a day from the 1870s, and who made up the backbone of Friendly Societies (from 1810) of cooperative stores (from 1844) and of working men's clubs (from 1852).[11] They were also the ones to pioneer what has become known as the "traditional" working-class family, an urban unit supported on the male breadwinner's family wage, dependent upon the wife's homemaking duties, and continued socially and culturally via the son's manual training (often secured through his father's connections) and through the

10. Skilled craftsmen were especially numerous in London, the center of luxury production, where in 1851 about three quarters of all firms had between one and five employees (See Jones 1976, p. 374).

11. By 1872, the Friendly Societies, which through a monthly subscription secured their members against unemployment and sickness and in old age, had some four million members, a figure to be set against the one million trade-unionists (Musgrove 1965, p. 72).

daughter's marriage to a "local boy" after some years of domestic service.[12] Artisans' sons and daughters were the first working-class children to leave paid labor and enter the realm of dependent childhood. Just as their parents pioneered a middle-class family structure, if not emulating its functions, so the young pioneered the general decrease in paid child labor that took place during the latter half of the century. Thus, in 1851 children under fifteen years of age made up 6.9 percent of registered employees. Ten years later the percentage was 6.2, and in 1881 it was 4.5 percent (Musgrove 1965, p. 74).[13]

Official counseling and intervention were not directed toward these self-supporting groups. The scanty autobiographical material and its reticence about sexual matters preclude any general and definitive conclusions about how strictly artisan children were raised. But the silences also about intimate experiences occurring in adult life suggest that they were subject to a rather firm regulation of childish whims and sexual practices (Burnett 1984, pp. 43–47). We know more about their later years. Boys, at least, would attend a private day school or perhaps a British or National school until the age of twelve or thirteen, while the education of girls, as in the decades before, would often be interrupted by domestic chores.[14]

Outside school hours, parents often sought to keep their children off the streets, protecting them from any association with the poor. The Sunday school, missionary societies, and, from 1847, various Bands of Hope (the youth sections within the temperance movement) all reinforced parental propriety and prudence. Reward books were given away freely and the printed word in general was held in high esteem as a proof of literacy and morality. For the artisan schoolboy, the young apprentice, or the printer's assistant this inculcation of respectability was reinforced through a strict hierarchy of labor. Thus, thirteen-year-old Henry Broadhurst, born in Oxford in 1840 and apprenticed as a stone mason by his father's employers, started by carrying out the most onerous tasks:

12. This common artisan pattern of raising children to the parents' own station, was tentatively broken in 1876 with the introduction of a national scheme of teacher training. After preparation in their elementary school as low-paid pupil-teachers from thirteen years of age, able young people from the age of eighteen were eligible to sit for so-called Queen's Scholarships at a training college. This scheme offered a coveted nonmanual career option to artisan and, especially later, to lower-middle-class children, not least girls (Hobsbawm 1964, p. 274; Crossick 1977, p. 31). In 1850, there were about 1500 certified teachers, a third of whom were women. Ten years later, the total was 12,500, but women now comprised more than three-quarters (Turner 1974, pp. 66–68).

13. Note, however, that during the same period, 1851–81, the number of domestic servants under fifteen (mainly girls) increased by 55 percent while the employed population as a whole increased by 38 percent (Musgrove 1965, p. 75).

14. Not only did boys attend school more regularly than girls, they were also taught a wider range of subjects. In 1851, an investigation demonstrated that, reading apart, boys dominated in academic and girls in domestic subjects, that is, mainly needlework (Hurt 1979, pp. 25–29).

> At eight o'clock in the morning I had to see that hot tea and coffee were ready for thirty or forty men. Then at ten I must start on my tour of "the shop" to see how many pints of beer would be wanted at eleven, and this task had to be repeated at three o'clock. There were plenty of public houses close at hand, but I must fetch the beer from one nearly a mile away, because the landlord was foreman of the yard—a position invested with large authority. (Burnett 1977, p. 313)[15]

As the apprentice gradually came to master his craft, deference to authority merged with self-esteem and personal pride. This contented work identity and communal feeling can be what culturally separated the adult artisan most distinctly from the white-collar worker who, in material and moral terms, ranged near the skilled worker. The white-collar worker, moreover, lived outside the artisans' established networks spun within urban surroundings whose pace and unpredictability both groups shared and to some extent shunned.

Still, during the formative years of adolescence both the office lad and the artisan apprentice, unlike the middle-class schoolboy, chiefly shaped their identities through work and its explicit conflicts. Material necessity demanded deference while the acquisition of marketable skills generated a sense of independence. The constant negotiations of these poles must have been a chief psychological concern with both groups of working juveniles. Hence, to them reading in itself offered an acknowledged space of independence, and through it they found an approved means of personal entertainment without forfeiting their sense of social propriety. Home reading became more enjoyable with the introduction of paraffin oil in the late 1850s. And by then the new public libraries, though still few and far between, were patronized by large numbers of adolescent subscribers, mainly "schoolpupils" and "errand and office boys." When graduating in the 1900s from the libraries' choice of boys' authors (Marryat, Henty, Cooper, and Mayne Reid), working boys seem to have favored magazine reading, and there is no reason to believe that their choice would be different thirty or forty years earlier (Altick 1967, 236–37). [16]

Literature offered a welcome and approved alternative to work. The buying or swapping of magazines was a social occasion and comparing the weekly change in the contents formed an interesting discussion topic. With literacy still a recent and hard-won accomplishment, fine distinctions between respectable novels, religious or political treatises, and magazines often must have seemed unnecessary extravagances to the adolescent reader. Similarly, few parents or employers who themselves had little schooling would censor the contents of

---

15. Henry Broadhurst later became a high-ranking trade unionist and in 1880 was elected to the House of Commons as only the third working man in history.

16. The first Public Libraries Act (1850) empowered local authorities to levy a ½d. rate for the provision of libraries (from 1855, 1d.). But in 1869 only thirty-five local authorities had adopted the act (Lawson and Silver 1973, p. 279).

juvenile books and magazines as long as the titles were not too alluring and the pictures not too indecent to look at. To the lower-middle-class and the artisan reader, then, the new boys' magazines, such as the *Boys of England* with its deletion of the wildest penny-dreadful traits, offered exciting and inexpensive means of useful recreation.

Semiskilled workers, making up about half of the male working class in 1867 and employed as machine-minders in industry, as miners or shop workers, experienced less regular employment, longer working hours, repeated spates of migration, and more fluctuating family relations than did their skilled counter-parts (Burnett 1977, p. 261; Cole and Postgate 1976, p. 354). Even if their children did attain a rudimentary literacy, schooling was short, and it was interrupted by periods of paid or unpaid work, the illness of a close relative, or perhaps by several moves to new towns or other parts of the city. These condi-tions were even more marked for unskilled laborers and their children. In 1861, the unskilled category comprised about a third of the male working class, to which must be added about as many women who as adolescents were employed mainly as domestic servants, and in adult life as milliners or seamstresses in small workshops (the "sweated trades") or as "outworkers" sewing sacks, glue-ing paper bags, or making artificial flowers at home in between the daily routine of their numerous domestic chores (Burnett 1977, pp. 27, 261).[17]

The more uncertain the social conditions, the more essential was children's labor. But their tasks were often varied and could be interspersed by games and pranks. Running to the pawnbroker, fetching water, or minding younger sib-lings offered versatile means of sharing experiences with other children, and in most semiskilled and unskilled families the streets, backalleys, and courts formed accepted social meeting places for adults and children alike. There was little time and not much incentive to read within this public culture whose collectivity and oral traditions were reinforced by boys' early entry into the factory, the mine, or the warehouse. For adolescent messenger boys and "hands," the penny gaffs (small theaters), the new music halls, as well as the Negro minstrel shows formed integral parts of their leisure entertainment. In 1852, one witness in a Manchester "singing saloon" observed that ten percent of the audience was under the age of fifteen, twenty-five percent between fifteen and twenty and most of the customers were out on their own (Bailey 1982, p. 183).

Moreover, these juveniles were often discouraged from any possible enjoy-ment of serious literature by their school experiences. After the introduction in 1862 of the so-called Revised Code, government grants to elementary schools were made dependent on a national standard of examinations in the three Rs,

---

17. One third of all Victorian women found employment as domestics, most between the ages of fifteen and twenty-five (McBride 1976, p. 14, and 1978, p. 53).

which put a premium on rote learning and which also made needlework a compulsory subject for girls. This system of "payment by results" deeply affected teachers' and pupils' attitudes to learning. In one elementary school in the 1860s, the master appeared "in his best suit" for the yearly examination, unable to conceal his anxiety in front of his pupils, who were so overcome with fear as they were brought to the Inspectors that "the boys howled and the girls whimpered. It took hours to get through them." When the examiners had disappeared "with a deportment of high authority," the master would bring out a rare consolation prize for all, a hamper of large oranges (Ashby 1961, p. 18).[18]

Given such pedagogical ordeals, it took unusual personal interest, an established cultural tradition, or considerable parental enthusiasm to continue reading for pleasure. When the semiskilled or unskilled juvenile did read, he most likely favored maximum emotional return. Unhampered by adult admonition, he would probably keep to the traditional penny dreadfuls, whose stirring events, sexual innuendo, vivid imagery, and narrative pace corresponded to the changeability of the reader's own life. Conversely, his sister, often engaged as a domestic servant, generally found a more serious censorship imposed on her by the mistress of the house, the parlor-maid, or the cook. To many servants, penny romances, more or less furtively enjoyed, seem to have been the most palatable form of fiction (Mitchell 1981, esp. chaps. 1, 7).

A final group of working-class juveniles were either too poor, too illiterate, or too disinterested in reading to care much for fiction, no matter how stirring its contents. As these children were most at variance with the middle-class ideal of well-ordered innocence, their morals and especially their sexual behavior (rather than its social roots) gave rise to vivid debates and vigilant action. At the same time, the combined effects of mechanization and factory legislation turned an increasing number of children out from the secrecy of the mills and the mines into the public gaze at the markets and in the streets.[19] By midcentury, a multitude of destitute children and adolescents carved out a precarious living by advertising, pilfering and selling everything from their own bodies to fruit, firewood, sweets, and toys. Most conspicuous in the cities but by no means confined to the most densely populated areas, hordes of urban street arabs, child acrobats, and girl prostitutes highlighted the degree of juvenile deprivation and,

18. In 1870, Joseph Ashby, having attended school from the age of five to ten, became a farm hand and then did two years of stone carting at a nearby quarry before joining the Methodists at the age of fifteen.

19. According to Best 1971, pp. 122, 92, there existed no "scientifically approved measurements" of urban poverty until the late-nineteenth century. Worsened housing conditions, substantial variations in diet, and a persistent crime rate, however, defy claims of a general improvement of working-class living standards and point to "a perhaps positively growing body of destitution and deprivation." This conclusion is amply confirmed, e.g. by Burnett 1966, pp. 113–66; and Wohl 1977, pp. 21–44, 63–64.

to the concerned Victorian, juvenile depravity. A Coventry Patmore would shrink from reading Henry Mayhew's interview with an orphaned sixteen-year-old girl in London:

> I met with a young man of fifteen—I myself was going on for twelve years old—and he persuaded me to take up with him. I stayed with him three months in the same lodging-house, living with him as his wife, though we were mere children, and being true to him. At the three months' end he was taken up for picking pockets, and got six months. I was sorry, for he was kind to me; though I was made ill through him; so I broke some windows in St Paul's Churchyard to get into prison to get cured. I had a month in the Compter [prison], and came out well.

The girl then took to walking the streets staying in the same lodging-house where "whatever could take place in words or acts between boys and girls did take place, and in the midst of the others. . . . Some boys and girls slept without any clothes, and would dance about the room that way" (Pike 1967, p. 354).[20]

Mary Carpenter's efforts under the aegis of the Ragged School Union (1844) were only among the better-publicized charitable and educational schemes proliferating in most cities from the 1850s with the express aim of alleviating the direst consequences of poverty. Despite individual compassion and much hard work, the voluntary schemes nevertheless proved insufficient bulwarks against what was perceived as a growing working-class depravity. In 1867, a quarter of the "youthful population" in a working-class district of Manchester could not read while in another poor area of that city thirty-five percent of the children had never set foot in a day school, and Sunday school attendance was decreasing. In the whole of England, it was estimated that between 250,000 and two million children of school age received no formal education (Altick 1967, pp. 170–71).

Since most middle-class Victorians saw basic education as the great lever of moral elevation, parents who were either too poor or unwilling to send their offspring to school had to be forced into doing so. After much Parliamentary controversy, W. E. Forster's Education Act became law in 1870, three years after Robert Lowe, on the passing of the Second Reform Bill, had deplored that it was necessary to "prevail on our future masters to learn their letters." The act was hastened by middle-class anxieties about the increasing power displayed by the skilled work force, anxieties that were further spurred by the first signs from Germany and the United States that Britain's economic and military supremacy

20. While Mayhew asserted that there were "nearer 10,000 than 20,000" street arabs in London, the Ragged School Union in 1861 estimated that there were closer to 100,000. The number of child prostitutes was equally hard to define. But in the fifty years before 1887, a quarter of York's prostitutes were eighteen years and under (Hurt 1979, p. 52; Walvin 1982, pp. 69, 144).

The *Boy's Own Magazine; An Illustrated Journal of Fact, Fiction, History and Adventure,* new series, 6, no. 32 (August 1865), facing p. 156. A. Ludovici's drawing accompanied W. B. B. Stevens' poem, "The Boy Bedouins of London Streets: A Social Problem." In accordance with middle-class notions of urban street life, the artist focuses on the deprivation and possible depravities of poor juveniles.

might not remain unchallenged. But the act was also clearly intended as a moral substitute for "deficient" family upbringing.

Publicly funded elementary schools, the so-called board schools, were erected as complements to the voluntary schools already in existence. In Forster's words, the act was "to fill up gaps," not only geographically, it turned out, but also morally (Hurt 1979, p. 59). The act was important in educational history chiefly because the state for the first time acknowledged its full responsibility to educate working-class children for their future station, albeit no further than that. In the longer term, schooling enforced a structural harmonization of working-class upbringing toward a middle-class ideal, while in more immediate terms the act secured the spread of literacy to poor children in general and to girls in particular. Thus, in England and Wales the literacy of adult males in 1871 stood at 80.6 percent, an average decennial gain since 1841 of 4.4 percent. And 73.2 percent of adult women were literate, a decennial increase of about 7.4 percent in thirty years. By 1900, 97.2 percent of adult males were literate, a decennial gain of 5.5 percent on average, against 96.8 percent of adult females, an average decennial increase of 7.9 percent (Altick 1967, p. 171).

The Education Act, however, created no sudden increase of juvenile readers, but rather a gradual extension of literacy whose full impact only became noticeable from around 1880 when compulsory attendance was enforced (free schooling became a possibility only from 1891). During the third quarter of the century, then, most girls, whether middle or working class, were raised within the purview of domesticity, either as mistresses or as servants. The middle-class reinforcement of femininity imposed severe restrictions on leisured and literate girls' fictional choices and hence discouraged indiscriminate magazine reading. For the majority of working-class girls, even from an artisan background, femininity still implied hard work and home responsibilities from an early age, although domestic service might allow some romantic flights into fiction. It was the boys, the middle-class, lower-middle-class and artisan adolescents, who between them shared what important magazine novelties came to light during the mid-Victorian decades. This readership, although marked by a "proper" childhood, encompassed a range of experiences, anxieties and aspirations. Similarly, the new magazines offered two distinct shades of male morality, mixing secular prowess and spiritual responsibility into different concoctions of excitement.

7

Serenity and Fortitude:
The *Boy's Own Magazine*
and the *Boys of England*

WHEN SAMUEL BEETON addressed the youth "whose glorious heritage it is to possess the Empire that their fathers have founded and preserved," both he and the readers of his new venture, the *Boy's Own Magazine*, knew that this youth hardly included girls or working-class boys (Hyde 1951, p. 50). The new type of quality paper appealed to the middle-class boy, and it did so chiefly by holding up a heroic past or an exotic present as illustrious indications of the reader's actual possibilities in his immediate future. As in the religious periodicals, biographies were used as ideal examples highlighting the moral tone of the magazine. But Christian martyrs and missionaries were replaced by secular adventurers such as Captain Cook, Daniel Defoe, and James Watt. In the first issue of the *Boy's Own Magazine* a story of Benjamin Franklin's estimable career is concluded: "Let one thing be remembered. Bright as is Franklin's fame as a philosopher and a statesman, it is brighter as a virtuous man. . . . let every young reader of this memoir resolve to follow the example; he will certainly become a happy and prosperous if not a great man" (1, no. 1 [January 1855], p. 7).

This was an unusually direct proclamation of the paper's blend of Christian and capitalist dogma. For although the author was still discernible as a moral judge, the *Boy's Own Magazine* generally worked its messages into the plots to a larger extent than was the case in religious and utilitarian ventures. Historical fiction was the most popular feature of the paper. The medieval crusades, the Norman conquest, and the British army and navy were inexhaustible reservoirs for serials about audacious but responsible heroes. In the long-running serial, "Cortes, and the Conquest of Mexico," the Spanish general is just such an ideal. When two thousand Aztec hostages are "hewn down with as little difficulty as corn in harvest," it is still Cortes' humanity which is emphasized: "The horses easily overtook the fugitives, riding them down and cutting them to pieces without mercy, until Cortes, weary with slaughter, called off his men" (1, no. 6 [June 1855], p. 174).

98

The general is clearly the readers' object of identification. His "serenity, fortitude, constancy and power of endurance" embody a perfect balance of moral and military superiority, which legitimates his imperial atrocities. As in the religious periodicals, the alleged barbarities of native religion—despite their unmistakable fascination—justify Christian intervention but with the important difference that the emotional emphasis is placed squarely on the victor, not the victim. The European point of view is personified by Cortes masterminding the action, which shows little reveling in gory details. The moral is integrated into the plot and not tagged on as a Protestant imperative at the end of a story otherwise glorying in "heathen superstition" or "Popish practices."

Yet, while a Spaniard might defend European standards in exotic countries such as Mexico, he would be equally sure to feature as a hotheaded opponent in tales set closer to the British Isles. In this, Beeton apparently found no contradiction. But observant readers might note a certain incoherence within the moral hierarchy of nationalities, even if one or perhaps two serials would generally dominate a yearly volume (twelve monthly issues) so that such clear inconsistencies between the different tales only materialized over several years. For example, "Antony Waymouth; or, the Gentlemen Adventurers. A Chronicle of the Sea," was a popular serial recounting the training as a "cosmographer" of the young Elizabethan Edward Raymond under the guidance of the naval officer Antony Waymouth. In the tale, the author, W. H. G. Kingston, justifies British antagonism against the Spanish exactly by the latters' religious warfare:

> Their black injustice and horrible cruelties to the natives of Mexico and Peru were to meet with just retribution. The cries of thousands ascending from their Inquisitorial prisons were not unheard. National sins were to meet with national punishment. They had been tried in the balance and found wanting. So it has gone on. The land of Spain, bountifully blessed by Nature, still holds a people grovelling in the dust of ignorance and superstition.

By comparison, even ordinary English seamen seem paragons of virtue, and in the Royal Navy, as Kingston assures his young readers, "religion flourished more than among most communities on shore" (New ser., 3, no. 14 [February 1864], pp. 123–24). However, within the ranks of the British themselves only the lower orders express open defiance of accepted norms. In J. G. Edgar's historical romance "Cressy and Poictiers; or, The Story of the Black Prince's Page," Arthur Winram—"a stripling of fifteen"—follows his young master, the Black Prince, to war with France in 1344. Significantly, the serial is set during the early part of the Hundred Years' War when the fortunes are still with the English. At one stage when the prince's party conquers the Castle of Poix, the French lord's two "very handsome" daughters are valiantly defended by Arthur in the face of his own soldiers who "were then highly excited with their triumphs, and in no humour to pay any excessive respect to female virtue." But even on the verge of committing rape, British footmen express themselves with a fair amount of gallantry in the *Boy's Own Magazine:* " 'Make way,' shouted another, with a hoarse laugh, 'and let me advance to console the fair ones in their jeopardy' " (New ser., 1, no. 3 [March 1863], p. 186).[1] At this opportune moment, an approaching knight comes to the assistance of the brave page and the French maidens are rescued. Apart from being an unusually explicit reference to sexual matters according to Beeton's standards, the episode serves as a catalyst in Arthur's process of maturation, his gradual harnessing of an adventurous spirit by cool deliberation and forethought. As an "accidental" reward for his personal purification, he is revealed to be a nobleman, dispossessed by scheming relatives of his title and his heritage. In the final installment of the long serial, Arthur reclaims both by winning a duel against his principal wrongdoer. Social status is justified by individual courage and self-determination.

The popular historical romances insisted on contemporary male ideals despite their remote settings. This integration of ideals served a dual purpose. For the middle-class adolescent, oscillating between feelings of present insecurity and portents of future authority, the descriptions of dangerous battles, vicious fiends, and nature catastrophes offered a fictional universe in which feelings of aggression and inferiority could be legitimately vented and played out. But at the same time the reader's identification with the manly hero and his personal development checked these feelings even while he was reading. This new adulation of the victor marked an important ideological change from the earlier ideals of religious submission.

Perhaps of more immediate importance to the adolescent reader, the changing emphasis seemed to alleviate his individual anxieties and conflicts. Unlike the martyr or the missionary, the manly adventurer embodied a contemporary male norm while performing norm-breaking actions such as manslaughter or rape. He at once confirmed and rejected the reader's own submission. An identification with this Janus-headed hero might seem to complicate the reader's acceptance of the male norm. But since an adulthood ripe with possibilities of action was an immediate prospect for the adolescent boy, the norm was probably acknowledged as a necessary precondition for power. The manly ideal was credible as an actual possibility.

This general credibility was repeatedly underlined through remarks such as "It is a remarkable, but well-authenticated fact" and "it is a sad fact." Together with proverbial comments and factual details, these direct authorial insertions stressed the truth value of the stories. The author acted as a guide toward a general ethos that was acceptable to adults and adolescents alike. The historical setting strengthened this notion of a general truth. Since a sound knowledge of

---

1. "Cressy and Poictiers" was reissued as the main serial in 1870 at the beginning of the "second new series" of the *Boy's Own Magazine*. The story came out in book form in 1865.

Britain's heroic past was a sine qua non of middle-class upbringing, the old heroes warranted that, despite obstacles and personal danger, everything could turn out right in the end both in fact and in fiction. This historical perspective, moreover, acted as a convenient source for imparting knowledge about the precise number of hostages taken, the exact construction of military equipment, and the social divisions of native societies—all aspects that clearly indicated Beeton's utilitarian heritage according to which fictional quality equated factual quantity. The same emphasis marked entries on "sports and pastimes" and "facts, fancies and phenomena," the latter comprising mainly entries on geography and natural history.

Nonfiction covered about forty percent of the contents in the *Boy's Own Magazine*, an unusually large part compared both with its Sunday school and its penny-dreadful competitors (Drotner 1977, p. 124). Painting magic-lantern slides, engraving eggshells, and melting coins in walnut shells were among the more serviceable pursuits to be advocated by the inventive editor who would also furnish the reader with more exotic accounts of the proper hunting of bears and kangaroos, the remote origin of gunpowder (and how to make it), along with the correct observation of earthquakes. Whether or not middle-class boys might actually use such information, many obviously enjoyed reading about it if the popularity of Beeton's numerous books on travel, nature study, and sports is any guide. This enjoyment seems less of a mystery when we remember that Beeton's was an age without film and television and his readers' limited life experiences made literature a chief source of knowledge about the world around them. The nonfiction entries seem to have filled the reader's immediate needs to employ his newfangled liberties within the family in an approved fashion, and the diversity of the topics indicates that boyish activities might stretch well into adolescence.

Prompted by our knowledge of the middle-class reader and the mid-century reforms of his education, one wonders where school crept into this first self-styled boys' periodical. School stories did appear, in fact Beeton serialized extracts of *Tom Brown's Schooldays* in 1858, calling this first truly popular school yarn "a volume of sterling merit . . . vigorous, manly, and thoroughly English" (*Boy's Own Magazine* 4, no. 7 [July 1858], p. 211).[2] Yet during its total run the magazine contained less than a dozen pieces about school life. Most of these were factual descriptions of organized games at Eton and Rugby in which the reader had to digest long-winded introductions detailing the historical foundation of these esteemed institutions. That the *Boy's Own Magazine* paid only a token tribute to the public school story as it was developed by Thomas Hughes and Frederic Farrar may be proof of Beeton's indifference to his readers' needs. But it may also indicate that the middle-class adolescent was already looking

2. According to Altick 1967, p. 385, the book sold 11,000 copies in the first nine months after its publication in 1857.

forbidding the young ladies from keeping lantern-flies. A great many of the species are very showy, and there is a fine collection of them in the British Museum.

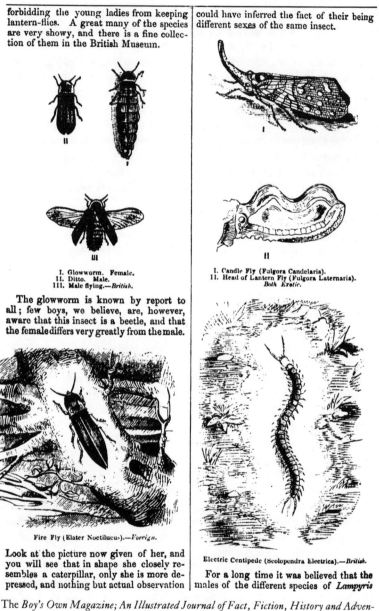

I. Glowworm. Female.
II. Ditto. Male.
III. Male flying.—*British.*

The glowworm is known by report to all; few boys, we believe, are, however, aware that this insect is a beetle, and that the female differs very greatly from the male.

Fire Fly (Elater Noctilucus).—*Foreign.*

Look at the picture now given of her, and you will see that in shape she closely resembles a caterpillar, only she is more depressed, and nothing but actual observation

could have inferred the fact of their being different sexes of the same insect.

I. Candle Fly (Fulgora Candelaria).
II. Head of Lantern Fly (Fulgora Laternaria).
Both Exotic.

Electric Centipede (Scolopendra Electrica).—*British.*

For a long time it was believed that the males of the different species of *Lampyris*

The *Boy's Own Magazine; An Illustrated Journal of Fact, Fiction, History and Adventure* 4, no. 11 (November 1858), p. 336. Illustration for a series, "The World of Insects." In the mid-Victorian quality periodicals for boys, large and often attractive pictures enliven information-packed articles emphasizing leisure pursuits outside the realm of sport.

ahead in life for solutions to his immediate problems. School life, whether real or imagined, might deepen his personal frustrations, but it did not appeal as a source of alleviating these frustrations. Conversely, the historical romance held sway because it successfully charted how exciting and often exotic adventure could be combined with "proper" behavior. It was left to Brett's *Boys of England* to develop this fictional formula.

This formula became evident in the opening story of the new periodical, and it was perfected over the years. "Alone in the Pirates' Lair" was a sea adventure written by Charles Stevens, the first editor of the weekly. It features Jack Rushton, a fourteen-year-old midshipman on "the good ship Titania" and a true British hero type: "he had frank, blue eyes and fair hair; he was merry as a lark, agile as a monkey, and brave as the aweless lion" (*Boys of England* 1, no. 1 [24 November 1866], p. 2). As the only son of a deceased naval officer, Jack has inherited nothing but his father's "good looks and sterling virtues, and self-reliance." These personal qualities are immediately put to the test when Spanish pirates attack the British ship. Jack, after he has put up a heroic fight, is imprisoned together with "the fair lady Marion" by the cruel but dashing pirate captain Don Pablo. Using his wits and strength, Jack escapes from the pirates' hideout and secures the rescue of Marion. In a final battle, Jack's friend Mark Ambrose, first outmaneuvers Don Pablo:

> They wrestled with amazing fury for the possession of a dagger which the pirate had drawn.
>
> With that repugnance which an Englishman ever feels at using the knife, even in an encounter of this sort, Mark forbore to seize the advantage, which presented itself more than once, of driving the poignard to the hilt in his foeman's breast.
>
> During the fearful struggle, Mark had prevented Pablo from shouting for assistance, by maintaining that iron grip upon his throat.
>
> At length, enraged and alarmed at the shrieks of lady Marion, and the cries of Jack, who appeared to be contending with the sentinel outside, Mark summoned all his strength, and, closing with Pablo, seized, with both hands by the neck, and tightened his grip till the face of the latter became horribly distorted, and he sank upon the earth limp and senseless.

Jack and Mark then face the entire pirate crew:

> A swarm of faces, white, brown and black, appeared at the end of the dark vista, and came sweeping towards [them].
>
> "Down!" whispered Mark.
>
> He sprang into one of the dark niches in the wall, and crouched low.
>
> Jack instantly followed his example.
>
> Then came a blinding flash and report like the explosion of a powdermill.
>
> A dozen muskets had been fired, and the bullets "ping" past, and thud into the yielding door.

> Once more was heard a tremendous crash.
>
> Lady Marion shrieked, and fainted.
>
> "Huzza! Down with the pirate villains!"
>
> With a stirring cheer the British tars came scampering in, like terriers bounding into a rat's run.
>
> The advancing tide of faces suddenly ebbed, and the pirates turned their backs and ran away.
>
> "Forward, men!" shrieked Mr. Middleton. "After the wolves!—down with 'em, lads!"
>
> And brandishing his cutlass, he bravely led the van. (*Boys of England* 1, no. 1 [24 November 1866], p. 13)

The pirates are defeated on their own ground and moral order is restored. The British turn up trumps, and Captain Middleton only appears on the scene when the decisive killing of Don Pablo has been done. Thus, the social hierarchy remains unchallenged while the accolade goes to our young heroes. This must have seemed both an acceptable and enjoyable balance for the young shop assistant or apprentice, who in their work had to face and to negotiate the intricacies of moral and social power.

With its rapid style and standard descriptions, "Alone in the Pirates' Lair" was typical of the *Boys of England*. Although Brett promised to provide his readers with "wild and wonderful, but healthy fiction," what dominated the tales initially was not much different from the penny dreadfuls. Unlike the *Boy's Own Magazine* and other quality monthlies, the new weekly spelled out in colorful detail not only violent actions but also the effects of these actions (for example, when Don Pablo was choked, his face "became horribly distorted"). "Healthy" attitudes appeared less as integrated aspects of the narrative and more often as authorial asides, as was also the case in the "Pirates' Lair":

> Perhaps it is necessary to inform our readers that the atrocities ascribed to the pirates are derived from fact, and that our purpose in giving a truthful picture of the lives and habits of such desperate villains is to disabuse the young mind of the false notion that there ever was or ever can be those chivalrous characteristics about robbers, pirates and other like pests of society which have been falsely portrayed in so many pernicious romances of crime. (*Boys of England* 1, no. 1 [24 November 1866], p. 4)

In time, Brett successfully combined morals and entertainment in the narratives of his *Boys of England*. The epitome of this success was the school fellow Jack Harkaway. It seems curious that a periodical run on commercial principles and catering mainly to a less well-off audience of apprentices and junior clerks should become the chief popularizer of the serialized school story. One reason for this is that the serial authors writing for Brett, such as E. Harcourt Burrage, Captain Mayne Reid, and Bracebridge Hemyng avoided the moral and psychological depths of *Tom Brown's Schooldays* when recounting school life. More important, they sought to lengthen popular tales by letting their heroes out of the school gates and into the Amazon jungle or the Australian bush.

To an upwardly mobile readership, school held an immediate attraction as a stepping stone to an improved status and wider options in adulthood. Yet the office, the warehouse, and the workshop occupied the everyday lives of such adolescents, and implanted in their minds problems of a tangible and immediate nature. In Jack Harkaway, the reader found a young hero with just the right combination of adventurous spirit and a down-to-earth resourcefulness.

From the outset, the *Boys of England* featured occasional school stories of a more conventional type such as Vane St. John's "Who Shall be Leader?" in the opening issue. But prompted by the success of the school serial "Tom Wildrake's Schooldays," which had appeared in the first issue of George Emmett's *Sons of Britannia* in March 1870, Brett in August of the following year introduced his audience to a new type, namely "Jack Harkaway's Schooldays" written by Bracebridge Hemyng (1841–1901). Hemyng, an old Etonian and author of the section on prostitution in Mayhew's *London Labour and the London Poor* (London, 1861–62), at once places Jack in the readers' minds as a high-spirited youngster endowed with a "high order" of "natural aptitude and intelligence" and a stock-in-trade mystery concerning his birth. Against Jack's will, his Dickensian guardian, mercenary and hypocritical, sends him to Pomona House, a small private academy like most educational establishments in such tales. The headmaster, Mr. Crawcour, is equally hypocritical but more mercenary ("there was a slight suspicion of the Jew in his appearance") and definitely more cruel (endearingly he describes his fifty canes as his "little persuaders").[3]

From the outset, then, a moral contradiction is established upon which the whole series builds: quick-witted justice is set against contriving brutality. Within hours of meeting Mr. Crawcour, Jack succeeds in tarring the principal's hands, filling his hat with a pound of flour, and putting black beetles in his soup before a final coup de grâce of chalking "Please kick me" on the unfortunate man's back. Unlike Tom Brown and other book heroes, Jack is morally and mentally superior from the beginning. Although some archetypal traits of the Hughes tradition are retained (the bully fight, the prayer at night, the football match), the serial is no bildungsroman in the sense that a protagonist gradually develops and matures psychologically before our eyes by overcoming internal and external adversities: in the Victorian school serials, not the hero but the scenery changes.[4]

3. The 1871 volume of the *Boys of England*, in which Jack Harkaway originally made his bow, his missing from the British Library. Quote from Brett ca. 1880, p. 7.

4. By contrast, Musgrave with his analytical interest in books rather than serials maintains that the hero's development is one of four characteristics defining the boys' school story (the other three are: the school is regarded as an organization, the plot is seen from the boys' point of view, and it has a moral or didactic element) (Musgrave 1985, p. 130).

On skipping life at Pomona House for a naval career, Jack and his true friend, Dick Harvey, soon find themselves shipwrecked on "Limbi," a coral island inhabited by a cruel tribe of "far-famed head hunters." Among them, however, the two British boys find a truthful black servant, Monday, who is "singularly quick . . . , and not bad-looking for one of his people." Having fended off impudent natives, mutinous sailors, and desperate pirates, the party returns to Oxford ("more swell than Cambridge"). Here, Jack's cricket and rowing championships, his revenge of murders, and his scaring of fake ghosts are topped only by his winning a double first in his exams along with his true love, Emily (Harvey and Monday are paired off with their respective girl-friends at the same time).

Unhampered by matrimony, Jack and his friends continue their perilous adventures around the world during the following eight years. In 1873, Hemyng went to America, so Jack in due course goes to the wild west, partici-pates in the gold rush, and fights the Indians. This caused some confusion since Brett, to fill out the gap left on Hemyng's departure, had sent Jack to Greece and Australia. Over the years, our hero acquired a son and even a grandson: Jack Harkaway the third was featured in the 1890s, for instance in *Jack Harkaway's Journal for Boys* in 1893 (the paper ran for only eighteen weeks), and he finished his career joining the Boer War in *Up-to-date Boys* (1899–1901), another Brett publication (James 1973, p. 96).[5]

Jack himself, though, remained unmarked by his years. Whether fighting his archenemy, the bully Hunston, or witnessing the "barbarous customs" of can-nibals, Jack always gets the upper hand by combining his superior intelligence with his gifts of ventriloquism and pugilism—both necessary requirements for any fictional schoolboy's survival before World War I. As in earlier tales, the hero is the emotional (and moral) point of identification. No violent details are spared; thus, when Jack witnesses a human sacrifice, the victim's head, "all smeared with clotted blood," is first kicked "wildly about as if it had been a football":

> The parts of the human body which are esteemed the greatest delicacies by these cannibals are first, the palms of the hands, and then the eyes.
> When the chief has gratified his choice, the others are entitled in turn to advance and cut out bits.
> The savage feast proceeded quickly, and the victim's shrieks and moans were pitiful to hear.

It is no wonder that it takes Jack some time to get "the sight of the hacked and bleeding form from his eyes" (11, no. 277 [2 March 1872], p. 227). With fascinated fright, the reader could indulge in bloody details while maintaining a

---

5. A bibliography of the Harkaway stories is given in Turner 1976, p. 83.

pure image both of his hero and of his own conscience: in a footnote on the same page the editor pays a token tribute to the veracity of the account by dutifully noting, "For confirmation of this revolting custom refer to Bickmore's and Pfeiffer's travels among the Battas of the East Indian Archipelago." The illustrations, larger and more plentiful than those found in the *Boy's Own Magazine*, served as a powerful reinforcement of the written excitements. While pictures in the Beeton periodicals, still rather static, displayed the manly hero on his way to battle or watching a beautiful and often exotic scenery, steel engravings in the *Boys of England* stressed the most thrilling parts of the action. With more background details, characters were caught in motion, the protagonist fending off a snake, killing a crocodile, or, in the common run of things, wrestling with a savage enemy. Captions also added to the visual message, presenting the reader with a moment of heightened emotion and an enticement to read on. Moreover, Brett profited on the improvements in illustration techniques; occasional notices in the paper promised "a colourful portrait" of a popular character with the coming issue—a simple but effective way of sustaining sales.

With or without color plates, the *Boys of England's* thirty-three-year run proved that Brett's fictional formula went over well with adolescents. The success relied on letting the reader have his cake and eat it too. In its overt morality, the *Boys of England* followed its better-class rivals: never sneak, never weep, never lie, and never trust foreigners were all maxims, equally applicable to the middle-class schoolboy, the office lad, and the apprentice. The underlying rationale of these maxims—fortune favours the brave—was accepted across a wide social scale, although it was invested with different connotations. But unlike earlier ventures, this overt morality was conveyed through violent actions and visual detail, often contradicting the manly ideals. The reader's emotional involvement was never impeded by religious justification nor harnessed by factual details concerning the weight of canoes or the distance of plains to be traversed. The exoticism of foreign countries and peoples served purely to heighten excitement.

This new type of fiction, with its clever mixture of betterment and excitement, must have been especially appealing to boys who had been raised to propriety and abnegation and were facing new demands and liberties. Jack Harkaway combined vigor and strength with an unlimited mobility, thereby harmonizing the boy and the man, the ordinary and the exceptional. He thus seemed to momentarily alleviate the conflicts of adolescent readers who themselves had to establish an identity through work. Their jobs demanded skill and dexterity while hopes for material security, even betterment, were continually limited by the uncertainties and fluctuations of their trades.

To middle-class adolescents, who had a narrower horizon of experience than their poorer contemporaries but had better prospects for travel and emigration, the paper's sexual innuendo rather than its violence perhaps provided the strongest attraction. While it is difficult to distinguish sharply between readers' reception of sexual allusions and violence—often rather sadistic violence—it can be safely assessed that both earlier and later editors of boys' periodicals made a sharp distinction between the two and banned all hints of sexuality. This taboo was exercised chiefly by excluding from the action all women or at least all under the age of forty. The sexual references in the *Boys of England* therefore merit closer examination.

Young Emily, Jack's sweetheart and later wife, looks like the perfect Victorian girl, "a pretty little brunette, with large lustrous eyes" (naturally she appears on one of the free color plates, rose in hand and with a demure expression). But in her behavior she is rather forward for her sex and for her "decent" background. Thus, in "Jack Harkaway, After Schooldays; his Adventures Afloat and Ashore" Emily is conveniently shipwrecked and imprisoned by Hunston on an island near Jack. She gets permission to see her beloved by giving her detested warder a kiss. She later confesses:

> "It felt like the touch of a snake, Jack dear," she went on.
> "So I should think. The brute, to think that he had a kiss when I haven't dared to ask for one. May I though, Emmy, may I?"
> "You know you may, Jack—a dozen if you like.
> And Jack did like.
> He construed this into permission to help himself, and he covered her pretty face with kisses.
> "There, Jack," she said, pushing him away; "that will do. Don't be stupid." (*Boys of England* 11, no. 287 [11 May 1872], p. 388)

Jack and the reader get their share of romance while preserving the ideal of prudent English womanhood. How Jack's son is conceived remains a mystery. The first hint of his existence appears in the beginning of "Jack Harkaway Among the Brigands" where we are informed that Jack's wife, Emily, "had been very ill, after the birth of a son, the only issue of their marriage" (*Boys of England* 14, no. 343 [7 June 1873], p. 2). Soon after, baby Harkaway enters the scene: he is kidnapped by the vicious Italian bandits, only to be rescued by a wolf, whom he expediently tames before Monday finds him and returns him to Jack and Emily. The observant reader can glean more information on sexual matters from Jack's former teacher, Mr. Mole, who allegedly impregnates his two native wives (one of them shows up in Oxford with their progeny). Perhaps the explicitness about Mr. Mole's behavior is allowed because native women in general were considered to be of a totally different nature, garrulous and aggressive. The usual manly courtesy could be suspended, and explicit violence is also permitted when native women are involved. Jack sees a witch being tormented by some of his black friends, the natives, who accuse her of having betrayed the British youngsters:

She was beaten with bamboos.

Fire was placed under her feet.

Red-hot stones were applied to various parts of her body, and a band of twisted reeds was tied so tightly round her forehead that her eyes threatened to burst from their sockets. (*Boys of England* 11, no. 285 [27 April 1872], p. 356)

This almost tedious, detailed description of torture clearly reveals that Hemyng's detached objectivity concealed hatred of—at least some—women and an almost sadistic pleasure in portraying their pains. More to the point, however, this portrayal offered readers a similar (subconscious) pleasure while morality was preserved through Jack. He objects, not to the killing of the suspect, but to the cruel methods employed. Thus, instead of being tormented by her tribe, the old woman is eaten alive by crocodiles:

There was a snap of the huge jaws, and a dreadful shriek.

This was repeated.

Nuratella's cries redoubled as first an arm and then a leg was torn away.

Other crocodiles, attracted by the smell of blood, approached.

Soon the cries ceased.

The witch was still, and though the cruel fangs of the monsters tore her flesh, she felt them not. (*Boys of England* 11, no. 286 [4 May 1872], p. 370)

Raised with the often harsh contradictions of sexualized purity, the middle-class boy could hardly fail to be aroused by such passages. With their total fusion of sexuality and violence, the descriptions, albeit rare, of female torture would trigger sadistic impulses toward women, which in real life the reader found little opportunity for expressing. To some boys, accounts of violence toward natives—like women a lesser race—may even have spurred their flagellation fantasies. At any rate, no simple impressions lay behind later reminiscences of the "heroic, Homeric" qualities of Brett's and Emmett's popular papers as expressed by an article in the *Times Literary Supplement* in 1918.

Love, of a more mundane nature, was also an important topic in the correspondence pages of the paper. Along with puzzles, charades and entries on sport, the reader would find answers such as: "You cannot compel a lady to love you. All you can do is to try, by superior devotion, manliness and personal worth to cut out your rival and win the prize." Advice on stunted growth, sparse beards, and wet palms also indicates the adolescent readers' preoccupation with personal appearance. Thus, "H. H. H." receives the following counsel: "Get some powdered nitre, put it on a damp towel, and apply it to the face, allowing it to remain some time. Persevere in this treatment, and the freckles will soon disappear" (*Boys of England* 14, no. 351 [2 August 1873], p. 143). What else might disappear in the process is not mentioned. Questions on smoking bring warnings against "the deleterious effects of the narcotic weed" and exceptional

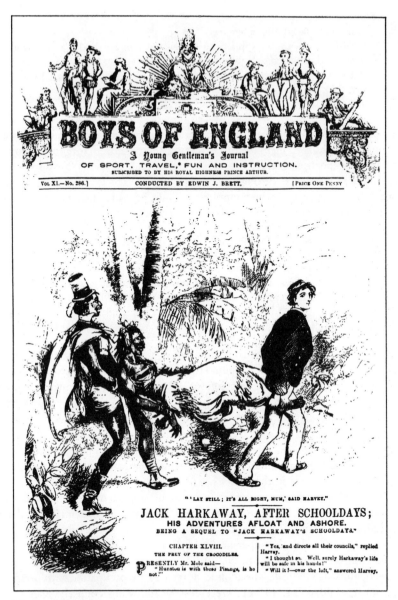

BOYS OF ENGLAND

A Young Gentleman's Journal

OF SPORT, TRAVEL, FUN AND INSTRUCTION.

SUBSCRIBED TO BY HIS ROYAL HIGHNESS PRINCE ARTHUR.

VOL XI.—No. 286.]   CONDUCTED BY EDWIN J. BRETT.   [PRICE ONE PENNY

"'LAY STILL; IT'S ALL RIGHT, MUM,' SAID HARVEY."

JACK HARKAWAY, AFTER SCHOOLDAYS;

HIS ADVENTURES AFLOAT AND ASHORE.

BEING A SEQUEL TO "JACK HARKAWAY'S SCHOOLDAYS."

CHAPTER XLVIII.

THE PREY OF THE CROCODILES.

PRESENTLY Mr. Mole said—
"Hunston is with these Pisangs, is he not?"

"Yes, and directs all their councils," replied Harvey.
"I thought so. Well, surely Harkaway's life will be safe in his hands!"
"Will it?—over the left," answered Harvey.

The *Boys of England; A Magazine of Sport, Sensation, Fun, and Instruction* 11, no. 286 (4 May 1872), front cover. Although "Nuratella" manages to keep her skirt at her ankles, her half-naked body and tied hands reveal the unusual fusion of sexuality and violence found in some commercial publications.

vocations are invariably snubbed at (*Boys of England* 4, no. 100 [16 October 1868], p. 351). To "Poor Ray" the answer reads: "We certainly do not advise you, or anyone else, to think of going on the stage. Strive rather to get into some good business" (*Boys of England* 13, no. 332 [22 March 1873], p. 271). In the editorial columns, we find the paper's conscious promotion of the healthy habits and the good bourgeois values that were so often undermined in the serials. The relative explicitness on sexual matters, also in the correspondence pages, is clearly a reminiscence of the penny dreadfuls and the romantic novelettes. Perhaps its presence also indicates that romance, if not sexuality, was deemed a necessary ingredient to wean a more worldly and less educated audience from their traditional literary fare.

In most other respects, however, Brett's *Boys of England* was a portent of future trends in periodical publishing for boys. Its serials, dominating the contents, popularized the school tale that would feature sustained characters such as Jack Harkaway, Tom Floremall, Ned Nimble, Dick Lightheart, and other schoolboys-cum-adventurers. One of these long-running yarns, featured in 1874–75, bore the title "Wildcap Will; or, Schoolboy, Lover, and Sailor." Muscular Christianity was attuned to the serials' demands for consecutive and hard-hitting effects, and the authors, called penny-a-liners, nurtured a short, clipped style coupled with much visual detail. That the format became bigger and illustrations more plentiful was in accordance with Brett's flair for using technical innovations for maximum self-promotion. This skill was also evidenced by his successful prize competitions in which neat essay-writing was discarded, in his advertisements for other Brett publications, the so-called companion papers, and the often intimate tone employed in his correspondence pages.

The *Boys of England* arrived at a time when a new adolescent readership appeared with money to spare and with at least some unsupervised time of its own. Such circumstances would induce customers and subscribers to choose for their leisure reading only what seemed most entertaining and enjoyable. The successful formula concocted by Brett paved the way for the commercial boys' weeklies of the Edwardian era. These papers, while catering to a younger audience, also had to strike a balance between profits to their publishers and pleasure to their readers.

PART FOUR

Commercial Morality
for Adolescent
Girls and Boys,
1870–1918

8

In Season and In Reason: The Development of Girls' Magazines and the Transformation of Boys' Magazines

ON 3 JANUARY 1880, the first number of the *Girl's Own Paper* came to light. It was published by the Religious Tract Society, which had come a long way in its editorial policies since the publication of the *Child's Companion* in 1824. This attractive penny weekly and its bound monthly issues priced sixpence became the first successful girls' magazine and also the most enduring, holding out under various titles and with changing fortunes until 1956. The periodical was brought out as a female counterpart to the society's then one-year-old *Boy's Own Paper* (1879–1967), itself the longest-living boys' magazine. Its fame, though, was challenged by the *Girl's Own Paper*, whose circulation soon rivaled the 200,000 weekly copies of the *Boy's Own Paper* (Altick 1967, p. 395). According to Dunae (1976, p. 151), the *Girl's Own Paper* remained the most lucrative of the society's numerous periodical ventures. By the late 1880s, the two weeklies were deemed by far the most popular magazines for adolescents. In a survey carried out by Edward Salmon among nearly two thousand pupils, more than half of the boys chose the *Boy's Own Paper* as their favorite magazine while nearly a third of the girls preferred the *Girl's Own Paper* (Salmon 1888, pp. 15, 23).[1]

It was the express aim of the editor, Charles Peters (1852–1907), to cater not only to the young lady of the leisured classes, but also to "girls of a less high position" who would receive instruction in "economical cookery, plain nee-

1. Only cautious judgments should be passed from Salmon's evidence on readers' actual preferences. His survey was limited to pupils, and their answers could easily have been influenced by the educational surroundings. Thus, one youngster professed a liking for the *Boy's Own Paper* because "knowing that, as well as simply reading, I shall also be instructed" (Salmon 1888, p. 20).

dlework, home education and health." Even servants should find in the magazine a guide "to their humble work . . . a counsellor in sore temptation" and an
advisor of "a pure and honest life." The readers were assured that there is
"honesty and nobility even in the kitchen" ("Answers to Correspondents," *Girl's
Own Paper* 2, no. 40 [20 October 1880], p. 15). It is doubtful that many
working-class maids would sustain the paper's weekly admonitions even if they
got sixteen pages for a penny. But for the middle- and lower-middle-class girls
there was lively fiction, two serials, several poems, and the occasional short story
or anecdote in addition to plenty of useful information. Detailed recipes, patterns, and instructions for knitting, embroidering, and dressmaking stressed the
practical rather than the extravagant aspects of homemaking. The fashion page,
called "Dress: In Season and in Reason" in the early volumes, would assist the
reader in keeping up with new styles by inexpensive alterations of frocks and
gowns. A regular correspondence page advised girls who faltered in these or
other female maxims and also offered guidance on school and career choice. All
was copiously illustrated by at least five or six large and many small engravings
in black and white with the occasional color plate. The imaginative layout of the
paper, the cutting up of the 7½-by-15-inch printed pages by pictures of birds,
fruit, and flower wreaths, gave the *Girl's Own Paper* a visual appeal that
undoubtedly added to its immediate success.

Many contributors to the periodical were women, among them well-known
contemporary authors such as Ruth Lamb, Rosa Nouchette Carey, Isabella
Fyvie Mayo, and Mrs. de Horne Vaizey (who published as Jessie Mansergh
during her first marriage). Although adolescence was still used as a specialized
term, the main part of the contents in the *Girl's Own Paper* clearly appealed to
readers standing midway between girlhood and adulthood. This period was
widening since marriage ages were going up. It was also marked by distinct
problems and possibilities. The *Girl's Own Paper* at once reflected a new female
self-consciousness and revealed the contradictions it involved. It thus prefigured
by about ten or fifteen years themes that were to be taken up in novels by authors
such as L. T. Meade (1854–1914), Evelyn Everett Green (1856–1932), and
Bessie Marchant (1862–1941).

Through most of the nineteenth century, social differences separated women
more thoroughly than divisions of age. While work dominated most working-
class women's lives, domesticity enveloped the entire existence of the middle-
class female. When the *Girl's Own Paper* appeared on the literary scene, this
domestic dominance was being shaken if not defeated. Thus, the use of "girl" to
denote an unmarried woman had not yet disappeared (the *Oxford English Dictionary* dates that definition of status back to 1530), and the modern distinctions
made according to physiological and legal age had not become universally
accepted. This duality seems to have posed few conscious obstacles to Charles
Peters, who shaped and selected the *Girl's Own Paper* for its first twenty-eight

VOL. I.—No. 1.]   JANUARY 3, 1880.   [PRICE ONE PENNY.

ZARA:
OR, MY GRANDDAUGHTER'S MONEY.

CHAPTER I.
AN ARRIVAL.

THE streets of a dreary London suburb were more dreary than usual on that December evening. A dense fog was fast gathering up its yellow vapour, making the shabby, tumble-down region only one degree less obscure than it would be at midnight. Jasper Meade, proprietor of the "Commercial Lodging House," stood on his own door-step, whistling a dismal refrain very much out of tune, but at the moment he was not thinking of melody — his keen, restless black eyes were striving to penetrate the mist. He watched every vehicle that rattled past, splashing through the sloppy mud, waking up the echoes for a short space, and disappearing into the obscurity beyond, and considered it another lost chance, a fresh disappointment. The secret of this was that Jasper's last venture in the world of speculation was not realising his expectations.

He had lately purchased the lodging-house before-mentioned, and found his

venture was of questionable advantage. It had been described in the advertisement as "ruinously cheap," having spacious, well-furnished rooms, good stables, every convenience for man and

beast, and doing a splendid business. Tempted by the delusive bait, he had rashly invested the whole of his capital in the purchase, awakening too late to the knowledge that much gloss and rosy tint is apt to be used in advertising, and that a bargain rarely comes up to the description given of its merits.

Rooms, many and various, there certainly were in the old house, but they looked as though generations of bygone travellers had tarried there, disported themselves without restraint, and then gone on their ways. The walls were sullied and grimy, the furniture worn out, the carpets ragged and faded, the whole place disreputable in the extreme. Jasper's wife — a pretty, bright-eyed little woman, charming with her Frenchified manner, born and bred a lady — had been driven to utter despair when Jasper took her down to that suburban establishment, and told her it was to be their future home ! The meanness and vulgarity of the place were repugnant to Phillis ; every instinct of her nature revolted, she

"WILL YOU COME TO MY LITTLE ROOM ?"

The *Girl's Own Paper* 1, no. 1 (3 January 1880), front cover. The masthead, depicting a Greek statue, "The Spirit of Truth and Love," sets the lofty ideals of this first successful girls' periodical, while M. Ellen Edwards in her illustration to the opening story captures a more mundane reality that the weekly also negotiated.

years. But to Flora Klickman, editor from 1908 to 1931—when a stricter differentiation between female age groups had been imposed—and to her successors, the ambiguities of adolescence were evident, as is indicated by the paper's rapid changes of title.[2]

The problems of definition make it equally difficult to trace the first girl's paper. The first attempt at creating a periodical specifically for a young female readership appeared in 1838. The *Young Ladies' Magazine of Theology, History, Philosophy, and General Knowledge* was a short-lived and unillustrated publication whose title suggested its semireligious contents and its didactic aims, and whose brief run indicated its prematureness. The "young ladies" of the upper and upper-middle classes simply had not developed as a separate magazine audience but still contented themselves with memoirs, novels, sermons, or household periodicals when they read. As for the younger girls of those classes, they relied, as already noted, on general children's books or on compound magazines, catering to the whole of the large Victorian nursery, such as the religious periodicals and later the *Chatterbox, Aunt Judy's Magazine,* and *Good Words for the Young.*

In the same vein as these lofty publications was the *Monthly Packet of Evening Readings for Younger Members of the English Church* (1851–98), edited until 1893 by Charlotte Yonge. A sixpenny monthly, it was chiefly aimed at the rector's and the professor's elder daughters, "young girls, or maidens, or young ladies, whichever you like to be called, who are above the age of childhood, and who are either looking back on school-days with regret, or else pursuing the most important part of education, namely self-education," as the editor stated in her "Introductory Letter." Miss Yonge expressed the hope, though, that her new venture would also "be pleasant reading for boys at the same age, especially school teachers" and that it would be found in "the servants' hall, or the lending library." The *Monthly Packet* was meant as "a companion in times of recreation, which may help you to perceive how to bring your religious principles to bear upon your daily life," and this endeavor was clearly thought of as a female prerogative (1, no. 1 [January 1851], pp. i–iv). Deeply imbued with Miss Yonge's Tractarian religion, the magazine over the years featured many of her uplifing stories in which feminine restraint and a Christian conscience were carefully nurtured within domestic surroundings.

In 1863 commercial publishers seriously began thinking of young women. The *English Girls' Journal, and Ladies' Magazine, The Ladies' Favourite Companion* was a penny weekly, published by Edward Harrison. Its sixteen pages

2. When the *Girl's Own Paper* became a monthly in 1908, its title was changed to the *Girl's Own Paper and Woman's Magazine.* In 1928, it became the *Woman's Magazine and Girl's Own Paper,* but three years later the *Girl's Own Paper* went independent under that title, then became the *Girl's Own Paper Heiress* (1941–50), and finally ceased its career as *Heiress* in 1956. The paper's popular yearly volume, the *Girl's Own Annual,* ceased publication in 1940.

contained a medley of short stories and serials of a romantic nature, elaborate fashion guides, and household notes ("The Model Housewife") as well as music scores, suggestions on embroidery, and a "Gossip with Correspondents" column. After fifty-nine numbers, the magazine was bought by the young and vigorous W. L. Emmett and formed the foundation stone of the Emmett family's later publishing successes. Although the weekly, which is not recorded at the British Library, probably ceased publication in 1865, Emmett later tried his hand with a follow-up more specifically directed at a younger audience, namely the *Young Ladies of Great Britain* (1869–71, then merging with *Dress and Fashion*). By 1864, the ubiquitous Beeton had already caught that idea, bringing out the *Young Englishwoman.* Harrison, on his part, was quick to rival Emmett with another and more successful penny weekly whose voluminous title, in the old tradition, formed a table of contents: the *Young Ladies' Journal, an illustrated Magazine of Entertaining Literature, Original Music, Toilet and Household Receipts, every description of Paris Fashions and Needlework, with magnificent supplementary volume containing full-size Patterns for Ladies' and Children's dresses, etc., and coloured plates of Fashion and Berlin Work direct from Paris* (1864–1920).[3]

The 1860s discovered the commercial possibilities hidden in a young and well-off female audience. This is also attested to by the success of contemporary novelists such as the American Susan Warner and, on a higher moral note, Elisabeth Sewell and Charlotte Yonge. Yet, the magazines straddled adolescence and adulthood, featuring for the bored girl palatable "fiction and entertaining literature," as Beeton expressed it, while also consoling the exasperated housewife with recipes for "curry fowl with cocoanut sauce" and detailed descriptions on the making of "pearl water" to whiten the reader's complexion.

In 1869 the *Girl of the Period Miscellany* appeared. A sixpenny monthly, it was a transient phenomenon lasting only from March to November. But its tone prefigured a new magazine trend, which the firm of Routledge took up in *Every Girl's Magazine* (1878–88?) and which the *Girl's Own Paper* was to popularize. The new monthly emphasized sensible instruction rather than uplifting moralism or extravagant directions and displayed self-reliant young heroines in its stories though none of them exceeded the golden mean of social acceptability— all were married in the end. That the 1860s was a period of transition in the history of girls' magazines need hardly surprise us when we remember the fierce rivalries that took place among mass-circulation publishers. Editors and proprietors looked for new groups of prospective customers among whom young middle-class women were becoming a distinctive unit.

The so-called Great Depression, lasting from 1873 to 1896, postponed the

3. Publishing information on periodicals not at the British Library is from Jay 23 October 1920, p. 172; 30 October 1920, p. 176; and 13 November 1920, p. 184.

commercial exploration of this new readership and highlighted its social presence. Cheaper industrial and agricultural products, especially from Germany and the United States, were threatening the British dominance on markets abroad and shattering the domestic equipoise of the mid-Victorian decades. Financial instability and social anxiety assumed new and poignant proportions for people to whom security was the be-all and end-all of life. In the 1870s and 1880s prices dropped on basic commodities like food and clothing, thus increasing the real wages of workers in regular employment and enabling working-class women to give up their jobs. The years of crisis for middle-class families, however, exacerbated the problems of keeping what Harriet Martineau called the "redundant women" in feminine idleness. The growing number of lower-middle-class women, who had never fulfilled the Victorian ideals ascribed to their sex, were already seeking new means of supporting themselves. The reform impulse in girls' education, evident as a moral and political issue from mid-century, was reinforced by strong economic arguments.

Nursing and teaching became female vocations combining economic independence with the spirit of philanthropy that was central to the Victorian conception of woman's sphere. The years of depression were gradually ousted by imperialist expansion and a renewed nationalist optimism. Trade picked up, and colonial administration developed while local and central governments widened their activities. The state increasingly assumed a responsibility to alleviate the worst excesses of poverty. The social scope of middle- and lower-middle-class women was further widened when positions opened up as health inspectors, typists, and secretaries. Thus, while women in middle-class occupations made up 12.6 percent of all workers in 1881, they constituted 23.7 percent of the labor force in 1911. Working-class women's gainful employment during the same period decreased from 87.4 to 76.3 percent of the total work force (Holcombe 1973, p. 216).[4] Even if most middle- and lower-middle-class women lived for hearth and home, the naturalness of a domestic destiny had been broken as a prospect for their daughters.

While the poorest Britons remained around thirty percent of the population and forty percent of the working class, much the same as in midcentury, the lower-middle class holding white-collar jobs rose relative to the labor aristocracy in the final quarter of the century. In 1851, salaried employees had comprised 2.5 percent of all male workers over fifteen years of age, but twenty years later that percentage had increased to 3.5, to 5.5 by 1891, and to 7.1 in 1911 (Hobsbawm 1964, pp. 284–85, 297; Crossick 1977, p. 19). A lower-middle-class outlook on life, shaped by the influences of job expansion and constant

---

4. Middle-class occupations, in Holcombe's definition, include teachers, nurses, clerks, civil servants, and shop assistants, the last group in some other studies being assigned to the working class.

economic fluctuation, was evident in juvenile publishing during the late-Victorian and Edwardian years. The first successful girls' magazines, the *Girl's Own Paper* and the *Girl's Realm* (1898–1915), were directed at middle- and lower-middle-class adolescents while not consciously excluding the working class.[5] Around the turn of the century serious efforts were made to capture the interests of young working-class women without losing touch with the lucrative lower middle-class market.

Throughout the nineteenth century, many poor and literate girls seem to have shared with their mothers not only the dominance of paid or unpaid labor on their lives, but also the fact that they had less time for leisure reading than did their male relatives. Popular family journals, penny novelettes, or inexpensive women's magazines had been their fictional mainstay. These choices might be supplemented or even supplanted by religious children's periodicals in devout households. But just as young middle- and lower-middle-class women became visible to the public eye in the 1870s and 1880s, so a growing number of their working-class sisters were forming a distinct consumer group twenty years later. The gradual development of multiple stores from the 1880s and the expansion of factory production, first to footwear (from the 1870s), then to clothes (1890s), and from the 1900s to consumer durables such as the bicycle and the sewing machine moved the industrial center toward the south east, and it also attracted as workers groups of unmarried women who had previously been employed as domestic servants or perhaps as milliners or straw-plait makers in the sweated trades.[6] Regulated work hours and higher payment offered the young shop assistants and machinists time and money for a conspicuous consumption, even if to modern minds this was still on a very limited scale.

Publishers, however, were quick to cash in on a latent trend. Of the new type of halfpenny and penny weeklies, the so-called mill-girl papers, some of the most popular were the *Girls' Weekly* (1912–22), issued by the young D. C. Thomson of Dundee, *Peg's Paper* (1919–40), which was brought out by Newnes and Pearson, and—published by Alfred Harmsworth (1865–1922), who first spotted the trend—the *Girls' Best Friend* (1898–1931, from 1899 the *Girls' Friend*), the *Girls' Reader* (1908–15), the *Girls' Home* (1910–15), and *Our Girls* (1915–19). Commercial publishing for adolescent girls now included all social groups, but their fictional needs were catered to in two separate

5. Other, more short-lived ventures included the Marshall Brothers' monthly *Schoolgirls* (1894–95) and the *Girls' School Magazine: Useful, Entertaining, Instructive* (1892–93), a penny monthly published by Glenn & Hall for the Useful Literature Company. This body also issued the *School and Home Magazine* ("equally suitable for boys and girls," 1892–93, then *School and Home*, 1894–1906), and the higher-class girls' periodical, the *School Monthly* (1892–94).

6. For a description of the transformations in home-market production and in the retail trades, see Fraser 1981, esp. pp. 110–33, 175–92.

The *Girls' Best Friend* 1, no. 1 (26 February 1898), front cover. The first of the so-called mill-girl papers treating mainly young working-class women to a mixture of romance, beauty, and fashion.

types of publication. In chapter ten, I analyze and compare the two types, centering on the *Girl's Own Paper* and the Harmsworth weeklies respectively.

In the history of juvenile magazines, the invention of the girls' periodical is clearly the most important innovation of the late-Victorian era. Out of a total of ninety-three titles, twenty-six, or more than a quarter of all girls' papers published before 1970, appeared before 1918 (six of these I have recorded as being issued before 1880). In terms of actual numbers, however, girls lagged far behind their brothers. The period between 1880 and 1918 was indeed the halcyon days of the boys' paper. Nearly half of the 307 commercial boys' magazines, 149 titles, appeared for the first time during those years.[7] A few of these newcomers continued to appeal mainly to a middle-class audience of adolescents who stayed on at school and saw professional or military careers as their coveted destinies. *Chums* (1892–1932) was brought out by Cassells and initially edited by Sir Max Pemberton, the *Jabberwock* (1905–07) was published by Chapman and Hall, and the firm of Newnes aimed the *Captain* (1899–1924) specifically at public-school pupils ("boys and old boys" as the subtitle had it), who became acquainted with P. G. Wodehouse's first school stories in this way.

The epitome of these quality periodicals, though, was undoubtedly the *Boy's Own Paper* (1879–1967). We have already encountered this penny weekly as the male precursor of the *Girl's Own Paper*. Published under the formal auspices of Dr. James Macaulay (1817–1902), the first issue of the *Boy's Own Paper* was given away at some schools in order to boost circulation (Warner 1976, p. 15). However, the magazine soon reached near-institutional status both with middle-class parents, attracted perhaps by the contributors' impressive titles, and also with their sons, enthused certainly with the breezy tales selected by George Andrew Hutchinson (1842–1913), the creator and daily editor of the paper for thirty-three years. While the magazine was the most popular one through the 1880s, Hutchinson's standards in the 1890s came under heavy fire from cheaper and more vigorously promoted publications. However, in 1888 the Religious Tract Society was optimistic enough to incorporate Routledge's *Every Boy's Magazine,* followed six years later by Sampson Low's *Boys* (1892–94). But in 1912, when A. L. Haydon was appointed as Hutchinson's successor, the *Boy's Own Paper* turned into a monthly, and in later years it was especially the bound yearly volumes entitled the *Boy's Own Annual,* which upheld the image of the Christian Englishman to a dwindling number of twentieth-century boys.

From its inception the weekly *Boy's Own Paper* combined the standard fare of "home employments and amusements" with a mixture of school and adventure

7. Number of titles are adaptations from Lofts and Adley 1969, pp. 9–18, 22–24, a bibliography that also includes girls' papers but does not list religious periodicals. While not attempting to complete the catalogue, I have added a few commercial magazines while excluding reissues.

stories. The odd poem, anecdote, and puzzle was thrown in for good measure. The paper embodied solid high-class fiction and Victorian notions of quality with its monthly color plates, its essay competitions (maximum age of participation sixteen) and its well-known authors, among whom were G. A. Henty, R. M. Ballantyne, Conan Doyle, W. H. G. Kingston, and Jules Verne, whose stories here made their first British appearance (Egoff 1951, p. 24). Most notable, perhaps, was Hutchinson's greatest find, Talbot Baines Reed, born 1854, whose public-school serials, such as "The Fifth Form at St. Dominic's" (1881–82), "The Master of the Shell" (1887), and the "Cock-House of Fellsgarth" (1891), became treasured classics (Musgrave 1985, pp. 112–46).

Although the *Boy's Own Paper* and its sister companion, the *Girl's Own Paper*, were both stamped by the moral ideals propagated by the Religious Tract Society, their editors were clearly not blind to the market mechanisms of publishing. Interestingly, much of the sizable revenue made from the two papers went to support orphanages and ragged schools at home, just as it assisted the society's missionary activities in India, China, and Africa (Dunae 1976, pp. 135, 154). However, despite Hutchinson's updating of Beeton's educative approach, the most innovative and, in the longer term, clearly the most successful publishers of boys' papers were found among those who continued Brett's and Emmett's more sensational style, which had proved so popular with lower-middle- and working-class juveniles. As noted in chapter six, the Education Act of 1870 gradually harnessed the three Rs for the last group of poor and illiterate English children. To an industry rife with rivalries, it became imperative to secure this group of boys and girls as readers. In their efforts to offer inexpensive reading matter and thus oust their competitors, publishers seized on technology. The introduction of the rotary press and the use of wood-pulp paper had facilitated the expansion in mass literature at mid-century, and the invention in the late 1880s of the Linotype machine, casting whole lines of type, forged the final link in fully mechanizing the printing process. Furthermore, the general expansion in retail trades created a national network of local tobacconists, sweetstalls, and cornershops to which adolescents swarmed on their way from school or work to get their Wednesday or Saturday weeklies.

While the copy price was brought down and the potential readership multiplied, mechanization drastically increased capital outlays and thus reduced the number of firms that were able to compete on the new terms. Small family enterprises such as Samuel Beeton's, in which one person was both proprietor and editor, were becoming a thing of the past. Publishers were also facing a growing competition from outside their own ranks. New racecourses, betting offices, and, to some of the more privileged, seaside resorts were added to the pubs and the music halls as commercial venues with decided appeal to many adolescents, not least those from the working class. Edwardian Britain was no longer a fiction-reading nation to the extent that mid-Victorian Britain had been.

Under these circumstances, advertising became an increasingly important source of income for institutional and commercial publishers alike. And although the development was less pronounced in juvenile magazines, the general reinforcement of commercialism nevertheless reverberated in their pages.

In 1888 a new level of competition developed in juvenile magazines. The established rivals—Newnes, Pearson, Aldine, Henderson, and Brett—were joined by a twenty-five-year-old free-lance journalist, Alfred Harmsworth. The phenomenal career of Harmsworth (he became Lord Northcliffe in 1905) highlights how the most farsighted proprietors secured their success by not only gradually including the remnants of a newly literate readership, but equally by sensitizing their magazine output to the varying needs of this readership. "If he was not the first to spot the growing new market coming out of the board schools he was the most thorough in exploiting it" (Cudlipp 1962, p. 188).[8]

As founder of the Periodical Publishing Company, which became the Amalgamated Press in 1902, Harmsworth's fame rests on his introduction into the daily press of what Matthew Arnold called "new journalism." Through his creation of the *Daily Mail* in 1896 and seven years later the *Daily Mirror*, Harmsworth promoted news as entertainment and turned the working man into a daily newspaper reader. But Harmsworth's successful formula, his journalistic blend of human interest stories, comic strips, jokes, and large illustrations, all generously garnished by advertisements, had been carefully molded through his initial, and less publicized, experiences with women's and juvenile magazines.

His first venture, *Answers to Correspondents*, was launched in 1888 as a competitor of George Newnes' popular *Tit-Bits* (1880), which mixed reader contributions with snippets from books and periodicals. Two years later *Comic Cuts* and *Illustrated Chips* followed; these halfpenny papers were originally aimed at adults but found a large following among working-class juveniles. Harmsworth was also an innovator of comics although he was not the first in Britain to issue them. The first comic-strip hero, Ally Sloper, had appeared in *Judy* in 1867 and got his own paper, *Ally Sloper's Half-Holiday*, in 1884. The first comic paper was James Henderson's *Funny Folks* in 1874. Harmsworth, however, was the first to spot the juvenile appeal of the new form. When he published the color comic *Puck* in 1904, its children's section, "Junior Puck," eclipsed the fame of its parent paper. The Amalgamated Press subsequently launched the *Rainbow* (1914–56), the first comic aimed specifically at young children, featuring the perennial hero Tiger Tim, whose exploits were to challenge the monopoly of the quality magazines for the very young (Gifford 1975, pp. ix–x).

8. For a detailed analysis of the differences in style and content between Beeton's *Boy's Own Magazine* and Harmsworth's *Boys' Friend* as examples of the nineteenth-century transition in commercial publishing for boys, see Drotner 1977, pp. 52–115.

Harmsworth's successful appeal to various sections of the comic-reading audience was repeated on the women's market. His penny weeklies, *Forget Me Not* (1891) and *Home Chat* (1895), both popularized the ideas of the modern woman's magazine with their blend of entertaining fiction, beauty hints, home furnishing, and housekeeping (White 1970, pp. 75–76). If the popularity of these weeklies, with their wide age group of readers, aided Harmsworth in discovering the market potentials of unmarried young women from the working and lower-middle classes, then his unparalleled flair for tracing boys' fictional needs must have prompted him to publish inexpensive papers for these young women.

A. A. Milne claimed that Harmsworth "killed the 'penny dreadful' by the simple process of producing a ha'penny dreadfuller." He did so through an unusually successful rejuvenation of Brett's blend of sensationalism and moralism at a time, moreover, when imperialist expansion reinforced middle-class concerns with working-class children's moral well-being, and when a growing number of lower-middle-class juveniles were to find their precarious positions in the social fabric. Harmsworth was not the first to publish a halfpenny juvenile weekly (this was probably the *Children's Missionary Record*, as noted, and, in the commercial vein, Brett's short-lived venture, the *Boys of the World*, 1869–70), but he was the first to reap the commercial benefits by undercutting his rivals in this way.

Harmsworth's first boys' paper, the *Halfpenny Marvel*, was published in 1893, and like its immediate successors, the *Union Jack* (1894–1933) and *Pluck* (1894–1916; 1922–24), it was allegedly invented in an idealistic attempt to debunk and destroy the morally vile and pernicious penny dreadfuls, which were, incidentally, published by some of Harmsworth's fiercest business rivals. Brett's old tactic of setting off his own new publications by a moral onslaught on his competitors was used by Harmsworth to captivate an audience whose daily lives were more often defined through family and school than through work as in Brett's early days. Nor surprisingly, the editor in the opening issue of the *Halfpenny Marvel* made an earnest request to the readers' guardians:

> PARENTS, if you see your children reading "penny dreadfuls," take them away and give them the "HALFPENNY MARVEL" LIBRARY books instead.
>
> If we can rid the world of even one of these vile publications our efforts will not have been in vain. ("The Editor Speaks," *Halfpenny Marvel* 1, no. 1 [11 November 1893], p. 16)

As Harmsworth's weeklies became firmly established, the attacks on penny dreadfuls subsided in favor of painstaking presentations of new, stirring serials, circulation-boosting competitions, and incessant praise of other Amalgamated Press papers. The editorial address, which was as stable a feature, if less heavy-handed, as in the quality magazines, gradually changed its tone (and its caption) to a more congenial attitude in an apparent attempt to enhance reader identification: many readers would object to any sign of overt authority in their leisure reading. Covert paternalism, though, still balanced youthful intimacy in the advice given to correspondents. As in the *Boys of England,* this advice included suggestions for suitable careers as well as consolations about overly severe school curricula. Thus, one dejected reader was told to "congratulate himself on being at an English school and not a French one," and he was then harangued on the hardships to be endured by French pupils (*Halfpenny Marvel* 1, no. 14 [13 February 1894], p. 16). But in the Amalgamated Press weeklies, personal concerns assumed an increasingly important role, and the detailed editorial answers included treatment of blushing and freckles, underdeveloped muscles, and chronic stammer, which was explained as being "simply a habit" whose cure "lies in applying the system with patient watchfulness and unbending steadfastness of purpose, and by never forgetting to fill the lungs before expelling the breath" ("'Stammering: How to Cure It,' by a Former Stutterer," *Boys' Friend* 1, no. 11 [9 April 1895], p. 90).

This curious blend of stiff upperlip and physiological insight appeared in the *Boys' Friend* (1895–1927, then incorporated with the *Triumph*). The weekly was printed on green paper (admittedly applied for its soothing effect on the eyes and not to make it distinguishable at the newsagent), and it was soon supported by two "companion papers," the *Boys' Realm* (1902–30, title varies), printed on pink paper, and the *Boys' Herald* (1903–12), printed on white paper. The magazines came out on different days, and such dispersion helped sustain the readers' interest and diminished the financial risks of entering on new magazine ventures. The popular triumvirate was firmly conducted by Robert Hamilton Edwards (1872–1932) who emphasized vigorous fiction, initially a mixture of adventure, public-school, and detective stories with a heavy bent toward exotic surroundings, rapid reversals of fate, and deus ex machina solutions.

Around the turn of the century, all self-respecting Harmsworth papers promulgated what the *Boys of England* had initiated in the 1860s. Britain's imperialism lent new credibility to fictional heroes' hairbreadth escapes in likely and unlikely corners of the globe. Their audacity no longer needed justification, secular or religious. The structure of the stories, though, still obeyed a certain chronological development with marriage and material riches to crown male daredevilry. Foreigners remained of an either belligerent or ridiculous nature, but girls took a more active part in the action even if they never challenged male supremacy, perhaps because they were always too busy keeping their skirts below the ankles. The many favorable judgments expressed by avid girl readers, duly published in the three papers, cannot but have hastened Harmsworth's creation of female correlatives to the popular boys' weeklies.

Harmsworth's successful marketing of companion papers for adolescent boys was topped by his gradual development of the single-genre perennial, which facilitated a further diversification of reader interests into detective, adventure, and schoolstory papers.[9] From its inception in 1894, the *Union Jack* was identified with the detective hero Sexton Blake, the "office boy's Sherlock Holmes," who had first made his entry in the *Halfpenny Marvel* one year previously (Turner 1976, pp. 127–56). From 1904 to its final appearance in 1922, the *Marvel* was the place to rejoice in the eternal adventures of Samuel Clarke Hook's "Jack, Sam and Pete." Jack was an Oxford undergraduate, Sam an American trapper, and Pete, clearly the most popular of the three, a black juvenile and multimillionaire from Zanzibar, who paired his racial quaintness with the good fortune of being a British subject, and who also excelled by being a first-class boxer and ventriloquist. Following the fictional footsteps of Jack Harkaway, as it were, the three youngsters spent their time roaming around the globe rather than exploring dusty lecture halls in Oxford.

However, Harmsworth's most famous single-genre papers undoubtedly became the schoolstory weeklies *Gem* (1907–39, then incorporated with the *Triumph*) and *Magnet* (1908–40, then merging with the *Knockout*). Within the serial framework of a public school, each paper spun out a weekly 50,000 to 55,000 word issue around a group of adolescent boarders who never got old, who were eternally sidestepping the school ethos or were busy in keeping others to the golden mean, and who therefore continually renewed what was basically an unchanging narrative structure. With Jack Harkaway, Brett had developed the static hero but retained different surroundings. The *Gem* and the *Magnet* took this one step further in that the schools also remained the same. What we might call the "flexible stability" of the two weeklies constituted a new narrative formula that subsequent juvenile papers have fed on.

This formula was the brainchild of a single author, Charles Harold St. John Hamilton (1876–1961), the first to enter *Who's Who* under the best-known of his pen names, Frank Richards, which he used in the *Magnet* (in the *Gem*, he appeared as Martin Clifford). During his long career, Hamilton created more than a hundred different school series with more than five thousand stories, as well as contributing extensively to the detective, adventure, and romantic traditions. All in all, he wrote about seventy-two million words. At the height of his popularity, when he churned out more than one-and-a-half million words a year, he had at least six stories and serials running every week under about twenty different pen names (Cadogan and Wernham 1976, p. 187; Richards 1952, p. 166).[10] Like Harmsworth himself, Charles Hamilton embodied a transforma-

9. In Harmsworth's early compound papers, reader preferences of various fictional forms were sometimes tested through opinion polls published in the weeklies but more often hinted at. Thus, the editor remarks of the *Halfpenny Marvel* (1, no. 13 [1893]) that the youngest of his correspondents seem to favor school serials while "adult readers" prefer adventure yarns.

10. According to Fayne 1962b, p. 4, this industriousness earned Hamilton about £3,000 a year. In 1913, there were "quite a score of men" in the business who earned from £500 to

tion in magazine publishing, combining the tradition of individual creation with an extremely systematic rationale of production—a combination that a later age would distribute over a number of writers, thus further enhancing the pace of production and minimizing the economic risk of being dependent on a single author.[11]

The success of the *Boys of England* suggested that the school theme was an untapped source of interest with magazine readers. This interest was later demonstrated by the popularity of papers such as the *Boy's Own Paper*, the *Captain*, and the *Boys' Friend*. It was to Hamilton's credit, and to Harmsworth's profit, that he managed to transform this interest into a popular narrative formula that would sustain two weeklies for thirty-two years and whose power would make an indelible mark upon thousands of boys from very different social backgrounds. Thus, Robert Roberts, in his famous autobiography of his Edwardian childhood in the poor area of Salford, records how "many youngsters in the working class had developed an addiction for Frank Richards' school stories. The standards of conduct observed by Harry Wharton and his friends at Greyfriars set social norms to which schoolboys and some young teenagers strove spasmodically to conform" (Roberts 1977, p. 160).

Some, apparently, continued to do so: on the death of Charles Hamilton, many adult devotees, whose enthusiasm for the old weeklies was as open as their purses, made suggestions to their fan paper for a proper commemoration of their idol with ideas including "a plaque, a statue, the foundation of a scholarship at some public school" (Fayne 1962a, p. 2). While no exact circulation figures are available, the *Magnet* seems to have been the more popular of the two companions, selling 250,000 weekly copies at its pinnacle before World War I (Lofts 1960, p. 325).

This development so far has received little analytical attention. Musgrave in his study of the boys' school story does refer to Hamilton's popularity: "What is remarkable is not so much that Richards wrote so much, but that he sold so many copies for so long." Musgrave writes off this banal but basic question by a reference to form: Hamilton's simple narrative style would make for success with the less educated readers (Musgrave 1985, pp. 224, 231). As chapter ten demonstrates, this style cannot be separated from Hamilton's structuring of the plots, and these, again, are very different from the contents found in *Stalky & Co.* (1899) and other contemporary boys' books about school. Despite minor differences in characterization and use of humor, the companions were formed

---

£1,000 a year (Rollington 1913, p. 85). For a complete list of Hamilton's fictional schools, see Lofts and Adley 1970.

11. For the Amalgamated Press, this risk was abated in 1920 when Charles Hamilton handed over his copyright of the school stories to the firm (Lofts 1961, p. 5).

almost single-handedly by Hamilton, and both were controlled by the same succession of editors. [12] Their joint development and enormous success cannot be understood without answering why school in the first place would come to occupy such a central role in the leisure reading of boys who were raised in widely different social circumstances.

12. The editors were Percy Griffith (1908–11), Herbert Allan Hinton (1911–16), John Nix Pentelow (1916–19), Herbert Allan Hinton (1919–21), and Charles Maurice Down (1921–40) (Beal 1976, p. 128).

9

Modern Girls and Masterful Boys: Childhood and Youth until 1918

DURING THE final decades of Queen Victoria's reign, adults began to think of children in terms of age rather than class or gender. The enhanced mechanization of British industry that made juvenile labor marginal to the economy coincided with renewed moral outcries against a perceived depravity of working-class juveniles, which, as noted, the hordes of vagrant children and the girl prostitutes in the cities only seemed to confirm. From the best of intentions, late-Victorian reformers curtailed the paid employment of children and adolescents and sent them to school instead. While only five laws concerning juvenile labor had been enacted during the first half of the century, double that number were created and enforced between 1850 and 1900. Similarly, some intellectual training of middle-class girls was now being acknowledged as necessary, although many men voiced their anxieties about women transgressing their proper sphere. Around the turn of the century, most children, at least in principle, lived similar lives: they were raised in a family with a male breadwinner and attended school in preparation of adulthood.

Under the influence of the intense debate over child prostitution, the age of consent for girls was raised in 1875 from its medieval twelve to thirteen, and ten years later it was raised to sixteen years of age (a legal age for boys, sixteen, was only designated in 1927) (Gorham 1978). For large sections of children, this formal prolongation of childhood also meant an actual extension of their social and economic dependence on their elders. In 1880, full-time school attendance between the ages of five and thirteen became compulsory although it was variously enforced. Children could be exempted at the age of ten until 1893 when the age was raised to eleven and six years later to twelve. The legal changes are indicative of a general trend to protect the morality of girls and to let the young stay longer at school not least in order to enhance a proper cultivation of their morals.

The Edwardian era also saw an all-time record in late marriage ages, namely, twenty-seven years on average for men and twenty-five for women (Thompson 1977, p. 71). Postponement was especially pronounced in middle- and lower-

131

middle-class circles where matrimonial bliss more than ever formed a goal, cushioned by a solid material security, that it now took longer to save up for.[1] All in all, the years between 1880 and World War I saw a formal unification of children's lives and a gradual development of adolescence among the better-off to signify the transition between innocent childhood and the adult responsibilities of work or marriage.

Some of the most ardent proponents of dependent childhood were found within the eugenic movement proliferating in the 1890s. Rather than forming a united school or a cohesive body of theories, the eugenists condensed what at the time was a widely accepted framework for understanding Britain's role in the world. The term "eugenics" was first used by Charles Darwin's cousin, Sir Francis Galton (1822–1911), who understood it as the study of inherited differences between individuals, groups, and races. The link to Darwin is important, for since the publication in 1859 of *The Origin of Species*, Darwin's ideas of natural selection had found a ready response especially with the growing section of middle-class intellectuals in need of a new philosophical and moral basis of existence, now that religion was breaking down as an all-powerful lever of social cohesion.

"Social Darwinism" is the term critics applied to the diffusion of Darwin's ideas into other areas of thought. Social problems and political developments were being understood according to the principles governing biological evolution and were being evaluated through methods taken from the physical sciences. Thus, imperialism was perceived not as an economic and political battle to secure raw materials and capture new markets but as a racial struggle in which only the sturdiest and most efficient specimens could secure the linear progress of mankind. Evolution equaled progress. Britain was seen as the apogee of civilization—but for how long? Pride mingled with fear made public attention turn toward the survival of the British people, which naturally put into focus the welfare of the young.

Contrary to traditional Social Darwinists who believed in the laissez-faire of biological selection, the eugenists sought to actively influence that mechanism. Thus, the eugenic movement at once reinforced an interest in child development and molded that development within the key areas of school and family life. While the eugenists, as biological mutants of the Hannah Mores a hundred years previously, were in the vanguard of impressing their specific version of childhood upon often recalcitrant juveniles, their efforts at the same time revealed that the formal unification of children's lives was full of contradictions, evasions, and loopholes. The structural similarities of real and ideal childhood concealed marked social and sexual differences. Perhaps the groups to experi-

1. Gillis 1985, pp. 231–59, gives a vivid account and succinct analysis of what he calls the "mandatory marriage," a pattern that is also gradually adopted by the working classes.

ence these differences most vehemently were adolescent middle-class girls and
the poorer working-class children. Their social situations clashed most sharply
with the accepted notions of a "natural" childhood.

"GRIM-VISAGED MAIDENS"

Most middle- and lower-middle-class girls growing up during the last quarter
of the nineteenth century experienced more tangible contradictions than had
either their mothers or their grandmothers. The possibilities of getting a formal
education and perhaps finding an independent career became dominant themes
in their adolescence because of the considerable changes that were taking place in
the social position of women during those years. Even at midcentury, when
Victorian domesticity was at its pinnacle and male emigration to the colonies had
begun, large numbers of adult women were forced or chose to challenge received
notions of femininity. The 1851 census revealed the more than 870,000 so-
called surplus women who would probably never marry and who thus had to
find alternative means of supporting themselves (Delamont 1978, p. 139).
From the 1830s until the outbreak of World War I, thousands of these wom-
en—about twenty thousand between 1884 and 1914—tried to solve their problems by emigrating to pioneer countries such as South Africa, Australia, and
Canada (Hammerton 1979, p. 176). Another twenty-five thousand unmarried
women had by 1851 found places as governesses in affluent homes (Banks and
Banks 1964, p. 31; Peterson 1972).

Not surprisingly, it was within this early group of gainfully employed middle-class women that the first steps were taken toward reforms in the education of
girls. Probably deliberately, the first reformers centered on educational subjects
with a direct occupational value. In 1843, the Governesses Benevolent Institution was established to protect the social and financial position of this group of
single women, and five years later this led to the foundation of Queen's College
in London for girls over the age of twelve. Its curriculum included English
grammar and literature, Latin, modern languages, mechanics, and geography
with geology. In 1850, a student from the college, Frances Mary Buss, founded
the North London Collegiate School, followed three years later by the Cheltenham College for Young Ladies, where Dorothea Beale became the headmistress
in 1858. Together with Bedford College, established in 1849, these private
institutions created girls' secondary education or a formal training of adolescents
who had acquired some basic skills.

The new schools from their inception deviated from the atmosphere cultivated at the small female academies, but they still balanced learning with feminine behavior. A more academic curriculum was implanted through pedagogical methods that reinforced the pupils' family upbringing in the direction
of unquestioning obedience and dutiful deference. "Anxiety in some shape was

always with us," said Molly Hughes of her first encounter as a diligent sixteen-year-old with the North London Collegiate School in 1883. "Marks were the life-blood of the school," she remembers. "No work whatever was done without them, so that a large proportion of time was consumed in assigning them, counting them, entering them in huge books, adding them, and checking them." The constant mental pressure on the girls was underpinned by a list of rules, some of which lingered as bad memories in the mind of the always observant Molly: "We were forbidden to get wet on the way to school, to walk more than three in a row, to drop a pencil-box, leave a book at home, hang a boot-bag by only one loop, run down the stairs, speak in class. As for speaking, it would have been easier to enumerate the few places where we were permitted to speak than those where talking was forbidden" (Hughes 1978, pp. 31, 29, 21).[2]

Such measures seem quaint to us, if not "rather excessive," as was also the verdict of Molly's liberal-minded mother. Their imposition, however, is indicative of the dilemmas facing the reformers of middle-class girls' education. Initially, few parents endorsed and financed the new schemes to directly prepare their daughters for a career. A main reason for the early success of the schools was a growing interest among middle-class professionals in raising the cultural standards of the home. For this task girls needed intellectual training (Pedersen 1979, p. 62). Curricular reforms, it was thought, should not prevent the pupils' preservation of feminine reticence and docility. In the words of Sara Delamont, the educational pioneers were thus entrapped in the "snare of double conformity" through their attempts to fulfill both the rigid Arnoldian ideals governing male intellectual pursuits and the obligations paid to ladylike femininity (Delamont 1978, pp. 140, 160). These contradictions, which have recurred in girls' education to this day, found different solutions in the dominant types of late-Victorian and Edwardian girls' schools.

Although many daughters from wealthy families were kept at home or went to one of the traditional female academies, many middle- and lower-middle-class girls were encouraged by the widening career opportunities to get some sort of intellectual training to fall back on. The modern types of school proliferated, and among the most successful were the so-called day schools modeled on the North London Collegiate School. Since many of the new institutions were organized on a shareholding or "proprietary" basis and charged moderate fees, they appealed to lower-middle-class parents who were in dire need of securing "decent" occupations not only for their sons but also for their daughters (Burstyn 1980, p. 26; Dyhouse 1981, p. 56; Kamm 1965, p. 216). Since 1877 a small number of public schools were established for a select minority of upper- and

2. Born in 1867 as the youngest of five children and the only girl in a family of unstable fortunes (her father was a stockbroker), Molly Hughes (née Thomas) went on to establish herself as a teacher and set up a teacher-training department at Bedford College, London, before happily giving up her independence for marriage and motherhood.

upper-middle-class girls. Like the boys' establishments, the schools were divided into houses organized according to the prefectorial system, and the pupils followed a rigorous curriculum emphasizing the classics, pure science, and organized games. While there were more than two hundred girls' schools by the turn of the century, there were still only eight public schools for girls by the outbreak of World War II (Pedersen 1975, p. 148).

No statistical evidence exists on the overall school attendance of middle- and lower-middle-class girls from this period. But autobiographies indicate that from the last quarter of the nineteenth century a rapidly growing number of girls attended the new forms of school, and they did so from a younger age (Gorham 1982, pp. 26, 35). Even for the girl who had never received any formal training or who had briefly attended a traditional academy, the reforms in female education presented new challenges. The schools highlighted what has since become a commonplace conflict for many adolescent girls, namely, the contradiction between family obligations and personal aspirations. H. G. Wells' Ann Veronica has come to personify what contemporaries saw as the "modern girl" whose longings would be recognized by many girls of her generation: "She wanted to live. She was vehemently impatient—she did not clearly know for what—to do, to be, to experience. And experience was slow in coming" (Wells 1968, p.11). The widening career opportunities for middle-class women offered possibilities of transgressing the domestic sphere and of experiencing a personal independence that was unknown and therefore often longed for as a coveted option. But it was equally an option that few girls were prepared for through their family upbringing.

Most late-Victorian girls grew up in families that were considerably smaller than just twenty years previously. While the mid-Victorian family averaged five or six children, their children in turn had under five, and the average couple marrying in the Edwardian era had just over three children. The decrease was most pronounced in middle- and lower-middle-class families. These groups used birth control as a solution to keen social dilemmas; they wanted to sustain a secure life-style under adverse circumstances. They also had to accommodate their strong beliefs in social order and economic stability to rapidly changing times. These dilemmas necessitated considerable investment of time, energy and money in the upbringing of the individual child, both boy and girl. The fewer children there were, the more individual attention they would get. But although the middle- and lower-middle-class girl of the late nineteenth and early twentieth centuries was thus generally closer to her mother than girls a generation before, it does not appear as if this proximity entailed more openness.

Few late-Victorian and Edwardian mothers seem to have acted as counselors or confidantes, helping to solve their daughters' key conflicts. Only a minority of women were able to pass on advice culled from personal experience on how to tackle problems at school, how to choose the right kind of career, or how indeed

The *Girl's Own Paper* 3, no. 122 (29 April 1882), facing p. 494. John Dinsdale's illustration accompanied an article on the North London Collegiate School. The physical education that was encouraged in many late-Victorian girls' schools trained both strength and feminine agility (as far as the pupils' heavy gym tunics allowed), thus highlighting the general contradictions in the education of middle-class girls. The exercises nevertheless developed a body consciousness that was firmly discouraged in other areas of female life.

to reconcile the contrary demands of work and marriage. Most mothers raised their daughters to become good Victorian wives and mothers at a time when the Victorian ideal of domesticity was being undermined. The adolescent girl, lodged between feminine docility and intellectual independence, found her mother no model of identification, and she rarely had an elder sister or a cousin close by whom she might emulate or consult.

The growing conflict between autonomy and dependence could have been particularly painful in relation to the girl's budding sexuality. The challenge to marriage as the only and inevitable female destiny in principle should have enhanced women's self-consciousness in sexual matters. However, reticence seems to have cut widely across the social scale. Thus, the nine-year-old Phyllis Bottome, born in 1882 and raised in the financial security of a clergyman's family, became "nearly frantic with rage and terror" when her mother revealed to her the facts of life. "The pains of child-birth—the greater physical strength of men—their far from greater moral strength—the white slave traffic—nothing was spared me." Similarly, Helen Corke, also born in 1882 but into a modest shopkeeping family, experienced revulsion on the onset of menstruation for which she was totally unprepared. "For the first time I wish, heartily, that I were a boy. My mother ignores this, and proceeds, hastily, to advise me of all the precautions and prohibitions relative to the monthly period that she had herself received at my age" (Gorham 1982, pp. 191, 198).[3]

Not much help was found in guidance books for the young on sexual matters, a type of literature that was just beginning to circulate. These manuals had a strong eugenic bias in their unanimous emphasis on the holiness of procreation in marriage and their complete neglect of extramarital relations. But while the knowledge imparted to girls was laced with lyrical expressions whose ornateness concealed more than it revealed, boys were informed in a more technical language. Thus, Professor Kirk in his popular book, *A Talk with Boys about Themselves* (1895), advised his young readers to prepare their minds for the delicate subject of sex by looking at fermenting hay in a microscope. In both this manual and its female counterpart, the information on intercourse was given in two different versions, with tear-out pages for the more sensitive children or their parents. In the frank version, the boy receives the following explanation:

> The penis passes up into the vagina in the union of the sexes which takes place after marriage. The spermatozoa then pass into the vagina.
> These then are the two sets of generative organs placed in male and female, each the complement of the other, which together form the wonderful vital laboratory in which the human being is built up. (Kirk 1895a, pp. A17–18)

Conversely, the explicit version in *A Talk with Girls about Themselves* (1895) reads:

> At marriage, when the man and woman closely unite in loving embrace, the life fluid passes from the man's sexual organ into that of the woman, the entrance to which is the passage in front of the body. This is used, as you know, for the passing out of the urine, but it also leads to the womb, which is the magic chamber into which the life-germ ascends. (Kirk 1895b, p. A47)[4]

Despite its striking differences of phraseology between the "vital laboratory" and the "magic chamber," the "Kirk Sex Series" was unusual in devoting a whole book to girls and another one to young children called *The Wonder of Life*, also in 1895. Other authors of guidance books followed the headmaster of Eton, the Reverend Edward Lyttelton, who gave only cursory information to girls since "the normal growth of animal desires, [is] far stronger in the male than in

3. That late-Victorian mothers merely passed on their own fears is indicated by an inquiry, performed in 1852 and revealing that of a thousand women 25 percent "were totally unprepared" for the onset of menstruation, 13 percent out of those "were much frightened, screamed, or went into hysterical fits," while of that group 6 percent "thought themselves wounded, and washed with cold water" (Trudgill 1976, p. 59).

4. In the same chapter, entitled "The Mystery of Life," the sex drive is defined as "the instinctive wish to unite and have children" (Kirk 1895b, p. 46).

the female, at least in England" (Lyttelton 1900, p. 10). The appearance of such manuals at once signaled the eugenic promotion of sexual knowledge as a means to preserve the race and revealed the limitations within which sexuality was defined. The conflicts over knowledge and sexuality were even more pronounced in the formal education of middle-class girls, an area in which eugenic advancement around the turn of the century exacerbated the contradictions facing the adolescent girl.

The eugenists eulogized motherhood, which was perceived as a biological bulwark set up against racial degeneration and genetic defilement. They saw an insoluble contradiction between women's intellectual aspirations and their biological and national obligations to bear children. On both sides of the Atlantic, the social critic Herbert Spencer (1820–1903) was the key figure in popularizing an evolutionary theory of motherhood. As early as 1867, he voiced his anxiety about the physiological damage that could result from women's academic endeavors. "In its full sense the reproductive power means the power to bear a well-developed infant, and to supply that infant with the natural food for the natural period. Most of the flat-chested girls who survive their high pressure education are unable to do this" (Dyhouse 1976, p. 43). According to the eugenists, intellectual and especially scientific training as well as physical exercise could cause anything from pelvic distortion to insufficient lactation and mental imbalance. Their evidence rested on the assumption that the human body relies on a "fixed fund" of energy and that adolescent girls needed most of that energy to establish a regular menstrual cycle, leaving little for intellectual improvement.

The male corollary to this reasoning was the repeated warnings against the dire consequences of masturbation. Seminal spending (note the economic term) was no longer prohibited on moral but on medical grounds. It would impair the boy's intellect and sap his male strength, which should rightly be saved for the matrimonial bed.[5] So while vigorous exercise of the mind and body was perceived as damaging to the middle-class girl's physiological development, intellectual pursuits and rigorous games were devised as health tonics for the adolescent boy troubled by nightly emissions and other sexual feelings.

Feminists refuted the biological theories of a fixed fund of energy, and women entering the professions disproved the eugenic assumptions in practice (not to mention the host of working-class women and girls whose funds of energy never entered the discussion) (Burstyn 1980, pp. 70–98; Delamont 1978; Dyhouse 1976, and 1981, pp. 151–69). The debate only invigorated the

5. The popular notions of a fixed fund of energy in the human body are indicative of the ways in which both Social Darwinists and eugenists applied to biology in general and to female physiology in particular accepted laws from the natural sciences, in this case the physical principle of the conservation of energy, first formulated in 1847 by Hermann von Helmholtz (1821–94) in his *Über die Erhaltung der Kraft* (On the Conservation of Energy).

antifeminist sentiments that were expressed as forcefully as ever in 1920 when the war had dispersed any ideals of the sanctity of procreation and motherhood. Arabella Kenealy conjured up her image of "a well-known Girls' College" that followed the trend to cultivate "the cult of mannishness" through physical exercise:

> And here are seen, absorbed in fierce contest during the exhausting heat of summer afternoons, grim-visaged maidens of sinewy build, hard and tough and set as working women in the '40's, some with brawny throats, square shoulders and stern loins that would do credit to a prize ring. All of which masculine developments are stigmata of abnormal sex-transformation, precisely similar in origin to male antlers in female deer. (Dyhouse 1976, p. 56)

By that time, however, the emphasis in the debate over girls' schooling had shifted from physiology to psychology. Educated women were no longer deemed unable, but unwilling, to assume the responsibilities of marriage and motherhood. This issue, which had been defined publicly as an individual problem, thereby became internalized as a mental aberration. With hindsight, we can hastily denounce as folly the antifeminism expressed by the eugenic movement, as yet another male defense mechanism put into operation to protect existing power structures that were being challenged by women's demands for legal and economic independence. But it should be borne in mind that the eugenists merely expressed, if rather more stridently, a pervasive social outlook shared also by many women and clearly seen by their adolescent daughters as pertinent problems.

The end result for many adolescent girls was an added insecurity. Education and economic independence had to be measured against the possibilities of social seclusion and occupational exclusion in a society in which women were still predominantly defined through their personal exchange value; that is, their sexuality. Like all "real" children, the girls perceived these conflicts as personal problems and shortcomings. The new girls' schools at once highlighted the social roots of their pupils' conflicts and reinforced individual solutions. It was at this juncture that the *Girl's Own Paper* and similar ventures entered publishing with their special appeal to an adolescent readership. Their relative success until World War I must be judged in relation to these real-life conflicts whose sharpening from around the turn of the century also influenced public policy-making.

Thus, the Board of Education in 1906 suggested that science "might be wholly replaced by an approved Scheme of Instruction in Practical Housewifery for girls over fifteen years of age." Rather than solving the problem of overstrain for secondary schoolgirls, the inclusion of domestic science added to their educational pressure, for they still had to fulfill qualifications similar to those required of boys if they were to enter the university or other types of further education. The Board's suggestions further increased the girls' difficulties, even if its directions seem slight compared to the firm regulations applied to working-class children's and especially girls' education in the so-called elementary schools.

"SELF-RELIANT AND PATRIOTIC"

In the opinion of the Victorian reformers themselves, the 1870 Education Act was an attempt to strengthen the moral fiber of the working class by rescuing its poor children from crime, vice, and depravity. It was also, if more covertly, a statutory concession to the need for a better qualified labor force, of men at least. But whatever the underlying reasons, the long-term endeavors to standardize all children's lives according to a middle-class childrearing pattern often clashed with immediate financial motives. Economic expediency repeatedly overruled moral concerns when juvenile labor was needed by parents, manufacturers, or large landowners, all of whom availed themselves of the contradictions existing between educational provision and factory and workshop legislation regulating children's paid labor. Until 1918, the half-time system persisted as a legitimate way of exempting youngsters from part of their schooling, and, especially in rural areas, the nominal compulsion to attend school was often leniently enforced in late-Victorian years, or it was circumvented through a variety of bylaws (Hurt 1979, pp. 188–213).

Not unnaturally, the neediest children generally worked the most. But even children from artisan and semiskilled families, attending school full-time and thus continuing the working-class tradition of intellectual improvement, often worked outside school hours. Their neat appearance and polite behavior secured them the best payment for the shortest time. But while boys were out in public doing their newspaper rounds, taking orders at the butcher's, or working as lather boys at the local barbershop, their sisters would mostly be confined to the home, minding a neighbor's baby, running errands for an older relative, or helping their mothers with the strenuous routine of cleaning, washing, and cooking. These jobs, regarded by adults as natural ingredients of female up-bringing, fetched little or no payment—merely a cup of tea, perhaps, or some food for the family.

Even parents, wanting their children, as Gwen Davies put it, "to let us have a better place in the world than they had, wanted to educate us you see to get on a bit," accepted sexual divisions in the home (Thompson 1977, p. 145). Compared with their sisters, boys would have more pocket money and more leisure time to spend on themselves; both coveted options would often be used for reading. Thus, the formal prolongation of working-class childhood during the final decades of the nineteenth century lodged children between the demands of school and work. These contradictory demands were most keenly felt by those who worked the most—the girls, who had few means of escaping duties, and the destitute boys for whom paid jobs, however casual, remained a key to independence, as they had always been for juveniles of this group.

Social and sexual divisions were largely reinforced through the educational system. To the private and charitable establishments attended by the better-off sections of working-class children, the Education Act of 1870 had added non-denominational board schools, which chiefly catered to children from more impecunious families. But throughout this elementary school system, the formal aspects of training mattered more than the substance of learning. Punctuality, order, cleanliness, and unquestioning obedience constituted the main objectives of schooling. Some pupils in the 1870s, like Frederick Willis, made school life bearable by internalizing these objectives as personal pride:

> We were taught to be God-fearing, honourable, self-reliant, and patriotic; to be clean and trim in our appearance, to be smart in our walk and actions, and always walk in step with a companion. I remember a master saying, "Never slouch, walk like soldiers." The best of us tried to follow this advice, and although our clothes may have left something to be desired, we made a brave show with clean collars, clean boots, well-brushed hair, and shiny faces when we assembled for morning prayers. (Willis 1948, p. 63)

To children brought up under the influence of a varied street culture and with peer-group solidarity, deference to teachers was at most a hard-won accomplishment and more often a source of subjection or resistance. As for the demands made to cleanliness, these put a heavy responsibility on mothers and sisters in charge of the onerous home chores. Far from alleviating this burden by offering the girls alternative perspectives on life, the elementary school curriculum from the 1880s further reinforced sexual divisions.

The sexes did share tuition in the three Rs. But, as mentioned, the so-called Revised Code from 1862 had specified that voluntary elementary schools must teach girl pupils needlework in order to qualify for grants. Not only did needlework for girls remain a compulsory subject after 1870, it was supplemented in 1878 by obligatory classes in household management. Four years later, public grants were made available for teaching cookery, and in 1890 laundry-work was added as well (Dyhouse 1977, p. 21). While girls were taking needlework, cookery, or laundry lessons, boys would do additional classes in drawing, geography, science, or history, subjects that were gradually introduced to widen the scope of working-class education.

In principle, therefore, the sex-specific curriculum better equipped boys for the new jobs that were being created in the expanding areas of industry and commerce, and it increasingly offered a set of interests that differed from those nurtured by most semiskilled and unskilled workers. In reality, some elementary schools were successful in reaching these goals, especially in large cities such as Sheffield, Manchester, and London where radicals and later socialists spurred curricular reforms for the benefit of older pupils.[6] But for a large part of working-class children, their teachers' manifest fears of losing authority, their insufficient or useless equipment, and the sheer number of pupils in each class (fifty to sixty around 1900) made lessons an experience to be endured rather than enjoyed (Smith 1930, p. 250).

In most schools, rote learning was still the order of the day, but it was often touched up with more modern aspects of discipline. Military drill had been first introduced into workhouse schools for boys in the 1850s, but it was also adopted in the elementary schools where it became integrated into the curriculum by the 1880s (Hurt 1977, pp. 169, 176). In accord with the expansion of the British Empire, ostentatious nationalism and martial masculinity in the drill exercises were stressed. But these ideals were not ameliorated by team spirit and a sense of cooperation as in the organized games of the public schools. The mental require-ments of the rank-and-file were subordination not self-reliance, and drill as an educational instrument spread to other subjects. Many children shared the school experiences of H. C. Dent, recalling that as a ten-year-old at his board school in 1904:

> I memorized, in rhyme, the names and idiosyncracies of the English kings and queens
>
> William the Conqueror long did reign,
> William his son by an arrow was slain . . .
>
> and I memorized (though not in rhyme) the names of capes, bays, county towns, mountains and rivers, literally all round Britain. And once each week I painted blobs (we called them flowers), and wove wet reeds into work baskets: the school's sole concessions to "activity." (Yglesias 1974, p. 368)

Dent, who in adult life became a professor of education and editor of the *Times Literary Supplement*, was among the most successful of the boys who benefited from the reforms of elementary schooling that came into existence with the Education Act of 1902. A formalized scholarship ladder had been set up for the top elementary school pupils, just as state-subsidized "county schools" were erected to provide these pupils with a secondary, more advanced but not more vocational, training. In 1904–05, there were five hundred of these schools but more than a thousand by World War I, when the number of pupils had also gone up from 64,000 to nearly 188,000. To these measures was added a so-called free-place system in 1907, making grants to all secondary schools dependent on an annual intake of at least twenty-five percent of elementary school children

6. For the development and subsequent demise with the Education Act in 1902 of these so-called higher tops and higher-grade schools teaching science, mechanics, and bookkeeping, see Simon 1974b, pp. 176–207.

who passed the prescribed entrance examination (Lawson and Silver 1973, p. 373).

The Education Act of 1902 marked the first serious statutory attempt to bridge the social gap between elementary and secondary education. In the years before World War I, then, the nineteenth-century explicitness about class and the aims of educating children to their proper station in life, and no further, slowly began to give way to a belief in educating all children irrespective of class but according to their individual abilities. The reasons for change were economic as well as moral. Competition from abroad revealed the necessity for a better qualified (male) work force in Britain. Also, in the 1880s mechanization and cheap imports such as French machine-made lace and Chinese plait meant the end to many rural cottage industries that had largely depended on juvenile workers exempted from school. For the male school leaver, technological change made apprenticeships and learning positions hard to come by, while dead-end jobs and casual employment also of schoolboys were on the increase and formed a conspicuous trend especially in large cities. Around the turn of the century, several public and private investigations of juvenile labor renewed the familiar outcries against working-class crime and degradation, anxieties that were now being strongly reinforced by eugenic fears of "race suicide."[7]

Consequently, an Employment of Children Act in 1903 prohibited children under fourteen from working between nine p.m. and six a.m. But implementation of the law was insufficient, and as late as 1910 it was estimated that about twenty-five percent of all London school children were occupied outside school hours, many of them illegally and most of them boys (Gillis 1974, p. 125).[8] Although the committee, on whose report the act was based, deplored that "the severest work, the longest hours, and the hardest conditions, are often to be found in the case of children who are employed without wages in doing housework in the homes of their parents," no provision was made to curtail domestic duties, which were largely performed by girls, as noted (Hurt 1979, p. 206). As in the case of education, legal regulations of work tied in nicely with the eugenists' elevation of motherhood. While numerous working-class women

7. Despite ample evidence, statutory attempts to better the physical well-being of elementary schoolpupils were made only when the Boer War revealed that, of all army recruits, an average of 30 percent had to be instantly rejected as physically unfit for military service (See Urwick 1904, pp. 258–59). From 1906, local authorities were empowered, but not obliged, to provide school meals for needy children, and a year later medical inspection in schools was made compulsory. But unlike social investigators, such as Charles Booth and Seebohm Rowntree, and socialist reformers, such as Margaret McMillan and Annie Besant, who had all revealed the social roots of ill-health and undernourishment, the state as yet only assumed its responsibility to alleviate symptoms, not find a cure.

8. In 1914, 10 percent of the families in some communities still depended entirely on their children's income (Gillis 1974, p. 124).

were being trained in hygiene and health matters at "Schools for Mothers," set up in 1907, their daughters of school age received an intensified tutoring in household management, efficiently renamed "domestic science" (Davin 1978; Dyhouse 1977).

Early in this century, then, a number of statutory measures heightened the problems, already facing many working-class children and adolescents, of negotiating the conflicts between work and education, working-class culture and middle-class norms. To many elementary schoolteachers, their pupils' formal possibilities, however slight, of bridging the social gap between elementary and secondary education seemed to confirm that individual competition could lead to social betterment. This awareness almost invariably entailed an intensification of discipline that was felt by all pupils irrespective of their intellectual aspirations.

The rigid enforcement of attendance meant that schooling took up a large part of the time and energies of the majority of children. Education assumed a growing importance in working-class childhood often not so much because of the lessons but in spite of them. School became a venue of social and cultural struggle. For some, this struggle was experienced as a personal problem, but for many others it was instinctively realized as a power game that could only be won, or at least opposed, through collective action. Thus, a bus conductress, born in Bristol in 1904, recalls, "If you wanted to 'ave a bit of fun in class it was important to be sitting next to your mates. . . . If you were a bit brilliant and yer mates was only average like, you wouldn't want to be moved up the class, you'd want to stay with them, so you'd deliberately get some of your spellings or your sums wrong" (Humphries 1981, p. 55. See also pp. 121–49).

The battle over territory and autonomy that boys especially had waged in the street was increasingly moved inside the school gates. While this eliminated some strategies of resistance and playful opposition, it also developed new social experiences. Pupils would pass notes and suck sweets in class, they would gain access to the girls' or the boys' playground, and they would relish the concealed trading of cigarette cards, skipping ropes, or well-thumbed magazines (five or six for a penny). But while schooling thus attained a growing importance with the majority of working-class children and some adolescents, they possessed different means of confronting the contradictions that this importance entailed.

Except in the most secure of artisan families where the mother, being a full-time housewife, allowed and perhaps encouraged her daughter's intellectual pursuits, most working-class girls tried to resolve the conflicts facing them by giving up whatever educational aspirations they may have entertained. While still of school age, they simply had too many duties and too strict adult supervision to get much time for or interest in leisure pursuits such as reading. Only when they left school did these girls taste a bit of personal freedom. For, according to Flora Thompson, who grew up in the 1880s in a village on the Oxfordshire-Northamptonshire border, boys could often find work near home while girls, going into service, had to strike out for themselves. "The girls, while at home, could earn nothing" (Thompson 1973, p. 156). A similar pattern prevailed when in the 1890s more adolescent girls changed their caps and aprons for work in shops and factories. Since they were inexperienced with these new types of occupation, their focal concerns would be how to settle in an unfamiliar work situation and perhaps in a new town, how to find their place among many workers from different localities, and, not least, how to handle the important subject of courting and sex without the strict regulations surrounding domestic servants.

To working-class boys, the conflict between work and education presented itself in a different manner. On the one hand, the elementary school curriculum gave them more variety and, at its best, encouraged their intellectual improvement. Consciously or unconsciously, most teachers transferred their professional interests to their male pupils. Boys were often the ones to be reprimanded most severely, but they would equally receive most of the attention and encouragement. On the other hand, the boy would also gain more than his sister from working. He was paid more and allowed to keep more for himself, and he was also out and about in the street listening to adults and playing with his friends between his duties. The poorest section of boys would be the ones to resist most forcefully any encroachments upon their traditional hand-to-mouth existence, whether these encroachments took the form of an attendance officer, a police constable, or a tradesman, enraged by their pinching of goods on display. Many boys exercised a considerable resourcefulness and resilience in circumventing adult rules and regulations. Thus, Thomas Morgan, who was born in 1892 in the poor London district of Southwark, repeatedly exempted himself from school:

> I used to get a button, you know, a bone button, and I used to press it in me throat just before I went into class see. And I used to go up to the headmistress and say, 'Mother said, could you tell me what this was?'
>
> 'Oh ringworms—oh'! I was away from school three or four months at a time. Over Covent Garden with a sack—sackful of broken up wood, you know—flower boxes . . . knock at a door. 'Firewood, ma'am?' (Thompson 1981, p. 26)[9]

To sons of the growing number of semiskilled laborers, whose families were less dependent for their survival on child labor, work supplemented rather than supplanted education. Even if they held few or no intellectual aspirations,

---

9. That the boys identifying most strongly with work were also often the most effective in resisting school is indicated by the more than 100 school strikes occurring between 1889 and 1939. Many ringleaders were half-timers who gleaned their tactics from adult relatives, not least in the nationwide spate of protests in 1911 and 1914. For an extensive treatment of these strikes, see Humphries 1981, pp. 90–120.

The *Boy's Own Paper* 9, no. 436 (21 May 1887), p. 544. Artist: L. Cunnis. The leisure pursuits of late-Victorian boys differed widely and fostered markedly different personalities in the opinion of the right-minded middle class.

schooling was a social pressure, a conscious cultural, even social, battle in which they invested considerable energies, if one can judge from their distinct memories of school organization and fellow pupils. Rather than being their center of identification, work became more a possibility of exploring areas and developing experiences not allowed at school. Ranking above the ice-cream vendor's assistants and the destitute boys collecting coal on the railway tracks, these youngsters had the time, the incentive, and the money to make the most of the new consumer amenities of which they had an expert knowledge. Thus, London-born Thomas Burke retained a clear memory of the luxuries—sweets and a weekly—that a prewar child could buy when having the quite unusual luck of getting 2½d. pocket-money on a Saturday morning instead of the usual ½d.: the *Funny Wonder* (½d.), a prize-packet (½d.), one ounce coconut toffee (¼d.), a clove stick (¼d.), a bag of wafers (½d.), and a capful of chestnuts (½d.) (Clay 1964, p. 50). Boys such as Thomas Burke made up the core group of the new juvenile consumers. Consumption, it seems, suspended the increasing demands made on them at school.

As in the generation before, the sons of artisans and of other skilled laborers were the least affected by communal street culture. Like lower-middle-class juveniles, these working-class boys often displayed a strong commitment to schooling whose standards measured up to their family upbringing. The traditional emphasis in their homes on book-reading and self-improvement was reinforced by required obedience and punctuality. These requirements seemed particularly relevant to the skilled workers in the expanding southeast, where the material and cultural superiority of the workers was threatened during the late-Victorian period by the combined forces of mechanization and commercialization. Children of these workers rarely displayed any open rebellion against education, as did some of the more indigent juveniles. Perhaps they did not consciously experience schooling as an area of collective cultural and social struggle, as did many semiskilled youngsters. To the compositor's or the engineer's son, educational contradictions existed and were keenly felt, but most likely they were assumed to be individual shortcomings, as was the case with middle-class children and adolescents. The skilled laborer's son often shared a pattern of life with middle-class juveniles, if under less secure circumstances.

Artisan children were mainly kept to their books, forbidden to play in the street at night, and boys were often encouraged to join one of the voluntary youth organizations, which encroached upon the Sunday schools as approved leisure pursuits. Like their religious counterpart, the new organizations were designed for the poor as means to combat street-gang violence, crime, and the alleged thriftlessness and fecklessness of working-class life. In keeping with contemporary strategies of education, militaristic means were employed to reach this goal.

The first of the movements, the Boys' Brigade, was founded in 1883, and it was followed eight years later by the Anglican Church Lads Brigade, which, between 1911 and 1930, was recognized as a Cadet Corps like similar establishments in public and grammar schools. But while poor boys could enjoy the annual summer camps and the splendor of the regular parades, they often viewed the all too familiar drilling and marshaling with suspicion. The new movements found their strongest supporters among lower middle-class and artisan juveniles (Blanch 1979). Middle-class youngsters were added to these groups in 1907 when Baden-Powell formed the Boy Scouts, followed two years later by his sister Agnes' pioneering of the Girl Guides. The scouts and guides, combining nationalism with an active outdoor life beyond parental control, flourished during the interwar years.

Alfred Harmsworth's commercial success and the concomitant developments in periodical publishing for juveniles assume a new significance when related to the changes taking place in the lives of children and adolescents in the late-Victorian and Edwardian years. The social position of adolescent girls changed markedly during this period. Young females became visible as a distinct age group and also as a potentially profitable consumer sector. But while middle-class and lower middle-class adolescents and women saw the ideal of domesticity cracking, if not crumbling, before them with the widening of educational and occupational options, working-class girls and their mothers found themselves increasingly destined toward hearth and home. Female aspirations differed widely according to social class. Not surprisingly, the secular magazines that developed during this period for the adolescent girl were of two distinct types. To middle-class and many lower-middle-class girls, reading had formed an important element of their upbringing. In adolescence, weeklies such as the *Girl's Own Paper,* which emphasized fiction of improvement and sound information on personal and occupational matters, found an immediate resonance with these girls, who were embarking on a future (or wanting to do so) for which their family upbringing made an insufficient preparation but on whose personal standards they nevertheless depended.

Conversely, educational improvement and career choice were issues of little importance to young women from a poor background. While more of them learned to read and to do so at an earlier age than their mothers, who had often acquired their literacy as domestics, most of them had the time, the money, and the motivation to use their literary abilities only on leaving school and facing an often unfamiliar life.[10] Hence, we find a proliferation early in this century of inexpensive mill-girl papers—such as the *Girls' Friend*—with their attractive mixture of romantic fiction of the novelette type, fashion hints, and personal queries.

Boys, again, fared differently. By the turn of the century, even the poorest had been introduced to the three Rs, and the majority of them possessed at least a basic literacy. But unlike their sisters and most working-class boys in the generations before them, many found opportunities to use their faculties at school age by the reading of magazines. Perhaps least susceptible to this were indigent boys who had to work hard for sheer survival and whose identification with traditional street culture made larking about with their friends the most coveted form of pleasure in between their heavy chores. When at school age they did read, they probably shared their elders' interests in comics, penny dreadfuls, and gory adventure stories.

Their social opposites within the working class, the sons of skilled workers, while rarely having regular employment outside school hours generally received pocket money for saving up. Some of their savings were undoubtedly spent on commercial weeklies whose contents not only seemed more exciting and accessible than books but whose very possession often formed a covert protest. Thus, Frank Benson remembers how, circumventing a parental ban on the *Magnet* and the *Gem* papers, he would "smuggle them into the house and read them in the privacy of my own bedroom" (Thompson 1977, p. 135).[11] Most of these boys shared an interest in schooling with the growing section of peers from a semi-skilled background. As noted, schooling was often more a social than an intellectual experience for the sons of semiskilled workers, and it was often acknowledged as a collective struggle. This perspective was framed by the boys' links to

10. For evidence of domestic service as a stepping stone to female literacy and the reading of penny novelettes, see Davies 1977, pp. 26–27 (around 1870); and Thompson 1973, pp. 109–10 (1880s).

11. Benson was born in the cotton town of Bolton as the son of a craftsman in the engineering industry.

paid labor. The fireman's and the machinist's son generally held a rather well-paid job outside school, and, while being raised in a well-ordered family life, this regularity rarely precluded his intense participation in the varied public life unfolding in the streets and the market places. This life taught him and his poorer contemporaries an enterprising sagacity combined with an acute consumer consciousness.

From their parents, these boys were imbued with self-esteem and pride in working-class culture. This self-consciousness was not unlike that found in artisan families where it found more organized and "approved" outlets. Being without bookish pretensions and traditions, boys from a semiskilled background, along with their fathers, constituted the ideal participants in the new forms of commercial entertainment that were filling a growing space between self-organized activities and voluntary leisure provision. The contemplation of the buying, the exchange, and the use of inexpensive toys, sweets, boys' weeklies, and, later, films made exciting experiences of enjoyment and entertainment, which for a time seemed to invalidate conflicts experienced at school and in other areas of life. These boys probably made up the majority of those, recalled by Robert Roberts, "so avid for current numbers of the *Magnet* and *Gem* that they would trek on a weekday to the city railway station to catch the bulk arrival from London and buy first copies from the bookstall" (Roberts 1977, p. 160).

Harmsworth's reworked ideological formula of commercial moralism thus found a ready response with a wide selection of schoolboys, straddling at least the lower middle-class, artisan, and semiskilled groups. Moreover, his development of the single-genre perennial and his popularization of companion papers secured a diversification of juvenile readership. This enabled the Amalgamated Press to cash in on both the large number of Edwardian boys whose personal interests and social experiences made them turn to school serials, such as the *Magnet* and the *Gem*, and then the section of juvenile readers who followed adult tastes in their preference for traditional adventure yarns touched up with novelties such as science-fiction stories, comics, and perhaps sensational newspapers. In magazine terms, the school perennial marked the most important innovation, confronting its readership's varying conflicts with remarkable success.

10

Cast upon Their Own Resources: The *Girl's Own Paper* and Harmsworth's Trendsetters

FROM ITS inception, the *Girl's Own Paper* stressed information. Compared to both contemporary boys' magazines and later periodicals for girls, the new weekly carried more articles dealing with practical and personal problems confronting readers in their daily lives. While novels catered to the middle-class girl's fictional needs in adolescence, the *Girl's Own Paper* seems to have succeeded in part because it provided a central forum for advice that was of common interest. This kind of advice had hitherto been scattered in diverse household manuals, educational or legal guides, and books on etiquette. Through the magazine, knowledge was imparted and judgments were passed, and the alleged applicability of the various topics consoled insecure readers who knew little about the world lying beyond the confines of home and possibly school. Throughout its advisory articles on health matters, etiquette, work, and education as well as in competitions and the sizable correspondence pages, the *Girl's Own Paper* emphasized mental and practical usefulness along with methodical work habits—activities that were seen as necessary bulwarks against feminine dissipation and inactivity.

In his editorial policies, Charles Peters clearly endorsed a middle-class elevation of women's cultural mission. This elevation demanded earnest preparation through formal schooling. Not unnaturally, then, numerous articles appeared over the years discussing secondary education for girls and suitable careers for women; not surprisingly these discussions reflected the contemporary contradictions inherent in those issues. Alice King, in an article called "School-life" deplores the girls who are raised with "a taste for not one single, solid, useful pursuit" and continues by praising school reforms: "Let us be very thankful for the vast educational advantages which our times offer to women, and let our girls take good heed that they do not misuse the talents entrusted to them." Girls should be educated, in Alice King's opinion, to become "in their way, quite as steady workers as our boys," for "woman is the God-given companion and equal of man, and, after all, half the work of the world falls upon her shoulders, though, of course, she labours in a very different workshop from man, and with very different tools." Alice King supports the traditional evangelical maxim of woman's role as being "equal but different," but she openly acknowledges that there have been some human changes of the casting:

> In the best ordered families even there may come days of trouble and disaster—days when, through a bank failure, or some other like mischance, the delicately-nurtured daughters of the house, who hitherto have been watched and guarded as rare, tender, conservatory plants that not a breath of rough wind must touch, are suddenly cast upon their own resources in a more or less degree, and exposed to sharp blasts of poverty and adversity. In such a case— and in our own days such cases have been far from being the dreams of romancers—how well and happy it is for a girl to be able, through some cultivated talent, or some thoroughly acquired branch of knowledge, to become at once a working bee who can bring back her share of honey to the home hive, instead of being a dead weight hanging round the neck of father or brother. (*Girl's Own Paper* 3, no. 99 [19 November 1881], p. 124)[1]

Through her description of women's paid employment, not as a new and exciting option to widen the female range of activities but rather as an unexpected misfortune and a necessary alleviation of male care, Alice King conveys a traditional Victorian view of unselfish femininity updated to meet contemporary demands without using these demands actively to further one's personal goals. Her suggestions for proper female vocations are "authoress," hospital nurse, and teacher—all occupations that preserve a distinct aura of domesticity and Christian philanthropy. Alice King's attempt to reconcile her own Victorian ideal of femininity with an open recognition of change is reiterated in the paper's numerous articles on women's employment. One of the early ones is called "On Earning One's Living" and bears the suggestive subtitle "Fruitful Fields for Honest Labour." Advocated among proper female fields of activity are china-painting, book-binding, and flower-making along with law-copying and the teaching of deaf-mutes and infants. Perhaps more appealing to the readers is the subtitle to a later article called "Girls as Pianoforte Tuners: A New Remunerative Employment," in which the anonymous author starts out on an encouraging note:

> WOMEN tuners! Why not? If a blind man can tune a piano . . . —if men without the least education, musically speaking, earn their bread by tuning only, and there are thousands who do, it would be strange indeed if a girl with good sight and some knowledge of music should find the art of tuning impossible of acquirement.

1. The article was intended as the first in a series called "The Four Periods" in women's lives, but the other three never followed.

To start on her way to success, the prospective piano tuner merely needs "an old grand" which "can be bought at any time" for four to five pounds, but how to secure that sum unfortunately is not part of the advice given (8, no. 382 [23 April 1887], pp. 465–66). While most of the articles on education and employment covertly sought to reconcile the readers' social contradictions and thus reinforced what we have described, in Sara Delamont's words, as the "snare of double conformity," other contributors openly advocated a widening of the female sphere to encompass medicine, chemistry, and dentistry. And as early as 1883, a series called "Work for All" ended with the anonymous author's plea for equal pay:

> It should be remembered that the work of girls is, as it were, on its trial. If it be found to be inferior to that of men it is but just that it should be paid for at a lower rate, but if equal or superior, surely it should stand upon its intrinsic worth, and be paid for accordingly. Every woman who does what she undertakes to do in the spirit of the true workman, rejoicing in it and doing it to the very best of her ability, is a benefactor to her sex—nay, more, a true patriot. (Forrester 1980, p. 39)[2]

Articles, voicing different opinions on these matters, certainly appeared over the years in the paper, and the views expressed no uniform "progression" or trend. Similarly, clear contradictions appeared to the conscientious reader going through the advice given in a single issue or volume. As is indicated in the numerous answers printed in the correspondence pages, health was one of the regular features that captured the readers' attention. For almost thirty years, these articles were firmly conducted by "Medicus" (the naval doctor Gordon Stables [1840–1910]). Perhaps because of his bracing background, Stables was no prey to eugenic views on overstrain debilitating secondary schoolgirls. Rather than regarding strenuous childbirth as a be-all and end-all to female problems, he was a vigorous proponent of physical exercise for girls during adolescence. Thus, he proclaims in "Can Girls Increase their Strength?": "Let me . . . state boldly and without fear of contradiction from anyone, that in the increase of strength will lie an increase of health, and therefore additional happiness" (15, no. 752 [26 May 1894], p. 533).

The fact that Stables was influenced by his contemporaries is revealed in his physiological determinism, which forms a medical variation on the "fixed fund of energy" theory. According to "Medicus," it is the lack of "pure blood" which is the cause of all female ailments from cold feet to bad complexion and "neu-

---

2. In the *Girl's Own Paper* (April 1882) a letter appeared from a reader ("aged 14 years and 7 months") who refuted an article printed a few weeks previously on "The Disadvantages of Higher Education." Apart from the odd poem or short story, reprints of such contributions were unique and must have formed particular points of reader identification (Forrester 1980, pp. 36–7).

rasthenia" (a contemporary term denoting nervous exhaustion). But unlike some of his colleagues he does not, even covertly, refer to this affliction as a symptom of masturbation. Blood circulation can be improved by sensible clothing (no tight-lacing), a cold "sponge bath" every morning followed by a brisk walk: "Do not stop to stare in at shop windows, but walk as if you meant doing something." Like a modern nutritionist, Stables bans pastry and sweets while oatmeal porridge and milk are recommended as being good to "the system," which also benefits from tomatoes "if ripe English ones, not pale sickly-looking Frenchmen." Having kept these simple rules, diligently written down in her notebook, the inactive reader, "without gasping like an asthmatical bantam," will be fit enough to join a "gymnasium" where exercise could be started in earnest (15, no. 752 [26 May 1894], p. 534).

For readers who had reached such physical standards, the *Girl's Own Paper* printed infrequent but informative descriptions of gymnastic exercises performed with chest expanders and dumb bells. (Accompanying illustrations would show the precise position of arms and legs.) Beginning in the 1890s, some articles followed (not written by Medicus) on new sports that had been taken up by girls: hockey, golf, and cricket along with the craze for bicycling. Depressive and nervous girls—that is, daughters in middle-class families with no paid employment—were advised by Stables to be gentle in their physical improvements. They should take plenty of rest, reading a book in the garden or playing the piano ("only the airs or pieces that touch the heart") in order for them to restore "pure wholesome blood to the whole system" ("Nervous Girls," *Girl's Own Paper* 15, no. 722 [28 October 1893], pp. 60–61). But no such precautions seemed necessary for the paper's prospective working-class readers "to whom health is, perhaps, the only capital they possess." The tired girls, after their eight or ten hours of sedentary work, should never take "the first Underground Railway carriage" home and thereby exchange "the carbonic acid gas of the workroom for the sulphurous gas of the underground tunnels." Instead, they need a sprightly walk to their destinations, at least "walking that part of the route which has the most trees about it." If the same procedure is followed in the morning—and this "can quite well be done by a little management"—the girls will soon "feel in a higher mood; difficulties will be brushed aside" ("Healthy Lives for Working Girls," *Girl's Own Paper* 8, no. 357 [30 October 1886], pp. 77, 78). Whether these difficulties included overwork and underpayment is not revealed.

While it is impossible to determine how many regular readers noticed the contradictions found in Gordon Stables' and other advisory articles, it should be remembered that a generation of magazine readers, which today craves certain types of reading matter for maybe two or three years, would then last considerably longer because reading was one of the approved leisure pursuits for well-behaved girls and young women. However, the center of their attention would probably be their own immediate difficulties rather than troubles besetting their sisters. As to health, menstruation and a budding sexuality were undoubtedly matters of interest to the many middle-class readers who, as noted, found little or no comfort and advice elsewhere. But these topics were beyond the pale of communication—the most direct references to bodily functions that I have found are "flatulence" and "indigestion."

However, assessed within the heated debate on overstrain for secondary schoolgirls and the eugenists' melodramatic eulogies of motherhood, Gordon Stables' articles to many must have acted as a welcome antidote, strengthening their beliefs in their own physical powers. Lacking sexual advice, it may have been a consolation just to consider one's own health in a legitimate way. Despite their indubitable Spartan overtones, the repeated suggestions to take physical well-being seriously as an important element in mental health provided at least middle- and lower-middle-class readers with a consciousness and a self-reliance that may not only have counterbalanced an excess of self-forgetting "good works," but that may equally in adult life have assisted former, or even continuing, subscribers to combat physical complaints and debilities.

Other parts of the paper certainly nurtured a more unselfish spirit in the readers. Articles appeared on how to start private reading circles, how to commence district visiting of the poor, and how to organize sewing sessions, or "mothers' meetings," for those "who reign in the home of our labourers and artisans, who now, in their children, are shaping the men and women of the future that will form the mass of the people" (Alice King, "About Mothers' Meetings," *Girl's Own Paper* 3, no. 97 [5 November 1881], p. 84). On a more regular basis, many prize competitions, until around the turn of the century when "puzzle poems" became popular, reinforced this uplifting morality. That the sewing machine was being introduced into many middle-class homes at the time made no difference to the emphasis in the competitions upon traditional needlework skills. Flannel petticoats, camisoles, and mittens were produced by diligent competitors of all ages for the benefit of bedridden spinsters, needy fishermen, and hospitalized children. When pronouncing on the prize contributions, the examiners found a welcome opportunity to sharpen their readers' Christian conscience, and they also used this opportunity to evaluate the contributors' domestic skills. "How often shall we have to repeat that the buttonholes should always be cut rather larger than the size of the buttons" was the exasperated verdict of two early prize examiners who did not doubt, though, that despite these unforgivable faults, the garments would be valued by the poor for whom they were intended (*Girl's Own Paper* 3, no. 95 [22 October 1881], p. 59).

In other competitions, the Beeton tradition was followed in attempts to widen the readers' mental capacities. Early on, for instance, prizes were awarded for

MY WORK BASKET.

PINAFORE, SUITABLE FOR A CHILD OF THREE OR FOUR YEARS OF AGE.

The pattern may be easily taken from any dress that fits on the shoulders, and the length must depend also on the height of the child. The pinafore should reach as low as the dress. It can be worn in

place of the dress in warm weather, being light, and easily got up in the laundry. White or *écru* sheeting is very pretty for this purpose. The pinafore is fastened in front under the band of embroidery, which is worked in marking stitch over coarse canvas tacked on the material before commencing the work. When finished, the threads of the

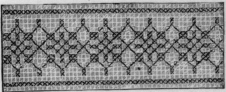

canvas are easily drawn out, if care be taken not to split them with the needle. The above design will show the pattern. Fine wool in two shades—of any colour warranted to wash—will suit the pattern and be quickly worked. The band across the back and pockets have a simple design in marking stitch on each edge, and are trimmed with narrow muslin embroidery. The sleeves and band

FIG. 3.

round the neck are worked to match the rest of the embroidery. The back of the pinafore is in three double plaits, on the top of which the above design is worked.

Cashmere, or any fancy woollen material, may be substituted for the sheeting.

SHADE FOR READING LAMP.

The material on which the embroidery is done is a thin, pearl grey sarsenet lined with stiff net. The designs are embroidered in satin stitch, with the finest white wool and white floss silk; the centres in gold-coloured and brown silks. The leaves are in soft shades of green wool, with veins and edges of floss silk; the stalks are in satin stitch; the scollops are worked in button-hole stitch, with white wool; the inner edge with gold-coloured silk.

The eight divisions of the shade are cut a-pattern without joins at the top, and the tabs are either left loose or tacked together half-way down.

KNITTED SOLE FOR SHOE OR BOOT.

Cut the pattern of the sole of the boot and knit with five thread black wool and large steel needles. Begin at the toe. Cast on about six stitches, according to the size required, increasing at the beginning and end of each row to the widest part of the pattern; then decreasing until you reach the arch of the sole, when you must begin again to increase to the round of the heel. After the knitting is done, work a row of crochet by passing the wool over a medium-sized pencil; fasten off the wool at each row. Leave two rows of knitting between row of crochet. This forms a very soft and warm sole for persons suffering with cold feet. The sole may be made in simple tricot, if preferred.

SERVIETTE RING.

This ring is worked on silk canvas in cross stitch. The canvas must be two inches wide and six inches long when made up. One row of cross stitches is in black coarse netting silk, with a steel bead in each square; the other row is in crimson floss silk. The ring is lined with white ribbon, stitched over the edges of the canvas with a row of beads, or plain stitches of crimson silk.

DETAIL OF LAMP SHADE.

FANCY WORK BASKET FOR "ODDS" AND "ENDS."

The basket is made of plaited brown straw, about nine inches deep and twenty-four inches round the top.

The design for the *lambrequin*, which is fastened a little below the edge, is made of fine cloth, either a darker shade than the basket or some lighter colour to contrast with the straw. It is cut in regular tabs in small vandykes at the edges, and worked in button-hole stitch, with yellow silk.

The stars are alternately pink and blue, in thick wool with leaves at each point, worked

FANCY WORK BASKET.

The *Girl's Own Paper* 1, no. 35 (28 August 1880), p. 556. Illustration for a regular entry, "My Work Basket," by Mary Laybourn. Detailed pictures add an aesthetic beauty to the periodical's firm instructions in traditional female pursuits.

the best essays on famous women from various centuries. Later, paintings and drawings became the vogue, often inspired by a religious motive. While these prize topics and their autocratic evaluations clearly underpinned traditional female accomplishments and deferential reactions, the competitions also offered adolescent readers a public outlet for their creative impulses, lending excitement and even reward to the successful competitors. Apart from gaining a certain visibility by getting their names in the paper, prize winners received sizable money rewards: early on, first prizes were generally three guineas and, starting in the 1890s, five guineas. Moreover, the large and attractive illustrations that generally accompanied these competitions, as well as the knitting and sewing instructions, served to balance the written notions of duty and decorum. Their aesthetic appeal seemed to promise that weaving, painting, or crocheting would also add beauty to the reader and her surroundings.

The printed results of the competitions give a good impression of the age range and the locations of the readership. Depending on the topic, of course, contributions would be sent in from girls as young as seven or eight. Contestants were dispersed widely across the country and, increasingly, across the world. Looking at the "Answers to Correspondents," we get an even clearer picture of this varied readership. The majority of queries came from girls in their teens, and while this group of correspondents does not necessarily parallel the main readership, it does indicate that adolescents were among the keenest fans of the *Girl's Own Paper*. That these readers were not limited to the British Isles is borne out by the growing number of correspondents from Germany and Austria, South Africa, Australia, India, and Ireland.

The regular correspondence pages were divided into subsections on education (including employment), art, handicrafts, and music complemented by the inevitable part "miscellaneous." Together, these sections offer a condensed image of the nonfictional contents of the paper, and the answers given therefore highlight the rifts in that image. Advice to correspondents was often detailed, sometimes curt, but very rarely intimate in tone. With editorial equanimity and diligence, addresses were provided on everything from good boarding-schools in France, female emigration societies, and new shorthand classes to hospitals and convalescent homes in which patients would gratefully receive readers' collections of used books, old toys, and cast-off clothes. That some of the "useful hints" can seem rather quaint to a present-day critic should not conceal the convenience these hints must have brought to readers living at a time in which the ideals of cleanliness and good housekeeping were upheld only through hard work and much inventiveness. That young readers sought advice from the paper on the cleaning of ormolu ornaments, alabaster, and marble together with white fur muffs, piano keys, and ivory fans gives us a vivid impression of the ornate Victorian drawing room; it equally indicates that middle- and lower-middle-class daughters living at home during their prolonged adolescence had to perform their fair share of domestic duties.[3]

While girls were expected to be working bees, they seemed equally anxious to nurture the ideal of the perfect Victorian lady. Correspondents, embarrassed by their red hands, were advised to wear gloves, and a freckled nose could be concealed under a veil. Recipes for tooth paste, face cream, and hair lotions also helped to further the girls' desired ideals. Charles Peters, apparently, shared with his readers a firm belief in etiquette: he readily provided them with articles on the "Classification of Handshaking" (1885) and the intricacies of greetings in the street (1881); he would warn correspondents not to walk under the same umbrella as a man unless he was an intended husband or a close, and preferably older, relative (1885); and they were told never to venture out on their own at night (1892).

In general, however, it is in the answers to personal queries that the most glaring contradictions can be found. In a single issue from 1882, for instance, "Winifred" is advised to ignore her mother's obvious preference for the girl's brother: "He is evidently spoilt, but you should not show that you see it." Conversely, "Perplexed 22" is urged not to remain silent, but to verify rumors about her fiancé: "Tell him candidly what you have heard, and that it has made you very anxious and unhappy; and ask him whether he would be content to give it up [gambling, drinking?] if you made him a happy home." With a lover, a girl's frankness could, apparently, overrule her feminine decorum—perhaps because in marriage she has more at stake than merely domestic discord. To "Humming Bird," the answer reads: "Pray daily for God's grace to aid you in your effort to restrain your hasty temper. Count sixty, or, still better, a hundred, before you reply to any observation that has made you angry." However, "Eocene" is tutored on fossil searching at Lyme Regis in Dorsetshire: "Latterly it has become rather more unsafe to walk under the continually falling surface of the cliffs than formerly, and you should be ever on your guard to escape at the first warning given by a few fragments. Climbing rocks in such researches is more dangerous than 'unladylike'" (*Girl's Own Paper* 3, no. 109 [28 January 1882], pp. 286–87). Hopefully, despite these contradictory warnings, conscientious readers would know when to be ladylike and count sixty and when to run for their lives. The ideal girl, apparently, was capable of both. The vul-

3. Phillis Browne [Sarah Sharp Hamer], a regular contributor to the *Girl's Own Paper*, was among a new group of successful authors who disseminated the domestic usefulness of late-Victorian girls as a social and moral imperative to the adolescents themselves. See, for example, Browne 1880, p. 50: "It would be a very good thing if young ladies would take an interest in home cookery, for apart from other considerations, one might hope their example would influence the servants. Unfortunately, servants in the middle-class houses have a perfect scorn for economy in cooking."

nerability, emerging from the personal queries, seems to have prompted the editor's full use of his authority. Misspellings and an ungraceful hand would invariably be remarked upon. "Your writing is unsightly; it looks as if a fly had walked over the paper after a swim in the ink bottle" (*Girl's Own Paper* 3, no. 109 [28 January 1882], p. 286). Or, less artistically: "Her Majesty the Queen has no surname. Do not write with red ink" (*Girl's Own Paper* 8, no. 381 [16 April 1887], p. 464).

This derogatory tone, which might dissuade any prospective subscriber, should be set against more imaginative attempts to convey information in an entertaining manner. Thus, an early serial by Isabella Fyvie Mayo, "The Other Side of the World," tells about two astute English girls and their experiences on emigrating to Australia. Twenty-year-old Bell Aubry, who is the daughter of a country surgeon, and Annie Steele, an orphaned elementary-school teacher of nineteen, together represent the groups of women who in real life were encouraged by the British emigrating societies to venture abroad, and they equally form fictional points of identification to readers with different backgrounds. Through the heroines' optimistic letters home, the author purveys a good deal of practical advice. And even if few readers actually followed this advice, Bell and Annie's ideal blend of self-reliance and duty undoubtedly captivated the sentiments of many adolescent girls: "The Bible says that woman was made to be the helpmeet for man, which means, I should think, that she shares and dares with him while he wants help, not that she comes in like a base camp follower after the victory to divide the spoil!" (*Girl's Own Paper* 3, no. 110 [4 February 1882], p. 291). While Bell Aubry's reflections reveal the contradictions between compliance and independence, her success in the new country justifies, in an entertaining fashion, that these contradictions can actually be mediated.

A fictional disguise was used more often in the *Girl's Own Paper* to impart less exotic knowledge. In " 'She Couldn't Boil A Potato'; or, the Ignorant Housekeeper and how she acquired knowledge" (1886–87), the author, Dora Hope, sends Ella Hastings off to nurse her invalid aunt for a year. Through her mistakes, the sensible but ignorant girl gradually learns the complexities of cooking, cleaning, and feeding the fowl while the reader, in the process, can add to her stock of recipes and menus. When Ella is beckoned home again on her sister's marriage, she returns a full-fledged housekeeper who even masters the art of booking rooms at a seaside resort without being cheated.

Personal improvement constitutes the main fictional theme in the *Girl's Own Paper*. But in general, practical as well as moral messages are integrated into the plot structures. These structures are found in two basic variants in the serials: one is the good girl who exudes her benevolent influence in the reformation of others; the other is the willful girl who matures by eventually mastering her adversities. "Aunt Diana," written by the prolific Rosa Nouchette Carey, is one of the numerous narratives in which the two variations are woven together. On her mother's death, eighteen-year-old Alison Merle is guided by the wisdom and humor of her aunt to overcome what on later reflection she sees as her "incapacity for responsibility, her morbid dislike to her surroundings," not least the "incessant whir and grind" of her father's nearby mills (*Girl's Own Paper* 6, no. 273 [21 March 1885], p. 386). She throws all her energy into being a good housekeeper to her father and four siblings, which proves particularly difficult because her sixteen-year-old sister Mabel, intelligent but vain, disrupts all domestic harmony.

The unselfish behavior of a Cinderella-like friend, Anna, "her little thin hands and bare wrists unrelieved by any whiteness," touches Mabel's heart and propels Alison's reformatory efforts. But the pert "woman-child" only repents and comes to her senses after being the indirect cause of her father's serious injury. Disobeying his orders, she goes off on a day's outing, merely accompanied by her best friend, Anna's socialite sister Eva, and the young Captain Harper. When her father follows to take her home, his train meets with an accident. To Alison, Mabel's repentance proves the justice of her own unselfish cause. She stands a wiser and gentler woman, ready to accept a proposal of marriage, offered her by the noble young Greville Moore, who with his "sunburnt handsome face" and his "gaity and natural exuberance covered a depth of feeling that would have astonished people" (*Girl's Own Paper* 6, no. 300 [26 September 1885], p. 818).

The reader never gets a chance to be astonished, however. From the outset, the male hero is an ideal blend of good looks, intelligence, and empathy. His love is the prize received as a token of Alison's maturation. She and her sister are clearly the readers' points of identification, and, as in other serials, they are the more complex characters. Typical too is the older relative, Aunt Diana, who is close without possessing the problematic intimacy that many readers would associate with a mother figure. She stands as the title figure of the serial, an adult ideal who promises an unproblematic transference of female experiences between the generations. A psychological integration of the heroines' independence and deference constitutes the epic drive of these narratives that would generally run for twenty or twenty-five issues. Illustrations served to reinforce this integration of independence and deference. Larger than in periodicals of earlier decades and with more imaginative use of frames and background, the pictures often showed the heroine in unusual situations: alone on a beach, traveling on a ship, or riding a bicycle. Yet in these situations she invariably embodied demure femininity with eyes downcast and with bonnet, gloves, and skirt all in their proper places.

The Edwardian *Girl's Own Paper* seemed more outgoing. By 1894, the initial masthead, a rather stern-looking engraving depicting part of a Greek statue, the "Spirit of Truth and Love," was replaced by a line drawing of two smiling girls in Greek draperies, one of whom is sketching, the other one apparently writing her diary. This outward modernization was also evident inside the covers. The weekly started to carry articles on famous female singers, journalists, and actresses, and fictional characters apparently became more liberated and self-assertive not least in the school serials of the paper. Compared to contemporary schoolgirl novels by L. T. Meade (1854–1914) and Sarah Doudney (1843–1926), the serial heroines seemed more independently minded. Thus, Pixie O'Shaughnessy is depicted as an irrepressible and not very pretty schoolgirl ("an extraordinarily plain child") in Mrs. de Horne Vaizey's most popular serial, which began in 1901 under the heroine's name and was later followed by "More About Pixie" and "The Love Affairs of Pixie."[4] As the titles indicate, the heroine is followed from her school days, through her engagement into marriage, and this development constitutes the story line. On her mother's death, Pixie's father, the major, sends her against her will away from the family estate in Ireland to Holly House in London: "It had been a quiet well-conducted seminary before her time, or it seemed so, at least, looking back after the arrival of the wild Irish tornado, before whose pranks the mild mischief of the Englishers was as water unto wine" (*Girl's Own Paper* 23, no. 1136 [5 October 1901], p. 12). One of Pixie's wildest exploits is jumping about the classroom at recess without touching the ground. Since her quick-tempered disobedience is balanced by good-natured loyalty, the Irish girl soon wins over even her strongest opponents.

Pixie matures not so much because of her school experiences as through the loss of her father, her subsequent life with her newly married sisters sharing their various difficulties, and finally her unrequited love for the young Stanor Vaughan, "twenty-four and as handsome as paint." At the end of the series, she stands a wise but still cheerful young woman ideally prepared for the responsibilities of marriage. She is able to "do at least three things at the same time with quite a fair amount of success. She could, for instance, write a business-like letter while carrying on an animated conversation with a friend, and keeping an eye on a small child tottering around the room. Brain, eyes and limb were alike so alert that what to slower natures would have been impossible, to her involved no effort at all" (*Girl's Own Paper* 34, no. 7 [March 1913], p. 417). Pixie's inner radiance overshines her lack of beauty, and she actually ends by proposing to Stanor's ten-year-older uncle, whose lameness has made him refrain from revealing his deep love for her. Pixie's high-spirited charm undoubtedly captured the interests of contemporary adolescent readers who themselves were under increasing pressure to conform. But she was no new type of heroine since her transformation ultimately followed the usual fictional pattern found in the paper.

4. "Pixie O'Shaughnessy" started in volume 23 in the *Girl's Own Paper* (no. 1136, [5 October 1901]) with its follow-ups commencing in vol. 24, no. 1190 (18 October 1902) and in vol. 34, no. 5 (February 1913). Book editions under the same titles were issued by the Religious Tract Society in 1903 and 1914, respectively.

A similar trend can be observed in the *Girl's Realm*, the sixpenny monthly brought out by Hutchinson and, when it first appeared in 1898, explicitly catering to middle-class girls brought up under the influence of "do" rather than "don't," as the editor candidly stated in the opening issue. "The modern girl . . . is tired of living in a doll's house, and, married or unmarried, she will never take a back seat." But as the budding Noras are quickly reminded: "The 'Do' attitude must be fashioned by reason, by common sense, and chastened by the imaginative sympathy" ("Chat with the Girl of the Period," *Girl's Realm* 1, no. 2 [December 1898], p. 216). In the new paper, readers are strongly advised to lead an active outdoor life and to excel at sports. But, as suitable, female occupations are advocated: "home-making, feeding, clothing, teaching and caring for children, nursing the sick, providing the graces and daintiness and beauty of life." By contrast, careers as doctors, dentists, or journalists, are deemed less sensible. As it says in Alice Stronach's article "How Can I Earn A Living" (allegedly written at the request of numerous readers), such professional occupations are unsuitable, because a girl's "muscles are less tough, her nerves more highly strung" (*Girl's Realm* 7, no. 74 [December 1904], p. 204). Maybe it was believed that in the long run gymnastics would redress the balance of biological differences and thus pave the way for equal career opportunities. Rather than being proof of any simple trend of liberation, then, the subtle changes that did appear in the Edwardian quality papers for girls indicate that the readers' real-life contradictions had become more difficult to harmonize in an entertaining fashion by following the well-trodden paths.

But while these paths in the papers' informatory articles clearly lead the audience in different directions, the serials seem to unite different strands into a harmonious female ideal. If excessive self-will is conquered or maturity is achieved, women's true independence could be reached in marriage, a relationship based on love and mutual respect. In a sense, this ideal of personal betterment follows the tradition that the Religious Tract Society had been instrumental in shaping. But there are important innovations. First, the ethical maxims are conveyed by the action, not the authors. Female characters are recognizable as fallible human beings, making their transformations all the more believable. Second, these characters' moral transgressions find mundane solutions, and death is no longer posed as an unavoidable alternative to disobedience. Instead, love acts as a moral lever either in the form of sisterly benevolence or male admiration.

Compared, then, to the religious periodicals or the domestic novels in the Yonge vein, the better-class girls' magazines offered readers a wider range of action and left them considerable space for the development of self-worth. Although schoolgirl heroines, as noted, became popular, and governesses, journalists, and nurses appeared as principal characters, it was the personal struggles as single women that were stressed, and the heroines' ultimate reward remained marriage. Thus, the mechanism of psychological integration at once concealed the social origins of the young protagonists', and the readers', contradictions and held up a dynamic ideal of femininity. Many middle- and lower-middle-class girls badly needed this ideal that, moreover, seemed feasible to emulate by sheer will-power.

The fictional double bind was reinforced by the element of romance. To readers going through the mental turmoil of adolescence but finding few legitimate outlets for their emotions, magazine reading prompted fantasies about men (whose looks were always described in loving detail). These fantasies must have brought a sense not only of enjoyment but also of relief since romance was veiled in the moral garb of the heroine's betterment. But the fantasies were equally directed toward matrimony as destiny, thereby ultimately reinforcing the emotional frustrations of readers who had not reached, or would not reach, this appointed goal.

The contents of the *Girl's Own Paper* were as contradictory as the lives of its adolescent readership. But since the fictional and the nonfictional sections of the magazine treated the girls' contradictory experiences so differently, it is hard to evaluate how the paper as a whole operated in the lives of these readers. However, it can be surmised that the lower-middle-class girl, needing personal and vocational information yet often lacking social connections to secure her future, would be a keen reader of the advisory articles and could thus spot their authors' differences of opinion. Rather than adding to her self-assertion, however, these differences probably exacerbated her confusion about how to balance on the social tightrope of her class. She therefore would have enjoyed the serials more despite their narrower range of female ideals. Conversely, the middle-class girl, already familiar with such fiction through contemporary novels, would have spent more time learning the advice on good health and the hints on perfect housekeeping. In general, she also had more opportunities to act upon the ideals of independence and self-support set up in some of these articles. Their contradictions would therefore have become catalysts to her self-realization, more so than to her impecunious sisters.

"FAME, FORTUNE, AND HAPPINESS"

Once Alfred Harmsworth had entered magazine publishing with his halfpenny papers, romance and female self-realization took a new turn in the history of girls' magazines. While the *Girl's Own Paper* and the *Girl's Realm* continued to stress "sensible" information and personal maturation, the new mill-girl papers featured chiefly exciting fiction. The main theme was no longer the heroine's psychological struggle but sudden reversals of her fate. Promises of happiness and a blissful marriage were repeatedly shattered by revelations of matrimonial deceit and broken engagements.

A serial, typical of the new papers, was featured in the first volume of the *Girls' Reader* in 1908. "A Lancashire Lass in London; or, the City Paved with Gold" recounts the experiences of the eighteen-year-old Molly Ferral, "a real, hard-working, light-hearted Lancashire lass," when she comes into a small inheritance and goes off to the capital to win "fame, fortune, and happiness." Here, she meets with stage-struck actresses and with theatrical agents who are attracted by her untainted beauty. The men try to lure her not only on to the stage where she soon enjoys being an understudy, but equally into the snares of metropolitan depravity where "well-cut afternoon gowns, and smart hats with plumes in them" are de rigueur with women. The reader gets a titillating description of theatre and music-hall life. These milieus highlight how a woman's sexuality is at once her strongest asset and her severest danger.

But Molly "had a natural refinement and quickness which made her able to hold her own" (*Girls' Reader* 1, no. 31 [19 September 1908], p. 250). The heroine's modest charm is balanced by her common sense, an ideal personality combination that enables her to avoid the pitfalls of city life, gain overnight success when she stands in for the leading lady, Miss Flenback, and finally conquer the opposition of her beloved Cecil Rawson's parents—the millowners from back home whose wealth and influence pale completely when compared to the status of Molly's London devotees. The now famous actress is in a position to accept Cecil's advances: "She held his hands in hers, and suddenly he lost his self-control, and caught her to his breast, kissing her madly, passionately." Molly "pressed her soft, red lips to his cheek for one instant. "There, now go," she said, flushing and half pushing him away" (*Girls' Reader* 1, no. 35 [17 October 1908], p. 282).

Molly's story, like many serials from the Amalgamated Press, was a variation on the rags-to-riches theme, a traditional ingredient in many Victorian melodramas and romantic novelettes. Her fate would appeal to a young working-class audience on several levels. Through the tale, the reader could revel in details about exotic and extravagant London life with its female gamblers and its artful and equally feminine liars faking telegrams to oust their opponents or giving false evidence to obtain a divorce; but since such devious women always met their deserved downfall on the final page, the reader could ultimately preserve her belief in the sanctity of marriage. Also, the theme of emotion and romance essentially treated her own problems of negotiating her sexuality within an often foreign environment, while the ideal heroine promised that the reader's inherent human qualities, regardless of her background, would prevail in the end. The identification with Molly and an enjoyment of her struggles against vice and deceit were not conditioned by the reader's belief in or attempt to attain moral betterment. The action rather than the protagonist reconciled her conflicts. The heroine's self-sacrifice, her good sense, and sweet smiles would always soften the sternness of honest employers and melt the hearts of handsome young men.

¶ LONDON AND LANCASHIRE ARE TALKING. ¶

THE GIRLS' READER ½ᴰ

~ The ~ Bright ~ Saturday ~ Story ~ Paper ~

Vol. I. No. 32. ONE HALFPENNY—EVERY SATURDAY. [SEPTEMBER 26TH, 1908.

OUR GREAT NEW SERIAL DRAMA NOW STARTING.

A LANCASHIRE LASS IN LONDON

Or, THE CITY PAVED WITH GOLD.

New readers should first of all read the synopsis of the commencing chapters at the foot of the next page.

THE LANCASHIRE LASS DANCES TO AN APPRECIATIVE LONDON AUDIENCE.

The *Girls' Reader; The Bright Saturday Story Paper* 1, no. 32 (26 September 1908), front cover. In the mill-girl papers, even exotic disguises cannot hide an unspoiled nature, leaving the reader free to enjoy a plethora of excitements while she retains a belief in the justice of ordinary fate.

Principal characters in these serials ranged from shop assistants, mill-girls, and milliners to artists' models, gypsies, and nurses; even for ardent fans it could be difficult to keep track of their whereabouts. The pink *Girls' Friend* came out on Wednesday, the green *Girls' Home* followed on Thursday, while the pink *Girls' Reader* was "the Bright Saturday Story Paper." Within their eight pages, these large-format, halfpenny weeklies generally featured three serials and a short story in addition to which came entries on beauty and fashion (paper dress-patterns could be bought to make "a maid's afternoon gown" or "a comfortable gymnasium dress," for example, and sizes ranged for those from fourteen to eighteen years of age). In the occasional puzzle contests, prizes included rings, trendy blouses, and manicure sets as well as clocks, hat pins, and hair combs. The emphasis on personal appearance, which clearly appealed to adolescent girls and young women who for the first time had a little money to spend on themselves, was reinforced in the papers by their illustrations (two or three per page): just as fictional heroines retained an attractive femininity irrespective of the dangerous or unusual situations depicted, so the fashion pages were adorned by large line drawings of neat young women displaying the hats, frocks or camisoles that could be made from the dress patterns. In a similar way, beauty and personal appeal were stressed through the regular correspondence pages that in their turn underpinned the advertisements.

With understanding intimacy, the fatherly editor advised the young girl on how to overcome jealousy, shyness, and faithless friends, male as well as female, how to improve the color of finger nails, how to develop the neck, and how to dress in order to improve one's height. Similarly, in the advertisements promises abounded to cure blushing and blotchy faces, "Pearlia" toilet water could make the "hands, arms, face, and neck a healthy white tint," and "Icilma Hair Powder" would cleanse the hair "without wetting, without trouble, and without danger." If the reader was still dissatisfied with her looks and, even more unlikely, had ten shillings left to spare, the "Toilet Emporium" offered to send her an intricate instrument whereby "the soft cartilage of the nose" would be "pressed into shape" if the mysterious machine was worn half an hour daily "for a short time." Having thus acquired a classical Grecian profile, only a minority would probably have the strength, and the audacity, to opt for Mr. Ambrose Wilson's Magneto Corset, "the Corset that Cures," not to mention "Dr. Vincent's anti-stout Pills," which were assured to "reduce superabundant flesh as much as 10 lb. in a week."[5]

Once the Amalgamated Press papers were established, they turned into six-

5. Dr. Vincent was probably among the successful manufacturers of abortifacients whose covert advertisements included the "Lady Montrose Female Tabules," the "Panolia" drugs, and Madame Frain's pills (McLaren 1978, pp. 232–40). The presence of such advertisements in the mill-girl papers indicates the trade's recognition of a broad readership.

teen-page (or thirty-two-page) weeklies, and the number of serials increased accordingly. Among them, the school tale was assuming an increasing status. The most popular, though not the first, in a series of irrepressible schoolgirl heroines was Pollie Green. Created for the *Girls' Friend* by "Mabel St. John" (Henry St. John Cooper (1869–1926), who was also a prolific writer of school and adventure yarns in the Amalgamated Press papers for boys), Pollie combines the standard qualities of kindness and beauty with an unusual degree of pluck. Called "the prettiest, the wittiest and the sauciest girl whom we know," the heroine spends her time fending off a series of impudent school-mistresses, romantic suitors, rascally devious money lenders, and other opponents who turn up in the series, which ends with her marriage.[6] As with Pixie O'Shaughnessy, Pollie's school universe offers excellent opportunities for innocent pranks and humorous incidents including Pollie's final geography examination in which she answers that Buenos Aires is "a street in Paris where students drink absence and dance a good deal" (*Girls' Friend*, no. 445 [16 May 1908], p. 467). But contrary to her middle-class contemporaries, changing milieus form no part of Pollie's personal development. They create fictional variation and give endurance to a tale that basically deals with romance as the other serials in the mill-girl papers. Although the new setting would form an immediate attraction to lower-middle-class and artisan readers who might still be at school, readers in full-time employment would also enjoy the astute heroine's repeated subversion of discipline and authority: both aspects were all too familiar from the shop floor and the retail stores.

The fictional careers of Pollie Green and other school heroines make interesting comparisons with the earlier development of Jack Harkaway as a prototype of the schoolboy protagonist in boys' magazines. While Jack, after marrying as a token tribute to conventional morality, keeps roaming around the globe, the exploits of the Edwardian school heroines suddenly finish on their wedding day. A perennial school serial, as developed in the *Magnet* and the *Gem,* is thus inconsistent with the theme of romance that dominated contemporary girls' papers. Their editors found a solution to that conundrum only during the interwar years, but the popularity of the school setting across a wide social scale indicated a route that seemed acceptable both to the readers, seeking optimal enjoyment for their pennies, and to the commercial publishers who wanted to rationalize production and maximize the size of their audience.

---

6. Pollie Green's exploits were reprinted in the *Girls' Reader,* the *Girls' Home,* and the monthly *Girls' Friend Library.* The titles of the original *Girls' Friend* series indicate the heroine's fictional destiny: "Pollie Green" (introduced in no. 426 [4 January 1908]), "Pollie Green at Cambridge" (no. 446 [23 May 1908]), "Pollie Green in Society" (no. 474 [5 December 1908]), and "Pollie Green At Twenty-One" (starting with no. 508 [31 July 1909]).

"A HARD AND CURIOUS CAREER"

The stable setting and sustained characters as they appear in the *Magnet* and the *Gem* clarify how a modern—that is, a commercial—juvenile magazine operates aesthetically as an ideological organizer of the readers' needs: which problems receive attention, which topics are neglected, and how is the process of fictional selection constituted? But unlike today, the basis of attention in the two weeklies is the written text—apart from a large eye-catching color picture on the front pages, only three or four small drawings enliven the tiny print. In the texts, the basis of the action is the school setting. Thus, Greyfriars is situated on the Kentish coast, "somehwere between Winchester and Harrow," as Robert Roberts and his friends estimated in an eager attempt to relate their beloved *Magnet* stories to reality (Roberts 1977, p. 161). Numerous queries from curious correspondents are met by printing exact maps of the immediate surroundings of the schools, thus enhancing the realism of the stories without losing the real geographical vagueness that is a necessary precondition for preserving Charles Hamilton's fictional liberty. This necessity is also met by giving few direct topical references in the narrative, an omission which led Orwell to conclude in an essay on boys' magazines that, as for the *Magnet* and the *Gem*, "the year is 1910—or 1940, but it is all the same. . . . Everything is safe, solid and unquestionable. Everything will be the same for ever and ever" (Orwell 1976, p. 518).

This is partly true, but in the stories it is of no importance; what matters here are the skirmishes and contentions, the romps and the frolics experienced by the boys themselves. The school is a self-contained community where rank, wealth, and heritage are apparently insignificant appendixes. Many major characters are of nebulous parentage, and none of the boys are tied down in their holidays by tiresome family obligations. Mothers and sisters are nonexistent, and brothers only crop up as nefarious nuisances in the lower forms at the school. Quite a few of the pupils, however, possess a host of rich and much-traveled relatives who willingly open their old mansions, Mediterranean yachts, and well-lined wallets to the boys. But social status and other external accidentals only play a part insofar as they act as catalysts to the action among the boys.

Within the pupil community, the "core boys," led by Tom Merry in the *Gem* and Harry Wharton in the *Magnet*, form a stable group of moral reference and a secure source of fictional continuity. The two form captains are the ideal embodiments of manly intelligence and responsibility combined with boyish pluck and strength. The other central characters emulate this ideal to varying degrees. Compared to stories with a single, and perhaps even an adult, protagonist, the fourteen- to fifteen-year-old boys offer a variety of easy identification possibilities: from the good-natured duffer and the athletic rebel to the studious thinker and the suave aristocrat. The boys can be types, but none of them are paragons of virtue, and all have their idiosyncrasies and their lapses into forget-fulness and deviation from their normal nature. No one in this group, however, recurs to prolonged transgressions of an ethos whose raison d'être they never question: truthfulness to oneself, loyalty to the group, and unswerving alle-giance to the school. That they miraculously manage to harmonize these qualities is the reason for their dominant position in the narratives.

The rest of the pupils deviate from this codified straight and narrow by being either overly aggressive or excessively dependent. This deviation makes the central theme in the serials a problem of role fulfillment. Any solution to rivalries depends on a reformation of miscreants who have to go through a phase of transformation. Since the core boys' own forms, the Shell in the *Gem* and the Remove or "lower fourth" in the *Magnet*, are placed midway between the junior and senior forms, controversies are not hard to find. Within the forms, fights abound with cheats and cowards, gamblers, grinds, and cads. Likewise, higher and lower forms are populated with numerous villains and sneaks, on the lookout for any opportunity to overthrow the leadership of the core boys.

Most of the real bullies are found in the senior forms: Sefton and Know in the *Gem* and, in the *Magnet*, the prefect Loder and Coker, "with the brain of twelve and the muscle of twenty years of age" and spelling "worse than badly" despite his status as a fifth former ("The Magnet Who's Who," *Magnet* 11, no. 513 [8 December 1917], p. 27). Lower-form boys can be equally irritating, but their greater alacrity and inventiveness are paired by ignorance and foolishness, making their occasional intrusion upon the hunting grounds of their elders an occasion for amusement rather than resentment or threat. The school hierarchy is completed by the masters who, if less prominent in the tales than the boys, are not sacrosanct to Hamilton's versatile imagination and quick pen.

The stable school setting with its elaborate power relations yields ample scope for personal conflicts. What I have called its "flexible stability" facilitates a narrative structure that is characterized by a series of "evolving cycles": one pupil or a group form the center of attention over a couple of issues, during which time they can improve so much that they lose the grip of fictional interest. They are then replaced by another set of problematic boarders who in turn initiate a new set of stirring or comical events. Hamilton combines the well-known novel theme of personal betterment with a rational updating of the serial "strings" that had characterized, for instance, Beeton's and Brett's ventures where fictional innovation had been dependent on new serials and new scenarios, respectively. Within Hamilton's narrative framework, the theme of role fulfill-ment is found in two common variations, namely the "bounder" episodes, in which the pupil community is morally right, and the less prevalent "scholarship boy" episodes, in which an individual boy is morally right.[7] When Jerrold

---

7. The two thematical variations mirror Tom's and Harry's initiation into their respective schools. While the other scholars initially misjudge Tom's true heroism because of his

Lumley-Lumley arrives at St. Jim's, experienced *Gem* readers immediately recognize that this willful son of a poor-man-turned-millionaire is a true bounder:

> The boy who was always called the Outsider at St. Jim's had nerve enough for anything. Pluck is a good quality, and he had heaps of pluck; there was no denying that. If he had had a sense of honour along with it, he would have been a very different character. But Lumley's training, and perhaps his nature, did not allow that. He had had a hard and curious career when he was of an age when most boys are at school, and he had come to St. Jim's with more experience than falls to most fellows of twenty-five. The lad who had roughed it among the street arabs of the Bowery, in New York, who had been forced to take care of himself in many strange places, and had learned a hard unscrupulousness in his contact with a hard world, was not the sort of fellow to pull easily with the boys of St. Jim's. And Jerrold Lumley did not seem to care whether he pulled easily with them or not. He went on his own way, cool, hard, and determined, and utterly reckless of others. ("Lumley Lumley's Luck," *Gem* 5, no. 134 [3 September 1910], pp. 2–3)

Lumley-Lumley, brought up on the inhuman jungle laws of the metropolis, arrives at St. Jim's, with its civilized loyalties, and makes Tom Merry and company take the field in a large-scale operation to reform the insolent newcomer. Disobeying all school regulations and disregarding fellow pupils, Jerrold follows his own adult habits of smoking, drinking, pub-hunting and poker-playing. Our friends conduct a nightly expedition to the nearby village pub to rescue the rascal and bring him back to the school and to a true boyish behavior. The headmaster, when learning about the affair, flogs Lumley-Lumley with prompt precision and puts him on bread and water, reproaches the rescuers, who have infringed his rules but with the right intentions, and orders all to bed.

Jerrold's self-willed exclusion from the other boys causes him some uncertainty and produces a certain self-reflection but no change of manners. Finally, danger brings about his sudden transformation. Lumley-Lumley's valiant rescue of a little girl from drowning provides him with an opportunity for intuitive action, thus revealing his finer boyish nature. But a sudden attack of a "nervous malady" prevents his final atonement and protracts the closing of his story. Over the next few issues, Lumley-Lumley is declared dead, then he is resurrected by a distant friend, who explains that he has merely had yet another bout of his strange paralysis, only to be finally removed from the scene of action by the kind intervention of his uncle. However, he occasionally crops up as a gray eminence of morality—a boy on the right way, but still a latent troublemaker holding the readers' attention: will he ever reform?

Most other characters of Lumley-Lumley's kind do not disappear physically

---

effeminate Fauntleroy outfit, Harry must first learn to harness his aggressiveness by judgment before being accepted by the other Removites.

from the stories, but merely fade into the background after a few issues to be pulled out of the wings again when the fictional need arises for new episodes of personal betterment. Such a resurrection technique naturally has its limits, and over the years a number of former bounders stop smoking and poker-playing as they are partially transformed into mixed characters—boys open to betterment but not wholly converted. The popular "bounder" plots, though, run the risk of conveying a view of group infallibility, gradually undermining the credibility of the schoolboys. But another type of story redresses the balance by proving that a majority of the pupils can be in the wrong.

In an early *Magnet* story, Mark Linley, a poor Lancashire mill-boy, manages to cross existing class boundaries through his extreme diligence. He leaves his factory job for a scholarship at Greyfriars only to find that most of the boys are opposed to his dialect, his heavy boots, and his tweed suit, made by his work-worn mother to last him a lifetime. But by the subtle guidance of the omniscient author, the reader, along with a few of the boarders (Wharton among them, of course), quickly detects the signs of a hero in the boy, the balanced opposition of inner qualities: "There was nothing at all bumptious about him, and, on the other hand, there was no sign whatever of any wish to curry favour. He was of a sufficiently strong nature to stand alone, if they let him alone." This last warning is not heeded by Bulstrode, who challenges Mark Linley to a fight. The bully, though "breathing fury," finds "a pair of hammerlike fists too hard to pass." To Linley: "punishment had no effect upon his spirit. His left eye was closed up, his nose was swelling visibly, his mouth was contorted with pain, with a thin stream of red running from the corner. But he was game to the backbone. And hard as his punishment was, Bulstrode's was harder" ("A Lad from Lancashire," *Magnet* 2, no. 45 [19 December 1908], pp. 13, 14 [marked 11]).

The poor boy's physical strength matches his studiousness, and he wins the fight. His social discomfiture disappears, and he is inserted among the trusty scholars of the Remove. Over the years, Mark Linley's fate is recapitulated by a number of other scholarship pupils, poor but honest lads who disprove the significance of class—but not its existence—by their outstanding personalities and their ready accommodation to the school ethos. Their social conflict and its individual upheaval is always described with earnest endeavor and a sincerity of tone that clearly indicates that such obvious objects of self-identification for the working-class readers cannot be treated amusingly, let alone be morally rejected like the bounders.

When class is humored the boys are rich. In stable characters belonging to the nobility, their benevolent quaintness and extravagant habits are stressed. Arthur Augustus D'Arcy (Gussy), "the swell of St. Jim's," is exceedingly particular about his pinstriped trousers and impeccable top hats, while his less prominent duplicate in the *Magnet*, "the schoolboy earl," Lord Mauleverer (Mauly), is known for his ample allowance, "too ample if Mauleverer had not been a youth of unusual good sense and good feeling." Conversely, when nouveau riche boarders enter the esteemed establishments, smiles are turned into full-scale merriment, dissolving any serious notions of social division. A similar role is played by foreign pupils. Every corner of Great Britain endows Greyfriars and St. Jim's with at least one pupil. As Amalgamated Press papers gain popularity in distant parts of the empire, boys arrive who are distinguished by more than red curls or a fierce temper. In 1908, the Nawob of Bhanipur, Hurree Jamset Ram Singh, or Inky, enters Greyfriars: "His complexion, of the deepest, richest olive, showed him to be a native of some Oriental clime, and though clad in the ordinary Eton garb of the schoolboy there was a grace and suppleness about his figure that betrayed the Hindoo" ("Aliens at Greyfriars," *Magnet* 1, no. 6 [21 March 1908], p. 2).

Inky is initiated into the core group and gradually acquires a highly stylish manner of expression that secures him a safe place in the tales as a merry intruder. Like a jester he comments proverbially on the action—"the still tongue goes longest to the well and saves a stitch in time"—and often with the same irreverent results: "the perspicacity of the instructor sahib is mar-velful. . . . He jumps to the rightful conclusions with extreme ludicrousness" is his verdict of the infallible headmaster, Dr. Locke. The Nawob was created by Hamilton with the express aim that he might contribute "to the unity of the Commonwealth, and help to rid the youthful mind of colour prejudice," and Hamilton believed that he did "some good in this direction" (Richards 1952, p. 38). Hurree Singh is followed by Wun Lung, a "heathen Chinese" possessing "the good qualities as well as the faults of the Orient," and by a host of less amusing, but equally colonial chums from Canada, South Africa, New Zealand, and Australia. While it is doubtful if Hurree's "the -fulness is terrific" removed any ethnic preconceptions, it seems certain that the colorful characters enhanced the readers' enjoyment, as well as the sales figures, of the companion papers in the commonwealth countries. The correspondence pages of the *Gem*, for instance, regularly quoted readers from South Africa, India, and Canada.[8]

Printed correspondence equally reveals that girls were avid fans of the two Amalgamated Press papers. Borrowing their brothers' reading matter seems to have been quite a common pattern for girls who wanted to explore more exciting vistas than the ones offered in their own magazines. Thus, in the early 1880s, Alice Pollock enjoyed the tales of Jules Verne in the *Boy's Own Paper,* while a working-class girl just before World War I would sneak the comic paper *Larks*

---

8. As noted earlier, foreigners appear in the religious magazines as objects of pity or scorn. In the commercial papers, they come to provide comic relief, such as Monday in the *Boys of England* and Pete in the *Marvel*. The oriental characters pioneer that development. From being cunning ruffians, they mellow in the 1870s into the cheeky inventiveness of the noble savage in a fashion set by Ching-Ching, the popular Chinese hero created by Burrage for Charles Fox' *Boys' Standard* (1875–92).

away from her brothers to read in the toilet (Pollock 1971, p. 54; Humphries 1981, p. 126).[9] "Girl chums" accordingly feature regularly in the narratives, especially in the *Magnet,* where Philippa Derwent, Clara Trevlyn, and Majorie Hazeldene are frequent visitors to sports arrangements at Greyfriars—they even accompany the Removites on unchaperoned bicycle adventures. While these boarders from the nearby Cliff House were destined to popularity with girl readers in the 1920s, as we shall see, their function in the Edwardian period is mainly to be in the utmost danger when boys are most in need of heroic deeds.

Sexual feelings, as those allowed the adolescent readership of penny dreadfuls and popular magazines in the 1860s and 1870s, were not stirred by girls or women in the Edwardian boys' papers. Orwell complained about this taboo on sex in the weeklies. Charles Hamilton, in his reply to Orwell's essay, stated that the magazines were intended for readers under the age of sixteen, and the less such youngsters thought about sex the better. Moreover, he claimed, it played no "stupendous" part in real life "among healthy and wholesome people" (Richards 1976, p. 533). To the *Magnet* and *Gem* audience, identifying with their family upbringing and surrounded by school, sexuality crept into their weekly narratives in more subtle and, also to the author, more unconscious ways; namely, through food. While study teas and excursions to the village "tuckshop" are always described in great detail, one character, Billy Bunter in the *Magnet,* epitomizes gregariousness ("Fatty Wynn," his understudy in the *Gem,* never assumed quite the same proportions, neither around the waist nor in the minds of the readership).

William George Bunter, arch-duffer and master schemer of the Remove, is quietly introduced as "a somewhat stout junior, with a broad, pleasant face and an enormous pair of spectacles" ("The Making of Harry Wharton," *Magnet* 1, no. 1 [15 February 1908], p. 6), but he gradually develops into the best-known character of the companion papers and indeed of all figures ever appearing in a juvenile magazine.[10] Billy Bunter is everything in the extreme. Not dim but vacuously inane, not plump but a mammoth of bulky flesh, not self-centered, but a vain snob and egoist, not crafty but possessing the slyness of an artful dodger. Like the core group of characters, Bunter is a compound of mental qualities, but in such exaggeration that the balance of "the ideal average" is

9. According to Edward Salmon's survey of schoolchildren's reading habits, the most coveted magazine option for girls next to the *Girl's Own Paper* was the *Boy's Own Paper* (it was preferred by about 9 percent), while Dickens, Scott, and Kingsley topped their list of favorite authors over Charlotte Yonge (Salmon 1888, pp. 21, 23).

10. In the end, the *Magnet* bore the subtitle "Billy Bunter's Own Paper," and when the weekly had been forgotten, Bunter kept appearing, first in the Amalgamated Press comic, the *Knockout,* into which the *Magnet* merged, and then in 1947 in the Bunter books published by Charles Skilton (there were 39 in all). Eleven years later, Maurice McLoughlin revitalized the Fat Owl on stage in "Billy Bunter's Mystery Christmas." The plays remained an annual attraction for 6 years (Richards 1952, p. 189; Lofts and Adley 1970, p. 233).

completely distorted into a unity of human extremes. Had Billy lacked his redeeming features of naive incompetence and foolish self-deception, he would have made an arch-villain. But his pointless deceit and futile scheming create laughter and amusement rather than fear and excitement. He provides comic relief whether he attempts to relieve a matron of her keys for the kitchen, tries to obtain a note from one of his completely imaginary female admirers, or, more commonly, wants his undue share in a study tea:

> Billy Bunter opened the door of No. 1 Study, and blinked in through his big glasses. There was a merry flow of talk in the study, and Harry Wharton & Co. and their visitors [from the nearby Highcliffe school] seemed in great spirits. But there was an injured expression upon the fat face of Billy Bunter.
>
> "I've come," he said, with dignity.
>
> "Oh, you've come, have you?" said Bob Cherry, "Then the next proceeding is to go."
>
> "Oh, really, Cherry—"
>
> "This is our prize porpoise," said Bob, presenting Bunter, as it were, to the visitors. "Warranted forty yards round the waist, and able to beat a boa-constrictor in his own line of business. His great gift is that he can smell out a feed at any distance."
>
> "I saw you come in," said Bunter. "You looked funny!" [Wharton and Cherry have just been "ragged" on their way home with chickens for the study tea]. . . .
>
> "Are you going out on your feet or on your neck?" demanded Wharton.
>
> "Oh, really, Wharton, if that's the way you talk to a chap you invite to tea—"
>
> "I—I—I—"
>
> "After the way you pressed me to come, I call it uncivil," said Bunter. "I hardly know what these Highcliffe chaps will think of you. Still, I dare say you're a bit ratty at having been made to look such a silly idiot, so I'll excuse you. I'm not a fellow to take offence."
>
> "Not at teatime," remarked Squiff.
>
> "Oh, really, Field, if you're finished, I'll have your chair—"
>
> "Thanks! I'm not finished."
>
> Bunter snorted, and stood. He would have eaten standing on his head, for that matter, rather than not have eaten.
>
> "I say, help a fellow to the chicken!" "Fancy coming home with chickens hanging round your necks! He, he, he!"
>
> "Are you going to dry up?"
>
> "Well, I suppose you're rather touchy about it," said Bunter cheerfully. "You looked such an awful idiot. He, he, he! Never mind; I'll let it drop. I don' want to rub it in. Pass the ham, Nugent. You might have a chair for a chap when you ask him to tea. But never mind." ("The Fall of the Fifth," *Magnet* 9, no. 374 [10 April 1915], p. 8)

Bunter's prime object in life is "grub." Apart from empty studies where he can secretly enjoy purloined sausages, jam tarts, and whole tins of sardines, Billy's favorite abode is the school "tuckshop," where he gorges himself as often as uninitiated newcomers will lend him a "tanner." Newcomers are persuaded by Billy's eloquent explanations about the mysterious delay of a long expected postal order with his remittance from his "pater," the famous stockbroker Bunter de Bunter. Its arrival, naturally, is as fictitious as his pedigree. In his indefatigable endeavors to raise enough cash to satisfy his oral desires, Billy creates his private interpretations of the school ethos, and the check-trousered gourmand invariably defends his shady actions with naive dignity. Surrounded by realistic characters who undergo changes to varying degrees, Billy Bunter remains his own disproportionate self.

In his steadfast stupidity, his unswerving loyalty to his massive self-deception, lay the source of Bunter's appeal and his continued popularity. Vanity, unscrupulous self-seeking, and overindulgence were socially derogative labels for basic human experiences, namely, the new-born child's insatiable need for pleasure and its unrestricted oral sensuality. To the infant, these feelings are neither egotistical—since it makes no distinction between "self" and "other," "internal" and "external"—nor are they sexual in an adult sense, since all bodily needs and mental desires form one all-embracing sensation. Through the descriptions of Billy Bunter's unrestrained pursuit of pleasure, his eternal "grub" hunting for which all social considerations must dwindle and disappear, readers could reenact their earliest feelings of sensuous omnipotence, an experience which would evoke pleasure. But, since these early desires are molded and suppressed during upbringing, their direct means of satisfaction had to find unconscious means of fulfillment.

For many Edwardian readers, as for today's children, their delight in living out Bunter's blatant buffoonery was unconscious, and it was overlaid by heavy impositions from the "social watchdog," the superego. The audience would experience pleasure, but it was a pleasure that in its evocation was being re-suppressed. In that tension lay the source of laughter. The boy, by laughing at Bunter, was unconsciously ridiculing his own desires while letting them out and thus recognizing their existence (suppressed laughter, giggling, consequently arises whenever the mechanisms of restriction seem overpowering). His laughter served as a mental safety valve. By siding ultimately with the executors of punishment, Harry Wharton and company, the reader sided with his "just" superego as a protective mechanism against his own unrecognized desires. These desires remained unconscious and therefore sustained the need for characters like Bunter, hence his continued popularity. Basically, the Fat Owl performed the same function as the "ideal average" boys. He fulfilled certain wants but in so doing concealed their origin. Laughter only made this concealment more effective.

The *Magnet* 9, no. 369 (6 March 1915), front cover. Billy Bunter is the best-known and most popular of all British juvenile magazine heroes. His naive egotism makes him an object of laughter rather than scorn or pity.

Even if skirmishes between the boys themselves formed the basis of excitement as well as laughter in the two companion papers, adults could also come under attack. While direct disobedience of their usual form masters is anathema to the boarders, the continental quaintness of German and French masters allows the boys more liberty of action, providing readers with a rare insight into the power struggles going on during school hours. Sometimes, however, substitute British teachers arrive whose behavior cannot be explained by their national oddness. By being either too strict or too weak, they fail to fulfill their prescribed role as responsible and experienced individuals, hence they deserve their pupils' resistance. Most importantly, their shortcomings set off the justice of the regular masters whose authority therefore seems natural, not because of their age or their status, but because of their superior human qualities.

The ultimate embodiment of these esteemed qualities is the headmaster, who symbolizes the pinnacle of the school pyramid. He is a punishing and a blessing force in one, and his faultless authority is proof of the stable continuity and justice of the school system. His power is unquestionable, but also immaterial to the readers. The solution is not to debate his status, as this would entail a complete upheaval of the pyramidal structure, but to disperse his authority. His lesser judges, the housemasters, can experience occasional conflicts with some of the boys, thereby admitting adult shortcomings. The ideal nature of the system is sustained by the fallacies of its humans.

During school holidays, fictional variation can be created by letting the trusted scholars use their energies beyond the stable school setting. Next to London, the two most criminal-ridden places in Britain seem to be the areas near Greyfriars and St. Jim's. Over the years, a host of scheming robbers, brainy spies, and plodding poachers are tracked down by clever detectives and less astute police constables, if the schoolfellows have not already performed their duty to law and order—and secured the headmaster's blessings in the act:

> "We've caught a burglar, sir!" said Tom Merry. "Stopped him from bunking with a fearful lot of loot, sir! He's Jim the Nailer!"
>
> "Merry, I see what you have done, though I cannot quite understand this. You have run a great risk, my boys." ("The Boy Detectives," *Gem* 2, no. 33 [26 September 1908], p. 22)

Jim the Nailer had caught the boys' suspicion by his "oily ways," thus having lived up to the rule that strange behavior and "a savage, evil-looking face" are the unmistakable—and internationally recognizable—signs of a criminal. During most holiday issues, the heroes of the two schools visit circuses and old castles when they do not go scouting or treasure hunting. Both at home and abroad, the quick comprehension of the boys stands them in good stead. Whether in West Africa, the United States, or the South Pacific, gold robbers and diamond thieves all look the same, and they are invariably caught by the sagacious scholars.

While these more exotic exploits enhanced Hamilton's fictional liberties, he only employed those liberties during actual school holidays, thereby sustaining the realism of his serials. [11] And regardless of the scenery, the basic narrative point of departure was described as a problem of role fulfillment. Boys as well as adults, foreigners as well as Britons, could be too aggressive or too passive, too violent or too stupid, according to the ideal golden mean set up within the school hierarchy. Sudden action, a deus ex machina of excitement or amusement, would resolve the contradictions of character by removing deviance, though often leaving fictional room for further improvements. If the tensions between norm and deviance originated within the school environment, the tendency was to transpose the solution, not only into sudden action, but into actions that had nothing to do with the origin of the conflicts. Thereby the essential school values were never called into question, let alone incorporated into a process of change. Conversely, when problems admittedly arose outside the educational domain, they would be dissolved through an adept application of the school ethos that was thus reconfirmed as a universal and natural norm.

The stories treated conflicts that seemed real to the readers but left out instances when these conflicts actually originated, namely, during lessons, in the family, or at work. The final mediations thus became at once realistic and entertaining. The obvious result of such social cleansing mechanisms was that concrete historial differences disappeared through the process of reading. The explicit message of the tales, voiced by the omniscient author and crystalized through the action, was an individual, biological egalitarianism. This message, however, rested upon an unacknowledged paradox, a rift in the ideological surface, aspects of which we have already encountered in other types of serial, but which in the school perennial emerged with unprecedented clarity.

The clearest indication of this paradox is that mental superiority is mysteriously connected with material superabundance. Although class is hardly ever mentioned, the scholars either belong to or aspire to a position within the professional upper-middle class. The fates of the poor *but* honest scholarship boys form perhaps the best examples of how an alleged individual equality is based on an underlying view of the middle class as a social norm whose moral superiority never has to be questioned. The same contradiction applies to the

---

11. The realism of the tales was repeatedly stressed: the editor was continually at pains in his correspondence columns to answer detailed questions about the characters' ages, relations, and former status at the school. Moreover, the maps of the school environment and the occasional meetings of the Shell and the Remove scholars lent a concreteness to the tales, and the author still deemed it necessary to explain the abundant leisure time of his characters by information about "extra" half-holidays.

treatment of girls and foreigners, who, as individuals, can redeem their deficiencies of gender and race through an acceptance of middle-class standards. But the clearest expression of the paradox is the school hierarchy itself. Formed upon a rigid division of social power, it nevertheless emerges as a natural framework for human interaction. Its rationale is never questioned let alone discussed in the tales.

Charles Hamilton's fictional universe, his belief in biological equality, rested on assumptions about an absolute truth and an indubitable justice. Individuals could be at fault, but the social fabric was never fallible, since its organization was natural. Such were the conclusions to be gained by his school stories. That their basis was not self-evident and natural could only be proved outside the framework of the papers, since within the tales any trace of alternative realities was transformed and finally dissolved through the process of narration. Characters might start out with their class, gender, and ethnic differences, but everybody would end up as human beings per se.

The readers' problems of individual role conflicts, of suppression, and of contradictory social demands, were taken seriously in the weeklies; they were even solved. But the fictional upheaval of specific problems into an eternal naturalness was caused by removing the most difficult areas of conflict and by idealizing and personalizing relations in the areas remaining. The justice of masters and the relish in independent boy governments remained experiences within fiction and caused no change in the readers' actual reality except when they bought a new issue of the *Gem* or the *Magnet*. The reading experience was real and ideal at one and the same time, and it was not fictitious but fictional, since the experience of harmony and enjoyment was basically linked to purchase.

Yet a wide range of Edwardian boys were attracted to the school serials precisely because of their fictional nature, which at once focused on pertinent problems and removed these from the scene of action. Through the reading process, serious concerns were transformed into exciting or amusing solutions. School had assumed a major presence in the readers' lives whether its inequalities and repression were openly acknowledged, as was the case with many sons of semiskilled and unskilled workers, or whether these experiences were intuitively felt as by most better-off readers, who were cushioned and guarded by their parents. The two common plot structures enhanced a broad acceptance of the companion papers. The "scholarship boy" episodes, in which an individual proved right against the group, must have held an immediate attraction to the timid or insecure boy who desperately wanted to get the upper hand with his fellow pupils or his masters. Conversely, the "bounder" episodes proved to the school rebel that lonely opposition was right if it was just.

The general theme of role transformation would probably have been rejected by the adolescent apprentice or the printer's assistant reading the *Boys of England* in the 1860s and 1870s and identifying with the versatility of work and adult life. But the theme was palatable to the Edwardian schoolboy because it mediated edification and entertainment, deference and independence—oppositions that marked his own life. Moreover, personal transformation in the tales was caused not by psychological maturation, as in many Beeton stories and in the middle-class girls' weeklies, but by pupil independence and rapid actions stressing masculine strength and resourcefulness. These qualities were already emulated through the boys' street culture, and they were further reinforced by the companion papers' adventure and detective yarns, which graced the final pages of each issue and whose plots prefigured trends that were to develop in boys' weeklies during the interwar years. [12] No doubt, Robert Roberts' verdict of the *Magnet* and its influence upon his generation of prewar boys could be reiterated by many: "With nothing in our school that called for love or allegiance, Greyfriars became for some of us our true Alma Mater, to whom we felt bound by a dreamlike loyalty. . . . In the final estimate it may well be found that Frank Richards during the first quarter of the twentieth century had more influence on the mind and outlook of young working-class England than any other single person, not excluding Baden-Powell" (Roberts 1977, pp. 160–61).

The very commercialism of these and other Harmsworth papers almost certainly added to the readers' enjoyment. Consumerism was still a newfangled attraction to these youngsters, an area of independence and communication to boys who at school had a little extra money for personal spending and who were increasingly allowed to choose for themselves. In the Amalgamated Press papers, an abundance of advertisements induced readers to buy a cornucopia of commodities: water pistols and stamp albums, binoculars, bicycles, and ventriloquists' "Double Throats" ("fits roof of mouth; astonishes and mystifies; sing like a canary, whine like a puppy, and imitate birds and beasts—sixpence each and four for 1s."). Catering to more mature tastes, there were goods like "Mousta" Brazilian moustache pomade, which would turn boys into men, and wondrous treatments to increase one's height or to cure red noses or even blushing. Every week "a proved home treatment" promised to remove "all embarrassment" for the unlucky "sufferers."

---

12. During the years up to 1918, the most popular writer of these adventure and detective stories was E. Joyce Murray. The *Boys' Friend* was the first to serialize his most popular creation, the adventures of "the famous millionaire and inventor" Ferrers Lord. Together with his friends, Prince Ching Lung, Rupert Thurston, and the Eskimo Gan Waga, he haunted the *Magnet* and the *Gem*, engaged in perennial combats with scheming crooks from the diamond dealer Nathan Gore to the Russian rascal, Prince Michael Scaroff, with American scientists and German ruffians as occasional opponents thrown in for good measure. Other minor series in the companion papers included detective tales with Frank Kingston and also with Sexton Blake and his assistant Tinker.

The range of advertisements could indicate that the readership included adolescents who were eager to acquire a new role of adult masculinity and who were sensitive to the least bodily blemishes. But the commercial variation could equally denote that public relations were still in their infancy and that editors would accept what ads were offered, irrespective of possible target groups. To the young readers, the variety merely added to the variation in their entertainment. Boy consumerism had come of age.

PART FIVE

Universal Entertainment
for Schoolchildren,
1918–45

11

Of an Entirely New Type: Magazine Developments between the Wars

D URING THE interwar years, the reading of commercial magazines became a common experience shared by almost all British school-children regardless of their class and gender. While the Edwardian era had witnessed the upsurge of periodicals for adolescent girls and a flourishing of boys' weeklies, the years after 1918 saw a sharp decrease in religious and other types of "improving" papers in favor of the commercial magazine emphasizing fiction and geared toward a whole generation of boys or girls at school age. Thus, the schoolgirl paper was developed by the Amalgamated Press while a northern upstart, D. C. Thomson of Dundee, Scotland, innovated the boys' weekly. When the *School Friend* was launched by the London giant on 17 May 1919, its editor in chief, Reginald T. Eves (1892–1971), rightly claimed, "It is a paper of an entirely new type, and cannot be compared with papers published in past years. Essentially the *School Friend* will appeal chiefly to the girl at school—the girl whose tastes have not previously been catered for" ("Your Editor's Corner," *School Friend* 1, no. 1 [17 May 1919], p. 15).

Having started as an office boy at the *Gem* in 1908, Eves could have lived, as Hugh Cudlipp suggests, as "an unsuspected intruder in a world of gymslips, dorm feasts, hockey sticks and adventure in the half-term hols" (Cudlipp 1962, p. 193). But his long experience nevertheless earned him a final position as director of the firm after World War II. By then he had been editor of all the Amalgamated papers for girls, which, apart from the *School Friend*, came to include the *Schoolgirls' Own* (1921–36, then merging with the refashioned *School Friend*, the *Schoolgirl*), the *Schoolgirls' Weekly* (1922–39, then incorporated with the *Girls' Crystal*), the *Schoolgirls' Own Library* (1922–40; 1946–63), *Schooldays* (1928–31, then merging with the *Schoolgirl*), and finally the *Girls' Crystal* (1935–53; from 1953–63 a picture-story weekly). But the *School Friend* was the paper to set the pace and for a long time it was perhaps the most popular. It existed until 1940, the last eleven years as the *Schoolgirl*.

A twenty thousand-word school serial was the main attraction of the new paper whose minor serials and short stories depicted adventurous girls at sea, in circuses, and at camp—all extramural localities that were in later years to assume an increasing importance in this and other girls' magazines. Snippets about cookery, needlework, and, later, fashion (but no problem page) rounded off the picture of the girls' weeklies. The papers were sold at twopence, and their immediate success proves that girls of school age formed a market potential that had hitherto been unexplored by magazine publishers, but which the new film craze of the war years had made apparent and which educational reforms after 1918 further served to unify.

After initial food shortages and a lack of work opportunities, World War I, through the extensive employment of women and working-class adolescents, brought unprecedented purchasing power and a new resilience to poor sections of the population. As more unskilled workers were needed in the munition and related industries, local bylaws granted exemptions from school to children at the age of twelve (eleven in rural areas). Thus, between 1915 and 1917 the number of "Labour Certificates" issued rose by a total of twenty-two percent, a figure covering considerable regional as well as sexual differences (Ministry of Reconstruction 1919, p. 8).[1] Even children who were too young or too secure to join the labor force were affected by new patterns of consumption that the war brought in its train.

Mass entertainment received a considerable boost through the popularization of the radio, the gramophone, and film. Of these, the movies undoubtedly became the most important venue for juvenile amusement between the wars. From the invention of Edison's motion picture camera in 1889 through a "shaky" British inception at the Regent Polytechnic in London seven years later, films "burst like a vision into the underman's existence," and into the under-woman and child's one might add (Roberts 1977, p. 175). The war years saw an unprecedented influx of working-class women and children to the "picture palaces," which to many came to symbolize their new self-assurance and a sense of personal control. After 1918, it is estimated that up to thirty percent of the film audiences were below the age of seventeen (Briggs 1960, p. 18).[2] Cinema proprietors initially vied for the pennies of the young by offering prizes, free day excursions, or at least a candy stick during the peak performances, the Saturday morning "penny rush," as described by Lil Smith, who was born in 1907 in the working-class area of Hackney in London:

1. During the war years, the total growth in the employment of juveniles under eighteen years was 351,000 (18 percent), covering 258,000 girls (a 38 percent increase) against 93,000 boys (a 7 percent increase) (Ministry of Reconstruction 1919, p. 89).

2. Just after World War I, tickets could be had for as little as a halfpenny if one sat behind the screen watching the film backwards (Newton 1974, p. 38).

We used to see a film and a serial with Pearl White in it every week—that is if you got your jobs done in time. When you went to the cinema, which was called the Central Hall, you had either an orange, a bag of sweets or a pencil given to you; but if you made a row when you got inside, you got a clump round the earhole and were slung out (HA)! Needless to say, being the eldest, I rarely went because I had too many jobs to do. But we used to send Jacky so he could take Jimmy in his arms and we could get rid of at least one noise.

Jacky came home from the pictures and used to tell us how Pearl White had got on, and if she was still hanging over the cliff or if she was tied on to the rails. (Smith 1975, pp. 3, 6)

As cinema-going became an established form of indoor amusement and especially after the introduction of the "talkies" in 1927, the free gifts ceased and tickets went up to between threepence and sixpence in the 1930s. A survey of children's leisure pursuits performed in 1933 in the St. Pancras area of London showed that while twenty percent of the informants had never been to the theater, 38.8 percent of the boys and 26.6 percent of the girls visited the cinema once a week (Engledow and Farr 1933, pp. 20, 22).[3] Moreover, many of them would collect and exchange cigarette cards portraying their celluloid celebrities just as they might join a "star club," prefiguring the idolizations of the rock era while still being conducted with scout-like authority.[4]

The enrollment of working-class women and girls as important leisure consumers was quickly seized upon by magazine publishers. The success of the film industry increased commercial competition and thus indirectly became responsible for the formation of girls' papers such as the *School Friend* and similar Amalgamated Press ventures reaching across the social scale. However, the continuing popularity of these weeklies was sustained by less spectacular but equally thorough changes in children's lives, for the juvenile consumer consciousness nurtured during the war also spurred educational reforms. "In arduousness of labour," declared the Ministry of Reconstruction in 1917:

in earnings, in character and outlook upon life a generation of young persons has been forced into precocious maturity. . . . When the artificial conditions of war are removed, habis will require to be changed, standards to be revised, expectations to be written down. The change from a high to a low economic temperature, from a world in which they are important to one in which they

3. A similar but more extensive investigation performed in 1938 demonstrated that girls aged 12–14 had largely caught up with the boys' film devotion: about a third of all children in that age group visited the cinema once a week (Jenkinson 1946, pp. 95, 237).

4. A typical performance, often attended by upwards of 1,000 children, was accompanied by the singing of the national anthem and the club song plus the club pledge: honesty, obedience to parents, kindness to animals and old people—all conducted in front of the screen by the cinema manager (Stewart 1948, p. 9).

The *School Friend* 1, no. 1 (17 May 1919), front cover. Artist: M. Dodshon.

may temporarily be superfluous, will in any case be immense. Only measures carefully designed to break the shock of transition can prevent it from being disastrous (Ministry of Reconstruction 1919, p. 51).[5]

H. A. L. Fisher's Education Act, entering the statute book in 1918, was a noble effort to combine humanitarian concerns with economic expedience. The war was thought to have caused severe physical, moral, and mental strain on many working-class children and adolescents. But it had equally hastened capital concentration and a rationalization of production, not least in the new aircraft, engineering, and motor industries, whose continued expansion depended on a redirection of the educational structure toward versatile, and hence general, technical and scientific knowledge. By raising the school-leaving age to fourteen and abolishing exemptions and the half-time system, the act marked the most radical rethinking of state education since 1870. For the first time in history, all English children, regardless of their class and gender differences, were to share nine years of schooling, though not at the same educational establishments. However, the contradictions of family life and school had become common denominators of childhood, also defining the lives of working-class girls and poor boys. These groups hitherto had often been marginal pupils.

While this shared set of experiences was initially reflected strongly in the new girls' magazines, the interwar weeklies for boys immediately ventured beyond the well-defined orbit of the school universe. Unhampered by a long and successful publishing tradition, the newcomer D. C. Thomson became the boy readers' faithful traveling guide on this fictional journey. D. C. Thomson was formed in 1905 by William Thomson, a wealthy Scottish shipping manager, and his two sons, David Couper and Frederic. Their publishing venture started, as Harmsworth's had done seventeen years before, by trade in exciting news and serial romance of the mill-girl variety. Their first papers were the *Argus*, the *Dundee Courier*, and, as noted earlier, the storypaper *Girls' Weekly*. The *Sunday Post* was added in 1920 and became the cornerstone of the successful Scottish enterprise.[6] By then, the energetic family hit upon the huge market of schoolboys between the ages of about nine and thirteen.

The entrance on the juvenile magazine market started with a test balloon, the *Dixon Hawke Library* (1919–41), focusing upon the rather conventional daring of a young detective, Dixon Hawke. Then, on 17 September 1921, the *Adven-*

5. According to Waldo McGillicuddy Eagar's evidence given in 1917 to the Departmental Committee on Juvenile Education after the War, the "marked increase in juvenile crime" was mainly due to petty theft, such as stall robbing performed by gangs of schoolboys, an indication, one might conclude, of the young culprits' longing for the consumer possibilities provided by a wage-earning status (Eyken 1973, p. 217).

6. In the 1971 edition of the *Guinness Book of Records*, the *Sunday Post* figured as achieving the closest to saturation, being read by more than 79 percent of the Scottish population over the age of 15 (Rosie 1977, pp. 26–27).

ture emerged from the Dundee printing presses, inaugurating D. C. Thomson and Company's decisive innovation of storypapers for young boy readers. Their concoction was a true mass commodity, both in its method of production and in its consumer appeal. The initial impact of the magazine is difficult to gauge as D. C. Thomson has been singularly secretive about both circulation figures and general publishing policies. But its popularity must have been considerable since it was followed within a year by the *Rover* (1922–61) and a few months later by the *Wizard* (1922–63). In 1930 came the *Skipper,* which ran until 1941, and three years later the *Hotspur* was added (1933–59).[7] These papers, the "Big Five" as their discerning devotees termed them, could all be had for twopence each, and they all looked alike—the same standard eleven-by-fifteen-inch tabloid format, a colorful front in photogravure followed by twenty-eight weekly pages of highly visual and stylized stories in a medley of different types including school, detective, adventure, and science fiction yarns:

> Monday's Mag—
> 'Adventure'
> Tuesday's Treat—
> 'The Wizard'
> Thursday's Thrill—
> 'The Rover'
> Saturday's Select—
> 'The Skipper'
> ("Tales for All Tastes," *Rover,* no. 517 [12 March 1932], p. 300).

This advertisement from the *Rover* was not merely a catchy form of sales promotion, it was also an exact summary of the economic raison d'être behind these new publications. They were produced and were to be consumed as one product, distributing the audience between them and minimizing the financial risks of printing. What had been initiated by Harmsworth was carried to its logical conclusion by D. C. Thomson and Company.

The rationalization of production was evident from the layout of the papers, the identical format of the line drawings (one or two per page), the likeness of characters and their movements, and the universal emphasis upon visual thrills. But it was equally typical of the fiction itself. Rather than relying on a single author for each story or series, D. C. Thomson employed a syndicate of writers to submit fiction on a commission basis (Lofts and Adley 1970, pp. 12–13).[8]

---

7. Apart from the Big Five, D. C. Thomson launched two other boys' papers during the interwar years, namely the *Vanguard* in 1923 and the *Red Arrow* in 1932. Compared to the phenomenal success of their longrunning counterparts, these two papers seem to have caught on less well and ceased publication fairly quickly (in 1926 and 1933, respectively).

8. In the late 1920s, writers working on a commission basis were paid an average of £1 10s.–£1 15s. per thousand words (Groom 1929, p. 74). According to Rosie 1973, p. 15, D. C. Thomson authors of the 1970s were paid about half the going London rate.

This facilitated a speedy and highly flexible method of composition, but it also necessitated an unprecedented coordination of plots and characterization if the method was to work. The image of the papers rested solely with the editor in whose office the stories would undergo any necessary adaptations, perhaps even being rewritten in order to comply with the production formula. The similarities within the Big Five undoubtedly sustained a versatile consumption pattern. They nurtured a collector's "instinct" in the readers, whether these bought, borrowed, or exchanged their papers as Jim Wolveridge did in the early 1930s: "I would buy a copy of Bullseye, and when I'd finished reading it I would swop with Abie Roberts for a copy of the Wizard, and after finishing that I would swop it with Robbie Hope for a copy of the Magnet. In this way I could read at least fifty books" (Wolveridge 1976, p. 29).[9]

The variety of tales in each paper facilitated casual reading, browsing, and a quick glance through between other activities. The prewar papers with their emphasis on character development over a number of issues and gradual reformation had not contained a similar degree of versatility. Readers of the Dundee ventures would identify with their purchases in toto rather than with individual characters or series, let alone with the authors who always remained anonymous. Moreover, the new-style weeklies featured regular comic strips in an obvious attempt to cash in on the success that "funnies" now enjoyed with a wide readership. Here, too, D. C. Thomson and Company were timely innovators, creating the unscrupulous Korky the Cat in the *Dandy Comic* (1937) and, in the *Beano Comic* (1938), Big Eggo the Ostrich and Biffo the Bear. As *Dandy* and *Beano*, both comic papers remain some of the top choices with British children. In emulation of the comic and the film techniques, exuberant and rapid action, technical detail, and visual appeal were the single most important features of D. C. Thomson's innovative entrance on the magazine market for young schoolboys. And action they got—so much so that the undisputed master, the Amalgamated Press, had to follow suit.

Despite the fact that the London firm was by far the largest magazine publisher in Britain between the wars (by 1939 it controlled more than a hundred papers and bought up smaller competitors), the Dundee daredevil proved a hard opponent in the juvenile field (Orwell 1976, p. 529). While the *Magnet* and the *Gem*, keeping to Hamilton's well-trodden paths, were falling behind in the race for youthful popularity and continuing profits, new Amalgamated Press periodicals were soon copying their Scottish rivals. The *Champion* was launched as a conventional Amalgamated Press storypaper in 1922, but quickly it underwent a rejuvenation treatment that made it one of the firm's most

9. Jim Wolveridge was born in 1920. Note that magazines were called books (by other children comics), denoting that to the young audience popular leisure reading had much the same function regardless of formal differences.

popular boys' weeklies, lasting until 1955.[10] When its companion paper, the *Triumph* (1924–40), was introduced, it bore the marks of innovation from its inception. All in all, the firm started twenty-eight storypapers for boys in the 1920s and 1930s, as well as the comic papers *Playtime* (1919–29) and *Tiger Tim's Weekly* (1920–40).

While Harmsworth's nineteen prewar weeklies for boys lasted more than fifteen years on average, his interwar boys' magazines only had about half of that life span. Increased competition from film and radio as well as from the Scottish paper entrepreneur certainly had an affect on the London giant despite the attempts at innovation. D. C. Thomson set a new trend in boys' weeklies that made the *Boy's Own Paper* almost the only traditional middle-class magazine to hold its bastions. Boys' papers, in general, had come to look more alike than ever before. But as entertainment they were not identical, and the readers clearly favored the style of the Big Five.

In 1933, an investigation published by J. H. Engledow and William Farr on schoolchildren's leisure activities in the St. Pancras area of London demonstrated that half of all pupils between the ages of eleven and fifteen read upwards of three comics or storypapers per week, while a third of these children managed six or more issues during that time. With girls, reading ranked as the best-favored pastime, with boys it took second place after "fretwork and carpentry." But boys read more magazines, and over four-fifths preferred "adventure papers" (Engledow and Farr 1933, pp. 13, 12).[11] These findings were confirmed and refined in 1938 by Augustus Jenkinson in what became the best-known survey of children's reading habits prior to World War II. His twenty-nine hundred informants clearly showed that storypapers and comics were the most popular types of juvenile reading matter, that boys read more weeklies than girls, and that, generally speaking, the magazine interest peaked with twelve-year-old children. At that age, the average boy would manage between 3.7 and 4.2 comic or magazine titles per month while the average girl read between 2.0 and 2.7 titles (Jenkinson 1946, pp. 65, 211).[12] Boys clearly opted for D. C. Thomson's the *Rover*, the *Hotspur*, and the *Wizard*, the last magazine being read by between half and two-thirds of all twelve- and thirteen-year-old schoolboys.

10. In 1940, when the *Magnet* ceased publication on a weekly output of 80,000 copies, the corresponding circulation figure for the *Champion* was 150,000 (Lofts 1960, pp. 325–26).

11. The authors made no internal popularity poll of the magazines, but simply enumerated the papers most read: Thomson's the *Rover*, the *Wizard*, the *Skipper*, and the *Adventure* as well as the *Bull's-Eye* (1931–34), the *Ranger* (1931–35), the *Champion*, the *Startler* (1930–32), the *Thriller* (1929–40)—all published by the Amalgamated Press—and then Hulton's *Boys' Magazine* (1922–34). Only 7 percent of boys by then read school storypapers like the *Magnet*, the *Gem*, and the *Nelson Lee Library* (1915–33).

12. The exception to this pattern was the least academic girls whose magazine interest increased until the age of 14 when they would read an average of 4.2 titles a month. Note that Jenkinson, unlike Engledow and Farr, counts titles not issues read.

While in 1933 girls clearly favored the *Schoolgirl*, the *Schoolgirls' Own*, the *Schoolgirls' Weekly*, and the *Schoolgirls' Own Libary*, twelve- to fourteen-year-old girls asked in 1938 chose the *Schoolgirls' Own* as the most popular, followed by the *Schoolgirls' Weekly* and the recent *Girls' Crystal* (Engledow and Farr 1933, p. 13; Jenkinson 1946, pp. 214–15).

Apart from amply demonstrating that the newcomers on the juvenile magazine market were also the best-liked choices, the reader surveys of the 1930s bore out that consumerism as a general aspect of children's reading had truly come of age. Now that all the young were finally enrolled into a "real" childhood, such as had been defined and experienced by bourgeois manufacturers and religious devotees more than a hundred years earlier, popular literature assumed an important role as an age- and gender-specific, but not a class-specific, organizer of the contradictions that this child life engendered. Paid juvenile labor, which for most of the nineteenth century had been acknowledged, even advocated, as beneficial to the moral and intellectual improvement of young minds, was finally deleted from the official agenda of childhood. It was denounced as a symptom of social deficiency and individual shortcomings. In reality, too, the restructuring of the economy had virtually eliminated children's possibilities of acquiring paid work with the variety and self-worth it often contained. Under those circumstances, consumerism became a medium through which the young could achieve what historically had been lost in other areas of life. With the inclusion into a childhood "proper" of the last groups of working-class children, the magazine story had come full circle.

Childhood for All:
Interwar Children

CHILDREN'S LIVES in the 1920s and 1930s were marked by an extension of childrearing trends to working-class girls and poor boys that were common in earlier decades with middle-class and with many working-class groups. This extension, far from being caused by a successful filtering down of middle-class morals, was brought about by changes in working people's daily lives, hastened by World War I. It acted as a catalyst to rationalize production and concentrate capital. These developments paved the way for a general rise in the standard of living after 1918, when the economy turned increasingly toward mass production for the home market.

Through the 1920s, before massive unemployment hit the country, these developments drove more working-class women back to their homes as full-time housewives and conscientious consumers. Large-scale production, as noted, equally necessitated a general training of the workers-to-be through full-time education. The paradox of childhood, the separation between learning and doing, between preparation for and participation in social functions, became the common basis for all British children's lives. This did not make their daily experiences identical, but it meant that social and sexual differences were sifted through the distinct agencies of family, education, and leisure—agencies that the commercial weeklies with their broad appeal could take as their general points of narrative departure. Of these agencies, school was perhaps the most important factor, structuring the major part of childhood and providing a "natural" division of the young into well-defined age groups, a division that was further reinforced through, for instance, the editorial policies of magazine publishers.

"THE RIGHT PLACE FOR EVERY MAN,
THE RIGHT MAN FOR EVERY PLACE"

Beside all moral considerations, H. A. L. Fisher's Education Act of 1918 marked a serious attempt to update the qualifications of the future labor force by formally extending children's access to education. The act thus highlighted what I have earlier described as the contradictory aims underlying state education, the struggle between general social skills and specific differentiated skills: the pupils must acquire a universal belief in the justice of democracy, while they are prepared for the social and sexual selection mechanisms operating within a capitalist economy. This paradox now became the basis of schooling for the overall majority of children. Informed by Freudian theory and progressivist trends in pedagogical thought, well-intentioned proposals for educational reform multiplied through the 1920s.

Although child-centered pedagogy was developed as a full-fledged educational practice only in a handful of private, coeducational schools catering mainly to an intellectual clientele, it did make some headway in the nonvocational primary schools, just as it spurred a general rethinking of state education. The propositions made in the so-called Hadow Committee's three reports became most influential. Its chairman, Sir Henry Hadow, followed the progressivists and some labor politicians in advocating a school-leaving age of fifteen and a unified system of education structured as an organic process and geared toward the pupils' individual interests and abilities. The labor movement's traditional emphasis on free education for all, a notion that had found its first feeble statutory expression with the Education Act in 1902, received a seemingly objective justification. An intelligence test and a written examination taken at the age of eleven were advocated as universal criteria of educational selection, after which children could be "streamed" into different schools nurturing either an academic or a practical training. [1]

Even if Hadow's recommendations were only fully implemented with R. A. Butler's Education Act in 1944, some important elements were eagerly adopted beginning in the late 1920s. Thus, a closer coordination of elementary and postelementary education came into being when a growing number of nonacademic elementary-school pupils over the age of eleven were channeled into so-called senior schools or senior departments. Also, the number of pupils in the academic secondary schools rose so that by 1938 they comprised just under fifteen percent of all elementary school children, a third more than in 1920. Almost half of the secondary-school pupils (45.8 percent) were scholarship winners (Simon 1974c, pp. 366, 364).[2] Both written examinations and especially intelligence testing since 1913 had been fervently advocated by the educational psychologist Cyril Burt: "The need is urgent; the field is vast.

1. The term streaming, so important to English education after World War II, was first used in the second Hadow Report, *The Primary School*, in 1931. The other two reports were *The Education of the Adolescent* (1926) and *Infant and Nursery Schools* (1933).

2. In addition to the state-aided secondary schools, there still existed the separate and highly selective system of private grammar and public schools charging about £250 in annual tuition fees and catering to about five percent of children (Stevenson 1977, p. 35).

Throughout the country there is a cry for a practical mental test—for a handy method which can be immediately applied by teachers, doctors and social workers." The function of test analysis, Burt wrote in 1920, was to yield a "scientific statement of his [the child's] special and general qualities . . . of intellect and character" and so "find the right place for every man, the right man for every place" (Selleck 1972, pp. 140–41). With their eugenic aura of inherent intelligence and objective methods for its measurement, the tests in reality were designed in such a way as to completely exclude any evaluation of emotional understanding, practical cooperation, and nonverbal skills.[3] Thus, the tests served to disfavor many working-class boys and most girls whose family upbringing stressed exactly those human qualities. But since the official basis of educational selection increasingly became one of individual attainment rather than one of class and gender, the bias entrenched in the process of selection was blurred. More and more children would regard their success rate at school as a result of their personal efforts.

This interpretation in individual terms of what remained social and sexual differences was reinforced for many juveniles by changes in their family lives. Between the wars, more working-class people began practicing birth control. By the 1930s only nineteen percent of all children grew up with two or more siblings, while less than a fifth of all late-Victorian families had under three children (Gittins 1975, p. 53). Improvements in transportation and new industries allowed young couples to move to the sprawling suburban areas, especially if the husband was a well-paid worker in regular employment or if he belonged to the swelling group of clerks, technicians, and supervisors.[4] While children's inventiveness would soon convert new housing estates a..d construction sites into playgrounds as exciting as the streets of the inner cities, the suburbs (with their new-style pubs, their cinemas, and a lack of older relatives) nevertheless favored a family life based at home or at least indoors.

Under these circumstances, the regulation of the individual child's sexuality—so crucial to the formation of a "real" childhood—became at once easier and more important. A glance at contemporary mass-circulating women's magazines reveals that efficient home management and diligent child care ranked among the most common topics. More lower-middle-class and working-class children received their mothers' undivided attention but equally their intensive

3. Sir Francis Galton, in *Hereditary Genius* (London, 1867), was in fact one of the earliest proponents of mental testing as an objective measurement of intelligence. A humorous and revealing example of questions given at the early tests is provided in Simon 1974c, p. 246. Simon in the early 1950s was one of the first to criticize the method of intelligence testing.

4. According to Branson and Heinemann 1973, pp. 166–67, there were three civil servants in 1938 for every two in 1929, and the number of insurance and bank employees rose by almost one-fifth in the 1930s. By 1938 nearly a third of all employed people were in nonproducing industries.

supervision. Many of these women, locked between the contradictory demands of love and coercion, found an ideal in the rigid pedagogical ideas of Dr. Truby King rather than in the radical sexual theories of Freudian psychoanalysis. King was already a famous figure in his native New Zealand when he came to England in 1917. His regular feeding schedules and methodical advice on toilet training were heralded in England as guarantees of good motherhood by insecure and socially isolated women, although his ideals were perhaps only fully carried out in maternity hospitals and welfare clinics.

The moves toward individualizing social and sexual divisions as personal differences, which had been evident in the last quarter of the nineteenth century, now affected all children. While many working-class youngsters in Edwardian times had access to paid and unpaid labor as a route to personal self-esteem, which helped them realize their educational "fate" as a social injustice, that route was largely closed to children growing up in the 1920s and 1930s. This closure did not mean that all children accepted with equanimity the contradictions between love and coercion, experienced at home or between the formal equality and real selection they felt at school, as natural occurrences and inevitable results of their own behavior. The poorest sections of juveniles, at least, found strong enough evidence of social and sexual inequalities to judge them by what they were: injustices. However, the marginalization of child labor, the privatization of much of family life, and the individualization of educational selection to-gether set up a normative structure that made it increasingly difficult for even the most resilient to find a proper outlet for their protests and insecurities.

The conflict between school and work—a keen dilemma to many working-class children before World War I—was largely replaced by a vague longing for adulthood as an unknown, and hence magic, solution to pressing problems. This longing was particularly felt by the interwar children who only made it to the lower rungs on the educational ladder. Of these, many boys, who could look forward to a wage-earning status, lost interest in school and all it stood for. Others, whose family upbringing traditionally stressed intellectual self-im-provement, reacted to their educational failure with deep anguish and personal disappointment.

This form of reaction was perhaps particularly common with working-class and lower-middle-class girls to whom the formal widening of educational op-portunities after 1918 seemed a way of escaping their fate of marriage, moth-erhood, and domestic drudgery—a fate that they recognized only too well from their sparsely educated mothers. The contradictions of femininity between job and marriage, between autonomy and deference, which in late-Victorian and Edwardian times had been confined to adolescent girls raised in relatively secure circumstances, confronted a broader range of girls and did so when they ap-proached the age of eleven and the decisive examination to enter secondary school. No matter what the outcome of this examination, pupils soon realized the

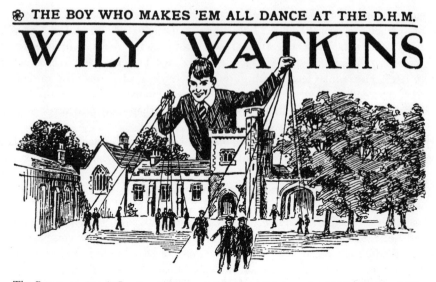

THE BOY WHO MAKES 'EM ALL DANCE AT THE D.H.M.

WILY WATKINS

The *Rover*, no. 201 (2 January 1926), p. 6. Masthead for the series "Wily Watkins." The boy's unrealistic but humorous command over teachers and fellow pupils by means of his magic strings capture the mixed sentiments of protest and resignation felt by many schoolchildren between the world wars.

conflict that it highlighted. Kathleen Betterton, for example, born in 1913 into a respectable working-class family in London, thought that school life at first was "fairly informal, and we were most of us on quite intimate terms with Teacher . . . [who] encouraged acting and makebelieve." But already at the age of eight, the pupils were graded as "Big Girls," and "life became more serious. We had entered upon the race for survival. Ahead lay the scholarship stakes: for the winners, free schooling till sixteen or over with the hope of a good job at the end of it; for the 'also rans,' a makeshift education ending at fourteen, and unskilled work that might end in unemployment and the dole" (Burnett 1984, pp. 205–06). Kathleen desperately wanted to be one of the winners and her highest wish was to go to boarding school: "The very word conjured up muddled visions of midnight picnics, sweet girl prefects, hockey, house-matches, and exploits that saved the honour of the school. . . . I was longing for a different world, less circumscribed than the one I knew. The prospect of going away to school seemed the merging of make-believe and reality" (Burnett 1984, pp. 207–08). Kathleen's daydream did come true. She found that her new school "absorbed us completely into itself, tolerating no other loyalties. Dimly we discerned a divergence between home and school standards but we could hardly help believing that the School was always right." Although Kathleen was an academic success at her boarding school (she was later awarded a place at Oxford University), she found that "the emotional shock of being uprooted was like being dropped into a wintry pond" (Burnett 1984, p. 209). The minority of children who entered the academic secondary school evidently felt an increasing pressure to compete successfully in what was now the only acknowledged preparation for material security in adulthood. To this vocational pressure came an ideological pressure to conform—maybe the most difficult aspect of schooling to sustain for the increasing number of scholarship winners. Some of them, like Kathleen Betterton, did acknowledge their emotional problems. Others resolved their difficulties like Annie Williams by identifying with the educational norms:

> I once won a scholarship with the highest marks in the whole of the valley, and I went to Country School, and I had to travel by train to school about twelve miles away.
> It was a very posh school. There were some kids that used to come up in big Rolls-Royces. But of course I was just a poor little scholarship girl, but never mind, I was all right. (McCrindle and Rowbotham 1977, p. 22)

Being "all right" for Annie Williams included an acceptance of her obvious feelings of inferiority (her father owned a small butcher's shop), the pressure from her home to succeed, and ultimately her approval of being transferred to a mixed secondary school when her parents' deaths ruined her security, such as it was. The onset of the depression in 1929 added further divisions to those already existing between the young. To the distinctions between academic and non-academic pupils, and between boys and girls, came the difference between children of the employed and of the jobless, between the prospering regions and the areas now threatened by devastation. "The Slump" lasting until 1932 caused mass unemployment especially in South Wales, the Black Country, Clydeside, and Northern England. In these former strongholds of working-class unionization and self-organized culture, children possessed few means of mitigating economic disaster through their own labor. Hubert Medland from Liverpool recalls, "It was common when we left the yard at dinner time to find outside the yard hoards of children with no shoes on their feet, begging, 'Any left, please, any left?' and that would be any left from our snacks, which we used to take out and give to them" (Barker 1978, p. 213).

Ill-health and malnutrition brought the nineteenth century forcefully back to memory. Seebohm Rowntree's poverty survey in 1935 confirmed this comparison only too well: forty-three percent of York's working-class children under the age of fourteen were living below his estimated poverty line (Rowntree 1941, p. 196).[5] But other children were also affected by economic stringencies. Education was a primary target for cutbacks during the years of crisis. Between 1931 and 1934, expenditure went down by two-thirds and, in

5. Of the working class at large, 31.1 percent lived below the poverty line—a figure that had kept almost constant for a hundred years (Rowntree 1941, p. 34).

1932, the official size of classes was fifty pupils. On the outbreak of World War II, more than a third of all schoolchildren were being crammed into class rooms with upwards of forty others (Stevenson 1977, p. 36; Jephcott 1942, p. 37). Overcrowding, derelict buildings, and deficient facilities exacerbated the dilemmas facing children even if their families were not hit by unemployment, and these dilemmas found no immediate solutions in the family, at school, or through work. Hence, the area of leisure—already an important factor in many children's lives—gained a key role as a testing ground for personal liberty and an enjoyable outlet for difficulties originating and experienced elsewhere. The expansion of the entertainment industries in an adverse economic climate through the 1930s merely confirmed the focal status that consumerism had already assumed for children across the social board after 1918.

A smaller family size, the decrease in working women's employment outside the home, and the proliferation of time-saving household appliances, such as new cookers and gas heaters in poor families or electric irons and vacuum cleaners with the better-off, all contributed to give young children, and especially girls, more time to spend on themselves. And if few had a regular income from their own work, most of them received weekly pocket money that was often doled out on Saturday mornings in return for help around the house.[6] "We'd do little jobs," Mrs. Harrison recalls her home duties as a child on a new council estate in Birmingham between the wars, "we used to do jobs to get our picture money . . . in those days you used to have to clean all your cutlery, we used to do that, just various small jobs, she never asked us to do a floor or anything like that . . . just small jobs" (Hall 1977, p. 78).[7] Children's domestic chores in this as in many working-class and middle-class families were regarded by the parents as a moral obligation rather than a material necessity. But it was still an obligation primarily imposed on girls. Relatively speaking, they were therefore also the ones to benefit the most from the interwar changes in family life.

Children growing up after World War I had more time for themselves, and they also had more options to fill their time. But their choices were made according to familiar patterns, some of which continued from early in the nineteenth century. Thus, the scout and guide movements remained popular largely with the middle and lower-middle class despite the enormous expansion of these organizations after the war and their redirection toward nature study and open-air life rather than military drills and parades.[8] A broader range of chil-

6. A survey performed in East London suburbs showed that 21 percent of all children received more than 2s. pocket money per week, 44 percent between 1s. and 2s., 24 percent from 6d. to 1s. and only 11 percent less than 6d. (Foot 1968, p. 43).
7. Mrs. Harrison's father was an engineer, and her mother worked as a clerk before her marriage.
8. Scout membership nearly doubled between 1920 and 1933, its interwar peak year,

dren used the growing number of sports fields and sports clubs that were established through private or public funding. Although group activities in these places, as in the scout and guide patrols, were carefully supervised by adults and were touched up with a good deal of individual competition, girls in particular often found that the sheer excitement of physical exercise overcame the drawback of authoritarian restrictions. This is clearly revealed in the pilot Amy Johnson's recollection of the yearly display at her local sports club: "Clad in navy nickers and white sweaters, about a hundred of us swung Indian Clubs, dumb-bells and bar-bells to music, followed each other over hobby-horse and parallel bars, and then—oh joy!—a chosen few would give a special display of high spring-board jumping, with or without a pole—my very special speciality!" (Clay 1964, p. 78).[9]

To these approved pursuits was added an important innovation of domestic recreation: radio. Although the invention had been patented as early as 1896 by Marconi, the radio industry only got under way during World War I. When the BBC started its transmissions in 1922, there were barely thirty-six thousand wireless licenses in England, while on the outbreak of World War II, over nine million people had a license (Walvin 1978, pp. 137–38). The stable radio slot for young listeners was "The Children's Hour," which occupied about six percent of the total program time and which featured radio plays such as the "Toytown" series along with the reading and dramatization of award-winning books.[10] The radio held an undoubted attraction to poor working-class children such as Robert Harvey, born 1925, who "liked to run home from school to listen to the plays in the dark until Mother came home for tea" (Harvey 1976, p. 18). But the selection of programs continued a traditional pattern of educative entertainment that clearly favored children with a middle-class background.

A similar situation was found in the provision of school and public libraries whose facilities improved between the wars. In principle, the libraries excluded no one, and their existence clearly benefited devoted working-class readers like Fiona McFarlane from Glasgow, who, during World War II, "was able to get a book every three days, which wasn't enough because I could read a book in a

---

when it was 461,740 (Springhall 1977, p. 134). In addition to the traditional movements, the interwar years also saw the development of small coeducational and nonreligious groups such as the Order of Woodcraft Chivalry (founded in 1916), Kibbo Kift Kindred (1920), and Woodcraft Folk (1925).

9. Amy Johnson, graduating from Sheffield University, working in a solicitor's office and training as a pilot in her spare time, attained the status of a popular myth in 1930 when she was the first woman to fly solo to Australia, a feat for which she won £10,000 from the *Daily Mail* (Graves and Hodge 1940, pp. 281–82).

10. In addition, children's programs broadcast a thirty-minute religious program every Sunday, occasional choral performances, even "little operettas" (Briggs 1965, pp. 35, 54, 121; Seaman 1970, p. 82).

night" (McCrindle and Rowbotham 1977, p. 222). She took out library cards in her mother's and her sister's names and even read library books concealed under her school desk. Less determined children would be unable to stomach the libraries' bulk of middle-class quality books, and some librarians' piecemeal introduction in 1905 of children's periodicals was of little help as long as the choices were limited to "improving" magazines such as the *Chatterbox*, the *Child's Companion*, and *Little Folks*, touched up with volumes of the *Girl's Own Paper* and the *Boy's Own Paper* (Ellis 1969, p. 139).

Children who were raised under close parental guidance and supervision often accepted the various leisure schemes provided from above whether by voluntary or statutory agencies. But this acceptance did not preclude their enjoyment of commercial types of entertainment containing a seeming freedom of choice. To the working-class children who were brought up with domestic lenience and fewer educational aspirations, such self-determination was often a precondition of pleasure. As the new Edwardian periodicals had indicated and as the phenomenal success of the film industry amply confirmed, consumerism had become a coveted arena for "real" children to acquire and display their autonomy.

In the 1920s and 1930s, an almost universal literacy, the increase in leisure time for the young, and the general provision of pocket money facilitated the enjoyment of popular reading for all children. The methods of production and distribution of the commercial weeklies, not to mention their contents, seemed to guarantee an entertaining freedom and an emotional release that were promised but rarely fulfilled by family and school and which made popular reading top the list of juvenile leisure choices. Those choices increasingly were the children's own. Since many of their parents had themselves been magazine devotees in childhood, they accepted the periodicals as part of growing up, and some even used the weeklies as rewards. "For being good boys we had comics," Robert Harvey recalls (Harvey 1976, p. 7).

Popular reading, then, held a strong emotional appeal to the generation of interwar children who had lost traditional areas of independence and who had not yet witnessed the entertainment deluge of the welfare state. This appeal is nowhere better demonstrated than in Richard Hoggart's description of a "typical" working-class street of the 1930s—seen through the eyes of "a boy of eleven going to the paper-shop for his Saturday magazine, for the *Wizard* or the *Hotspur*." When characterizing women's magazines from the same period, Hoggart focuses on their smell, "strongly evocative to me now, because it is also that of the old boys' magazines and comics" (Hoggart 1977, pp. 64, 122). Critics today may find that such keen consumer consciousness ties in only too nicely with some publishers' standardized products. The success of these products no longer depended on a single set of characters or a specific type of narrative: the magazine as such created the pleasure of reading. But Hoggart's almost tangible memory reveals that to the interwar children themselves popular reading meant more than the newsagent's weekly reaping of their precious pennies.

The magazines had become, as even parents realized, an integral element of childhood, cutting across social class but, significantly, not across gender differences. For if modern boys' and girls' papers displayed a reversion to the tactics employed in some of the earliest magazine ventures—they appealed to a whole generation of children through a medley of entries—no interwar publishers attempted to bridge the gender gap that had become firmly established in juvenile literature. Since all children now had as their common basis of experience a "real" childhood with its opaque power relations and its oblique reference to social structures, it remains to focus on the treatment of these aspects in the most popular of the interwar weeklies.

13

Worldwide Roving and Daring: Weeklies for Girls and Boys

THE INITIAL success of the first schoolgirl paper, the *School Friend*, rested on its main feature, the Cliff House saga, by one "Hilda Richards"—in fact Charles Hamilton, the veteran author of *Magnet* and *Gem* fame. The new serial was set in the well-known surroundings of Greyfriars, focusing on a nearby boarding school for girls. Most of the girls had been known to the *Magnet* audience for ten years. Since Hamilton also remained faithful to his Edwardian conception of forthright but feminine womanhood, the pen name of "Hilda Richards" was discreetly handed over to Horace Phillips after six issues. Phillips was the first in a sequence of male authors to retain Hamilton's versatile narrative formula of "evolving cycles," but he remodeled the Cliff House characters into an altogether more resourceful cast.[1]

Foremost among the Cliff House boarders was a group of resourceful and independent-minded fourth formers, actively shaping their own fortunes while keeping safely within the unwritten laws of the school: respect for superiors, loyalty to fellow scholars, and devotion to the weak and infirm. The leader of these "core girls" was the form captain, Barbara Hilda Redfern, or "Babs," harmonizing in her fourteen-year-old personality the contrasting female ideals of modest beauty and sporty independence. "Pretty, dark, with wavy brown hair, deep blue eyes, and olive complexion," she was "always ready for innocent mischief" but also "exceedingly generous by nature, and ready to do almost anything even for a girl she [did] not like" ("Who's Who at Cliff House," *School Friend* 2, no. 30 [6 December 1919], p. 15). The other girls in the group formed variations on this ideal embodiment of empathic self-reliance, with

1. In 1921, Reginald S. Kirkham took over the Cliff House authorship from Horace Phillips, and from 1924 to 1929 the serial was written by L. E. Ransome. The existence during the interwar years of two different sets of Cliff House characters, one in the *Magnet* and one in the *School Friend*, testifies to the gender differences in popular reading: while girl readers craved independent-minded heroines, preadolescent boys seemed uninterested in such female traits. The following analysis of interwar girls' papers is based on Drotner 1983.

"Jolly" Jobling and Bessie Bunter making up the two extremes within this moral frame of reference: Jolly's ultrafeminine aspirations to become a famous actress were balanced by her sharp wit, while Bessie's unladylike obesity was mellowed by her unintentional jokes. The variation in types offered a spectrum of possibilities for self-identification to readers from different backgrounds and with differing fictional tastes.

Throughout the 1920s, most Cliff House stories centered on conflicts within the school setting and had as their basic theme the accommodation of a girl who deviated from the accepted code of behavior. This theme as well as its resolution was closer to that of the prewar weeklies for boys than to either the mill-girl papers, in which romance predominated, or the *Girl's Own Paper* variety, in which personal maturation constituted the epic drive. As in the *Magnet* and *Gem* stories, a "sneak" outside the core group or a new pupil would create havoc within the orderly school gates of Cliff House and be the focus of attention for several weeks until the ploys of Babs and company or a dramatic event caused her to adjust—often, however, leaving a streak of insubordination for the author's convenient use in later tales. Another character would then appear on the scene, again deviating from the code. Within this plot formula, the process of reconstruction would take two forms, "the good girl wronged" or "the bad girl righted."

"Only A Scholarship Girl" merges the two motifs. Peggy Preston, a poor girl from the north of England, arrives at Cliff House, and with her "pretty blue eyes" outshining her shabby clothes, which "had seen so much wear that in places they were actually patched," and her boots looking "as if they had been mended with home-made stitches," the newcomer is the personification of poverty-stricken honesty. She is placed in the same study as her social opposite, the millionaire heiress Augusta Anstruther-Browne, who is introduced as "a tall figure, very expensively dressed, [with] a thin face that looked very pale and cold, gloved hands, the flash of a diamond brooch" ("Only A Scholarship Girl," *School Friend* 1, no. 21 [4 October 1919], pp. 3, 4). As "the spoilt child of indulgent parents, her nature has been allowed to run wild," and she now lives "to enjoy herself rather than make happiness for others."

Peggy and Augusta represent a fierce conflict between moral right and material riches. Despite being accused of theft and realizing that her family's poverty has been caused by Augusta's father, the scholarship girl remains boldly defiant. At the height of Peggy's predicaments, one of the innumerable school fires at Cliff House gives her an opportunity to rescue her archenemy. The scholarship girl is then reinstated in her rightful class position (Mr. Anstruther-Browne returning his illicit acquisitions) and is secured a future at the school and in the paper. At the same time, Augusta's animosity is replaced by an unprecedented altruism and kindness, although her own father has to go bankrupt before she finally atones. An essentially social conflict within the school system has been instantaneously resolved by an individual act of courage for which Peggy is awarded a gold medal:

> In this the proudest moment of her life, she knew that these friendly smiles and applauding cheers were tokens of firm friendships, more than atoning for all the pain and loneliness of the past.
> No longer the despised scholarship girl!
> No longer shunned by her Form!
> No longer the girl whose guilt as a thief was proved beyond all question!
> Time had vindicated her as it had vindicated her father! ("The Girl Who Had No Chance," *School Friend* 1, no. 23 [18 October 1919], p. 15)

Time, or fate, or the "natural" development of events would ultimately bring justice and truth to those with superior morality, whether rich or poor. Peggy Preston becomes socially recognized because she as an individual embodies the moral qualities of a core girl: she has shown a strong integrity when wrongfully opposed, but has also displayed self-sacrifice in the resourceful rescue of her study mate. Augusta, on the other hand, has to undergo social degradation because her nature lacks the kindness and human consideration necessary to ameliorate her excessive independence. The series of Peggy and Augusta stories is typical of the *School Friend.* It introduces a social conflict between rich and poor, describes it in psychological terms as a conflict between individuals with different human qualities, and solves the problem through personal action.

The *School Friend* series brought about an enormous boost in sales for the new weekly and established the scholarship girl as an important character in future magazine plots (Cadogan and Craig 1976, p. 233). Indeed, the story of Peggy and Augusta must have held an immediate attraction for the new generation of working-class and lower-middle-class schoolgirls. Despite their initial fascination with school, as we saw, many of them were unaccustomed to the middle-class norms and standards of a prolonged education that required more than docility and obedience for success. Academic self-assertion would feel strange for a working-class reader who had been groomed in domestic duties and who identified with them or with work, which the war had established as an important symbol of female independence. A lower-middle-class background, stressing educational aspiration as an economic necessity, might lessen a girl's social estrangement within the school. But as a female she would often lack sufficient self-assurance to endure what was then (as now) a male-defined and -oriented education. For both groups of girls, the result was a feeling of social or sexual insecurity, sharpened by the knowledge that their fortunes could not be changed until the age of fourteen.

To such readers, and they made up the majority, the initial fascination of the story rested on its recognition of the schoolgirls' real-life experiences of social and sexual depreciation and on its construction of these experiences as personal insecurities. Sustained interest in the tale lay in its reinforcement of the readers' potential for resistance, conveyed, for example, by the emphasis on Peggy's lonely strength. But the ultimate success of the story was secured by its offer of an individual solution to the readers' collective adversities through selfless behavior. The central achievement of this type of fiction was to harmonize individual desires and social restraint. The reappearance in the *School Friend* of this central conflict, which we have encountered in the *Girl's Own Paper*, indicates that the dilemmas of femininity had become evident to girls at a rather young age. But in the new-style girls' papers, the conflict never materialized as overt contradictions. Social and sexual opposites were harmonized in stories such as the one about Peggy Preston, thus at once justifying the readers' latent need for protest and strengthening their dependence.

By acknowledging social role conflicts as the basis of the action, and at the same time neglecting their importance in the fictional solution, the stories fulfilled the real desires of many, especially working-class, girls to see their own feelings of inferiority conquered. However, it also obscured the social basis for these desires. That the social conflict evoked decisive overtones of gender limitation—in the power struggle between defiance and deference—served to reinforce the fictional possibilities of identification for the lower-middle-class girl. Reading, then, made these girls' more or less conscious problems tangible, and it gave their individual uncertainties and insecurities a temporary solution. But it did not help unearth the social and sexual roots of these problems.

The general ideology promoted by the adjustment tales of the 1920s was thus a version of the bourgeois belief that the individual was separate from, and above, social circumstances and economic impediments. This belief permeated the social fabric and appeared in educational policies, as we have seen, as a democratic emphasis on individuality that helped mystify the paradoxical purposes intrinsic to state schooling. The ideology of individuality was further endorsed in the *School Friend* through the harmonious fusion of contrary female ideals in the model schoolgirl, her unity of empathy and self-reliance, motherly understanding, and girlish independence.

By the late 1920s, it seems as if the psychological troubles of scholarship winners and unhappy millionaire girls were losing interest with the readers. In 1929, the editor of the *School Friend* announced a radical reshuffling of his paper. It was to be given the less patronizing title of the *Schoolgirl*, and its "predominant note" was to become one of "drama and romance" ("Between Ourselves," *School Friend*, new ser., 9, no. 229 [27 June 1929], p. 737). Soon Cliff House was dropped altogether until 1931 when John Wheway reintroduced the school with a much invigorated cast roaming about on daring foreign tours, holiday camps, or mystery expeditions. Adventure and excitement found beyond the confines of school were to dominate girls' weeklies through the 1930s, but the trend was initiated by some papers as early as the 1920s. For example, the *Schoolgirls' Own* specialized in leisure stories about circus life and, particularly, about girl guides.

The girl guide patrol offered possibilities for characterization and group conflict similar to those displayed by the school serials. But with their numerous contests, camps, and hikes, the guide stories provided a greater fictional freedom for the author and more variety for the reader. Their appeal testified to the need for active outdoor amusements and indicated the few possibilities that many girls had of transcending the limits of parental supervision. Guide stories found a ready reader response as is evident from the fact that the *Schoolgirls' Own's* narratives were bolstered by a "Girl Guides Corner," firmly conducted by a "Guide Captain," answering a plenitude of questions from young enthusiasts on everything from stain removals to Morse coding and map reading.

Exciting adventures were also provided by the girl sleuth, who was popularized by, though not invented in, the *Schoolgirls' Weekly*. By 1899, the *Girls' Best Friend* had introduced the female detective Martha Wray as a young woman "with ruddy hair, a fine clear skin, and deep-grey eyes. No strong-minded female this, in mannish clothes, with a grating voice and clumsy ways. Simply a bright, fresh, natural English girl." The anonymous author in his description was clearly at pains to distinguish his heroine from the established tradition of pipe-smoking, hyperintelligent masculinity; and the Amalgamated Press was equally cautious in stressing the truth value of the new type of tales: "A good many people may think these stories trash, but the clever people must be compelled to admit that they are cleverly and brightly written. Besides they are founded on fact" (*Girls' Best Friend* 2, no. 62 [29 April 1899], p. 88).[2] Although Miss Wray moved only in the best circles and limited herself to the solving of classy mysteries such as the unmasking of Russian pearl thieves (her debut), the tracing of abducted child princes, lost wills, or stolen diamonds (murder cases from the outset are anathema to female sleuths), her cerebral pursuits seemed incompatible with the mill-girl papers' predominant note of love, and she found no sustained career.

In the interwar schoolgirl papers, the prospect of marriage never formed part of the action. Astute young heroines were more in demand. In the first issue of the *Schoolgirls' Weekly*, "Sylvia Silence—girl detective" appeared as one of six stories. Written by "Catherine Greenhalgh," whose real name was John W. Bobin, the story characterized Sylvia Silence as "a girl in a thousand—a girl who unravels problems and sets wrongs right. Her object is to help those who suffer, and she acts as quickly as a flash of lightning." Aided by her Alsatian dog,

---

2. Over the years, other serial heroines like Martha Wray made intermittent appearances in the mill-girl papers—e.g., Milly Carson, the journalist-detective featured in D. C. Thomson's *Girls' Weekly*.

Wolf, the first schoolgirl detective in British girls' fiction, though by no means the last, solved mystery after mystery in the initial two volumes of the *Schoolgirls' Weekly*. Her ploys, however, were dominated more by feminine altruism and charitable endeavors than by quick-witted contrivance, and the serial was overtaken by school and adventure stories.

After a short serial about the schoolgirl detective Lila Lisle featured in the *Schoolgirls' Own* in 1930, the figure of the girl sleuth was revived in the *Schoolgirls' Weekly* in 1933 when J. W. Bobin, now "Adelie Ascott," created the eighteen-year-old Valerie Drew and her Alsatian dog assistant, Flash. Although Bobin was an experienced chronicler of Sexton Blake, the popular detective who had made his bow in the *Marvel* in 1893, his immediate inspiration was undoubtedly the American Nancy Drew books written by "Carolyn Keene" (Harriet S. Adams and Andrew Svenson). The heroines' names were nearly identical, they both enjoyed driving a "speedy sportscar," and they started their careers in the same way ("The Secret of the Old Clock" in 1929 was turned into the English "That Amazing Room of Clocks"). With Valerie Drew, moralism was replaced by rapid action, although the plots were initially governed by chance encounters and happy coincidences rather than by Valerie's keen intelligence. Female opponents invariably use heavily scented perfume while most male crooks, smoking either a pipe or a cigar, generally seem forgetful enough to leave model airplanes and mauve moccasins, blue spiders, or green parrots as convenient clues to their crimes.

Unlike early school story heroines such as Barbara Redfern, the much-traveled Valerie with her "red-gold hair" and "pretty violet eyes" easily manages the repair of stalled speed boats, damaged radios, and ruined telegraphs—by 1937 she even grapples with television ("Seen in the Glass Screen," *Schoolgirls' Weekly* 29, no. 744 [23 January 1937]). Her technical skills were balanced by a selfless devotion to her dog, Flash, a relation which clearly prefigured the postwar popularity of pony tales and girl readers' fascination with the control of animal strength. Valerie's weekly exposure of callous counterfeiters, international smugglers, and scheming jewelry thieves turned her into the leading character of the *Schoolgirls' Weekly*. When the paper merged with the *Girls' Crystal* in 1939, Valerie Drew was transferred to the *Schoolgirl* (the reshuffled *School Friend*).

The *Schoolgirl* kept its place among the leading schoolgirl weeklies of the 1930s. In 1931, a "schoolgirl census" chose cinema stories as the most popular in the *Schoolgirl*, and during the early 1930s the schoolgirl-turned-film-star saturated most of the Amalgamated Press weeklies for girls. Star biographies, almost indistinguishable from the fictional accounts, sustained the illusion that it was really possible to make it in the celluloid dreamworld; and the emphasis on the unspoiled naturalness displayed by the idols secured their identification value for the young readers:

Four years ago Loretta Young was a schoolgirl in a navy gym dress and a little round hat, and to-day—at the age of eighteen—she is one of the leading stars of Screenland.

Just think of it; in less than four years from shutting the class-room door Loretta had accomplished what it had taken other girls years to realise! You might think that Loretta would be spoilt; but she isn't. For no one could spoil Loretta. ("A Star at Eighteen," *Schoolgirl* 4, no. 99 [20 June 1931], p. 19)[3]

"The Schoolgirls' Film Service" completed the picture by answering inquiries about Helen Bow's real hair color, the length of Lila Lee's eyelashes (were they genuine?), and Joan Crawford's favorite colors (blue and pale green) as well as by keeping its audience up-to-date on the cinema celebrities' latest holiday travels, marriage plans, and boyfriends. The new medium certainly influenced the topics of the girls' papers, not only directly but also indirectly through its brisk recounting of events and its emphasis on romance.

When John Wheway revived the Cliff House serial in the *Schoolgirl* in 1931, his revitalized *School Friend* cast appeared as an altogether more dashing and daring lot. The threat of explusion loomed large when their nightly mystery-solving expeditions took them on hazardous car rides, or when their film enthusiasm and dance delirium carried them beyond their prescribed schoolgirl duties. Most of the fourth formers' time was spent outside the orbits of education, and during holidays they ceased staying at old manor houses or enduring a discreet but careful adult chaperonage at prestigious seaside resorts. In the *Schoolgirl*, they went hiking and camping on their own, with Babs' uncle Cedric luckily still operating in the background as the wealthy provider of the schoolgirls' caravans "complete with staff and drivers," so that the fourth formers were free to enjoy their holiday suspense without being concerned with the baser necessities of life.

Such autonomy had already been pioneered in the last volumes of the *School Friend* by one of the Cliff House core girls, Clara Trevlyn—a new type of girl heroine who had no need for adult authority. During the 1930s, the "madcap" motif multiplied in the girls' weeklies. Clara Trevlyn replicas came as godsends to bored pupils at old-fashioned boarding schools in tales like "The Rebel Schoolgirl," "The Madcap's Mystery," "The Tomboy of the Family," and "The Unconquerable Josie." In these stories, the vivacious inventiveness of the new heroine brings about drastic changes, such as the introduction of hockey, high-heeled shoes, and Russian boots along with new fashions in hairstyles.

Gradually, many of these stories began to stress comic situations and verbal amusements. In 1934, "Rhoda Fleming" (Ronald Fleming) introduced readers

3. For the juvenile film devotees, the Amalgamated Press published special weeklies such as the *Girls' Cinema* (1920–32, then incorporated with *Film Star Weekly*) and *Screen Stories* (1930–35, then superseded by the *Boys' Cinema*). For women, the firm brought out *Woman's Film Fair* in 1935.

of the *Schoolgirls' Weekly* to "Patsy never grow up!" who successfully evades "the dodgy business" of turning into an adult woman with adult responsibilities: "Though turned sixteen and nearly grown up, Patsy had fought shy of the process known as 'sobering down,' which is supposed to occupy girls on leaving school" (25, no. 647 [16 March 1935], p. 541).[4] Patsy's climbing of rails and sliding down drainpipes and her formation of a secret society to outwit the "spiteful escapades" of a boys' club were all exploits that were easily rivaled in other tales by girl ventriloquists and girl impersonators using their clever disguises to defy their elders and betters. Thus, "Gipsy Joy, the Rich Girl Romany" describes the exuberant feats of Joy Sharpe, an ordinary English schoolgirl who, each week for fifty-four issues in the *Schoolgirl*, disguises her "normal self" as "Nakita, the gipsy girl." Hoaxing her absent-minded grandfather and obdurate governess, she changes "her life of discipline and restriction for freedom, jollity and pleasure," an existence whose attraction to the reader depended less on its morality or probability than on its merriment and unchecked liberties. Realism and psychological introspection were rapidly being outdistanced by entertaining action, which was accepted as an end in itself.

While "madcap" schoolgirls were adeptly transforming the tedium of their domestic lives, other heroines ventured farther afield as international swimming champions, lion tamers, racing drivers, or airplane pilots. In the opening issue of the *Crystal*, "Gail Western" starts a series about "Tony the Speed Girl." A tomboy not only in name, the young heroine is as successful at solving mysteries as she is winning races in her "big, gleaming thunderbolt of a car," the Silver Phantom. Her deeds were soon emulated in series such as "She had to Race in Secret" and "The Schoolgirl Speedstar." In the *Schoolgirl*, "The Flying Sisters," Joan and Kit Fortune, displayed their aerial expertise beginning in 1933. Written by "Ida Melbourne" (L. E. Ransome), who was undoubtedly inspired by Amy Johnson and her husband's transatlantic flight of that year, the series describes the two girls' search for their older brother in Africa; a necessary, but insignificant, precondition for weekly accounts of their near-escape from savage pygmies, weird oversized apes, and half-crazy Europeans stranded in the jungle. The sisters' skillful maneuvering of their plane, the Sky Queen, always sees them through, and to ordinary British schoolgirls their mobility must have seemed thrilling: "Kit was feeling elated on being free, up in the blue once again, and able to roar away whither she pleased. She was like a girl just released from school, and in real whoopee mood" (*Schoolgirl* 10, no. 235 [27 January 1934], p. 19).[5]

4. The serial of "Patsy Never Grow Up!" started in vol. 23, no. 590 (1934) and ended two years later in vol. 28, no. 720.

5. The series about "the girl air aces of the African jungle" returned a year later in the *Schoolgirl*, starting in vol. 13, no. 320.

Perhaps because Canadian readers took a particular interest in the Amalgamated Press papers, the careers of cowboy and lumberjack were added in the late 1930s to an already impressive list of girls' professions, a list in which "schoolgirl" now ranked near the bottom. When the majority of the schoolgirl weeklies ceased publication during the war, allegedly because of paper shortage, their heroines, whether foiling conceited adults, tracking down crooks, or perhaps fending off wolves, had come a long way, it seemed, since Peggy Preston had first entered the gates of Cliff House more than twenty years previously.

The appeal of the *School Friend,* as I have suggested, originated in its sensitive portrayal of real-life conflicts, and its continuing success was based on its effective transformation of these conflicts through a process of fictional harmonization resulting in a momentary alleviation of the reader's anxieties. Central to this process was the schoolgirl heroine who balanced the contrary female ideals of independence and deference into a norm of empathic self-reliance. A superficial reading of the magazines' development through the 1930s might suggest that all harmonization of class and gender conflicts disappeared as heroines became increasingly buoyant and insubordinate and their actions ever more exotic. A closer scrutiny, however, reveals that the girls' papers retained their function of conflict mediation but by other means and with different results.

The resolution of social contradictions and the alleviation of psychological insecurities were no longer worked out in the *process* of narration but became elements in the narrative *structure* itself. Personal, social, and financial obstacles, for example, seldom trammeled the latter-day protagonists, and when they did, such impediments were overcome as unimportant and often amusing trifles in an entertaining tale. Sustained repression and personal anguish were also abandoned in the traditional school serials. Headmistresses, the former wielders of punishment and symbols of power, receded into near oblivion, joining the ranks of fictional parents, especially mothers, who ever since the inception of the *Girl's Own Paper* had been conspicuous by their absence in girls' weeklies.

At the same time, form mistresses, the day-to-day executors of adult authority ("fifty lines, Bessie!") exchanged their hefty sternness or motherly understanding for feminine modernity. This new role would occasionally allow young mistresses amorous encounters with handsome coaches or substitute masters, thus circumventing the editorial policy of R. T. Eves who ruled out overt descriptions of sexuality along with religion and swearing (Cadogan and Craig 1976, pp. 231, 242). As in the film stories, covert references to sexuality in the form of romance at once recognized the existence of sensuality and molded its expression.

Of greater ideological significance, perhaps, than the structural concealment of social power relations was the newly static personality of the heroine: she never married; her self-possessed merriment and dashing resilience were displayed far from any surroundings recognizable to the reader; and her actions involved no

The *Schoolgirls' Weekly* 23, no. 573 (14 October 1933), front cover. In the 1930s, magazine heroines display increased independence and unrestrained mobility that are never checked against the reality of growing up.

maturing process, not even a sudden self-realization as in the early stories in the *School Friend*. Like the screen's assertive career girls and clever female spies, the principal characters in the girls' papers of the late 1930s could retain their independence simply because they never grew up to be women, never had to acknowledge the sexual constraints and social demands of an adult existence where hoydenish insubordination was in little demand. The weeklies sustained the readers' need for physical mobility, sensuality, and social power, but in doing so they obscured the real impossibility of fulfilling those needs. Although their techniques had been transformed, the storypapers still harmonized individual independence with social and sexual deference. This process, however, had become even more invisible than in the early 1920s when the heroine herself had symbolized the happy golden mean, the fictional and the ideological harmony between different demands.

Reasons for this fictional change in the interwar girls' weeklies are not hard to find. The gap between the educational ideal of equality and the educational realities of class and gender differentiation widened rapidly during the depression years of the 1930s. Middle-class and lower-middle-class girls probably experienced mainly the sexual aspects of this discrepancy, since their upbringing, with its emphasis on individual competition and verbal communication, made them more successful aspirants to enter secondary school than girls from the working class. It was working-class children, and especially working-class girls, who were the most likely to lose in the game of educational meritocracy, exactly as they had always done. In their educational position relative to that of middle-class children, they were no different from their nineteenth-century sisters, but they were in their experience of school. What was novel to working-class girls in the 1930s was the individualization of their situation: educational limitation had been turned into a personal problem rather than a social injustice.

Essentially, the school stories of the 1920s held a wide appeal because they captured and successfully harmonized, for working-class and lower-middle-class girls in particular, the real-life dilemmas caused by innovations within the school system. For example, the upsurge in entertaining leisure stories and exciting career adventures coincided with the onset of the depression, which severely restricted even middle-class women's occupational opportunities and left the middle-class and especially the lower-middle-class girl with little incentive to continue her academic efforts. This historical change, of course, was never uniform and linear, some readers (the scholarship winner, for one) being sufficiently adapted to the educational standards to retain a self-identified interest in school as a fictional basis.

But the popularity of the "accommodation" series wore off when the readers' dilemmas became too poignant to endure harmonizing within the confines of the school setting. It proved difficult up through the 1930s to postulate an individual resolution of recognizable contradictions, and to do so in an entertaining manner, when there was every evidence against such a resolution. Girls had gradually become too disappointed with their own school experiences to see them perpetuated in their leisure reading. Their dilemmas, however, remained, and so a new correlation between text and audience evolved.

The omnipresent career girl and her amusing feats or exciting adventures offered less painful means of mediating what conflicts the readers felt between social demand and individual desire. That the sensitive schoolgirl changed into a madcap or a self-assertive air ace was no portent of female liberation. The development indicated that the real dilemmas, both present and future, had intensified for the majority of readers, leaving them few means of individual solution, let alone collective resistance, to the social and sexual causes of the limitations on their lives:

> She walked into her friend's house, and found that she was busy doing her mother's housework. This girl's mother went to work all day so she had to do her mother's housework. . . . While her friend had been working, she had been sitting in the armchair reading the Girl's Crystal. She liked reading about all these boarding schools where the schoolgirls were always getting up to pranks, and having midnight feasts in the dormitories. This was another world to her. (Lowe 1976, pp. 11, 12)[6]

Rose Lowe's experiences between the wars are shared, even today, by a large number of preadolescent girls. Significantly, their most coveted books, such as Enid Blyton's *St. Clare's* and *Malory Towers* series, are modeled on the fictional formula that developed in the refashioned school story serials of the 1930s. Today, as then, "the school story is most 'relevant' when it seems most 'unreal'" (Frith 1985, p. 133).[7]

Leisure reading during the interwar years added an important aura of independence to young girls even of the poorest class. This is further evidenced by the editorial endeavors to encompass yet more of the readers' interests. From the mid-thirties, there was an upsurge of beauty and fashion columns in the schoolgirl weeklies. The fictional image of the omnipresent heroine was balanced by "Aunt Amy's," "Patricia's," or "Penelope's" ideal of natural appeal and girlish jollity.[8] Reducing expenses, ease, and fun are the main considerations of the

6. The title of Lowe's autobiography refers to the Burtt Brothers, who provided free meals for needy children at the Hoxton Mission Hall in London.

7. Frith's article, which appeared after the publication of my own research on interwar girls' papers (Drotner 1983), is based on interviews with mainly working-class schoolgirls whose answers illuminate many of the conclusions drawn in the present chapter. Interestingly, neither Frith nor Musgrave (1985) comments on the marked gender differences in the current appeal of the school genre.

8. In the *Schoolgirl*, the beauty and fashion columns were written by Isobel Winchester, one of the only women on the editorial boards of the interwar girls' papers (Cadogan and Craig 1976, p. 230).

columns. Readers are told how to turn last year's coat into a "snappy affair in an eyetwinkling," how to make inexpensive scarves and belts, pin cushions or pencil cases, and "a striking necklet" or "a charming trimming."

Personal affairs receive an equally lighthearted treatment. In relation to boys, it says in 1934, "there are several little problems which may crop up" for which the principal advice is "don't be selfconscious or affected, worrying over your hair, your nose, or your hat. Boys . . . above all like the natural type." Naturalness is not regarded as an end in itself, a way in which a girl may accept her individual looks. It is rather emphasized as a psychological preparation for the winning of future boyfriends without mentioning sex. And if the reader remains unsuccessful with her male "chums," she may always turn to the adjacent beauty hints to gauge how her hat or her hair can be improved on after all. An unacknowledged vacillation between unpretentious friendship and feminine attraction recurs when a chance encounter with a boy develops into closer contact. If asked to play tennis "enjoy your game—win if you can—and then home." Here mother is probably ready with an after-tennis tea for the two players in which case the politeness of the boy may induce him to hold the girl's chair before sitting down. "Do allow him to do this for you. . . . Remember he may feel a little strange, and your understanding will be a great help" ("Schoolgirls' Book of Friendship," *Schoolgirl* 11, no. 279 [1 December 1934], pp. 14–15). Equality on the tennis court should obviously not be taken so far as to eradicate an ever-present female sensitivity to male moods.

The ideal of a natural appeal concealed these contradictions to the readers and did so successfully because even personal problems were treated as entertainment; they were trivial, if never insignificant, occurrences that could be overcome by a little humor and individual inventiveness. No glaring contradictions as in the serious advice purveyed by the *Girl's Own Paper* and no entertaining, but acknowledged, grooming of femininity as in the Edwardian mill-girl papers. The alleged elimination of all conflicts under the watchword of entertainment made it difficult for the young readers to discover these conflicts of femininity, let alone to disentangle their underlying reasons.

The commercial schoolgirl weeklies certainly reinforced the readers' oppression by internalizing and individualizing social conflicts. Specifically, they reinforced new educational ideologies by obscuring overt class divisions and patriarchal power structures and by presenting every contradiction as an individual problem. The fictional forms of oppression, however, were submitted to voluntarily, for reading was leisure entertainment. "I loved everything about *The Schoolgirl:* its smell, its crispness," Mary Cadogan remembers. "Our elementary school playground was a positive arab bazaar of comic and magazine exchange—in spite of headmistress's regular edicts banning such periodicals from the school precincts" (Cadogan 1974, p. 5).[9]

9. Perhaps the school censorship on magazines made them even more attractive. Cer-

The unerring interest of girls in these magazines through the 1930s indicates the complexity of their function. As tokens of friendship as well as objects for trading and swapping, the papers created an indisputable, and much needed, collective reassurance. As for the reading process itself, it overtly affirmed the readers' self-reliance, while the weekly repetition of hair-raising plots lodged that self-reliance within a framework of predictable and safe exhilaration. On a conscious level readers bought the storypapers for their entertainment value, not to have their problems solved, but the papers' fictional transformation of unrecognized contradictions also formed an unconscious reason for purchase. If the fiction in the girls' periodicals formulated illegitimate sensations and had a subversive potential, then the fiction ultimately repressed its readers by covering up its own textual transformations of social contradictions.

This contradictory function of the schoolgirl weeklies was perhaps most clearly highlighted during the war. It brought about an immediate and effective elucidation of class differences that had hitherto mainly been reserved for the underprivileged living in the "black areas" of unemployment. Unlike World War I, which chiefly affected working-class children, World War II affected all the young. To both the large number of city children evacuated in the autumn of 1939 and the ones living in the reception areas, their involuntary meeting made tangible existing differences in speech and dress, peer-group customs, and family traditions. Although most of the evacuees soon returned to their prewar homes, children and adults alike lived in constant fear of new air raids or a possible German invasion.[10]

Significantly, this fear never became an explicit theme in the *Girls' Crystal* or the *Schoolgirls' Own Library*, the only schoolgirl papers to survive the war. The *Schoolgirl*, before it ceased publication in 1940, would feature occasional entries in its editorial columns on how to economize on coal and water, matches, tea, and sugar or make "A New Case for Your Gas-mask," followed by an obligatory reminder to place advance orders for the weekly at the local newsagent. When war did appear as a fictional topic, its treatment followed the familiar pattern of independent girlhood. Thus, "Elise Probyn" (John McKibbon) in the *Girls' Crystal* serial "A Girl Against the Nazis" concentrates on the young heroine's, Kay Royston's, clever disguises and subtle deception of the enemy in her search

tainly, after the war the best bargains at school were made through the trading of popular reading matter (Opie and Opie 1977, p. 152).

10. The first large-scale evacuation of children during World War II began on 1 September, 1939 (in London the operation was completed in three days). Altogether, about three million children moved to safer areas, but around Christmas nearly half of them had returned home. In 1944, another massive evacuation took place. Compared to 1914–18, few children had their childhood status changed during World War II. Only from 1942 were local authorities empowered to exempt children over 12 years of age from school to work in agriculture for 36 hours per week (a maximum of 7 hours a day) for up to 20 half-days per year (Gosden 1977, pp. 2, 18, 83).

for her lost brother in Germany. Her brief imprisonment in the concentration camp of "Grechamps" (with its "sinister gate" and its "fierce, relentless glare" of searchlights) offers the reader a rare glimpse of the hardships to be endured by the defiant English girl: "Kay tried to accustom herself to the suffocating shock of imprisonment, whilst two blankets were served out to her, a straw pillow, and a list of rules and regulations. . . . Icy-cold water to wash in, beds to be made, the hut scrubbed out from end to end" (16, no. 411 [5 September 1943], p. 418).[11]

The description would remind many readers more of tedious Saturday morning cleanings than of the ongoing war or the fears it produced. Similarly, the German officers, either ridiculous duffers or dumb bullies "rasping" or "roaring" their orders, are easily foiled by Kay's superior reasoning, which the readers never doubt will secure her reunion with her brother and her return to England. By reducing the fiend to inept or authoritarian props and by removing the scene of action to the continent, the war becomes a manageable, even quite enjoyable, but not a humorous affair. Fear is packaged as ordinary entertainment, not treated emotionally through horror or laughter. Within the recognizable universe of serial girls' fiction, the war, apparently, could not become a regular theme without impairing either the entertainment value of the stories or the protagonists' credibility as basically unspoiled English girls. A successful fictional mediation of the dangers incurred by warfare necessitated a transformation of the papers' fictional basis. This transformation took place only in the interwar boys' weeklies.

"A KICK IN THE FACE FROM A DEAD MONKEY"

If the schoolgirl magazines of the interwar years gradually discarded realism, then the most popular boys' papers did away with reality. The editorial address printed in D. C. Thomson's first boys' weekly, the *Adventure*, started off on a conventional note: "We can't all go off on daring stunts, but we all like to read of them. And week after week in these pages I'm going to give you the finest stories of daring, breathless adventure in every walk of life, and in every country under the sun" ("You and Your Editor," *Adventure*, no. 1 [17 September 1921], p. 2). But already with the publication of the *Rover* and the *Wizard* one year later, a chummy intimacy and a breezy directness balanced the papers' standardized, if lively, format. The editor of the *Rover* characterized his new venture by describing himself: "I've blistered off the Guinea Coast, and I've been frozen to the wheel round Cape Horn. I've visited every continent and sailed every one of the

11. The serial ran from vol. 15, no. 390 (10 April 1943) to vol. 16, no. 416 (9 October 1943).

seven seas. . . . That's the spirit you have of this new paper you have in your hands to-day—world-wide roving and daring" ("Chats with Your Editor," *Rover*, no. 1 [14 March 1922], p. 13). The editor of the *Wizard*, appearing six months later, was no less promising: "Real go-ahead lively yarns, with a kick in them. . . . That's what you want, isn't it? Sure! And you're getting them. The pals you will meet in these stories are real hustlers. They don't think about things—they do them" ("Step Right in! And have a Chat with Your Editor," *Wizard*, no. 1 [23 September 1922], p. 2). Riveting recommendations and a sense of participation were backed by a plethora of "free gifts," "special offers," and prize arrangements. The gifts invariably came in series: twenty-five different motor crests or medallions, pictures of popular soccer players, warriors, or strange animals ("Speedsters of the Wild," "Dandy Dogs," "Queer Animals"). Complete sets would, of course, secure the reader's participation in a competition for even better bargains such as "crystal sets" or fountain pens, "steel puzzles," table tennis and pocket tool sets, or maybe an album with pictures of "a hundred and twenty famous footballers" (probably the leftovers from the "special offers" in the weekly issues). The perennial prize schemes, indicating readers' ages to be between nine and thirteen or fourteen, bore no traces of editorial selection or moralizing. The arrangements were subtle acquisition appeals, nurturing the consumer consciousness of the audience and the young schoolboy's wish to possess a whole series of prizes as a new means of gaining social status at school or in the swapping games among peers in the street.

While prizes remained much the same, the editorials changed over the years. Snippets that seemed like random selections from the *Guinness Book of Records*—the fattest man, the tallest building, and so forth—gradually gave way to anecdotes about astounding human feats or strange natural phenomena. "Dear Chums, How would you like a kick in the face from a dead monkey?" begins a short description of death convulsions in an ape. A slightly more down-to-earth notice reads:

> There's a certain worm of the Annelid family, found in South America, that absolutely defies death.
> ### HALVE IT—AND IT DOUBLES.
> If its head is cut off, the body simply begins to grow a new head, and the head sprouts a new body! Instead of one worm, there are two, both alive and crawling!

Still, the editor adds in his comforting—or perhaps discouraging—final comment: "This doesn't happen with the common worm found in this country, so don't be digging up the back garden for the sake of trying experiments!" ("The Editor's Wide-World Chat," *Rover*, no. 507 [2 January 1932], p. 13). The distinction between facts and fiction, between informatory editorials and imaginary tales, became increasingly blurred. This growing emphasis on the exceptional and the exciting, on speed and masculine daring, was reiterated in the D. C. Thomson papers' main attraction, their fiction.

In the first issue of the *Adventure*, readers had been promised yarns from "every country under the sun" and from "every walk of life." This promise was fully kept in the Big Five. Compared with the school setting of the *Magnet* and the *Gem*, as well as other Amalgamated Press papers centering on single types of narrative, the fictional universe of the new Dundee weeklies was broadened and diversified. Reading through an issue of twenty-eight pages, the reader might travel the world, from the Brazilian jungle, New Mexico, and Florida to the Yukon Mountains in Canada, the North Pole, Monte Carlo, Gibraltar, or Morocco, ending up, perhaps, in the Khyber Pass on the Afghan border or at the Great Wall of China.

In this geographical mobility, the D. C. Thomson papers resembled the mid-nineteenth-century commercial boys' magazines. But the young reader of the 1920s followed several characters each week, and these were regularly replaced by new heroes. His range of imaginary action seemed much wider than his adolescent predecessors', and he did not have to await any personal maturing process in his protagonists for them to move to a new site. In fact, chronology and character development were remote to the speedy youngsters in the interwar tales—they simply never grew up, never reformed, but remained in vogue for shorter or longer periods with a possible resurrection following oblivion.

Not surprisingly, recalling that many interwar schoolboys nurtured vague longings for adult status, unusual male occupations held a prominent place in the papers. Some heroes had their base in the middle of the metropolitan hurly-burly and relied on the technical refinements of developed capitalism in their exciting jobs: "Mile-a-Minute Mike—the live wire of the G.P.O.," "Speeder Vic" (a racing driver), "Johnny-on-the-Spot—the youngest cameraman in the news film service." Other characters spread their activities and scientific knowledge to vast frontiers and woods, delved into fathomless seas or conquered precipitous mountains. "Railway Ralph—as cute with the willow as he is with the oil can," "Deep-Sea Delaney," and "Roving Rupe" with his "wonder horse Western King" were all early examples of these energetic youths who, regardless of their occupations, excelled by their unusual presence of mind, their extreme mobility, and their defiant battles against rascals who appeared wherever they went.

The young heroes were often employed as assistants to a police inspector, a super diver, or a famous mountaineer. "The Wireless Tecs" is one such long-running serial whose motifs originate in the city and whose protagonists are the renowned detective Morris Ward and his second-in-command, Sam Stretton. Their professional success owes much to modern technology—Morris Ward invariably comes up with a wonderful invention to escape his enemies in the nick of time, or his ingenuity serves as an initial ferment to get the action going.

Thus, at one point he creates "a new method of sending a brightly lighted scene by wireless rays." It immediately attracts a gang of "international crooks, mostly American" (just as its perfection, television, was to attract future generations of children). The detectives, "disguised as commercial travellers of the poorer kind," chase the gang to its hideout, "a rather disreputable apartment house, in the last stages of disrepair." Here, the leader, Lopez, stupidly falls into his own trap, an "electrified doormat," and with "a fearful scream" he is changed into a "twisted blackened body full length beside the door" (*Rover*, no. 222 [1926]).[12] With the head of the villains thus disqualified, it is an easy task for our heroes to pacify the other opponents and secure Morris Ward's invention.

Over the years, the main enemy of the wireless detectives became "a half-mad Jap," Fang, "the world's worst crook" (many rascals vied for that title in the D. C. Thomson papers). The heroes' search for this much-traveled rascal took them round the globe several times and landed them with additional adversities such as avalanches, shipwrecks, and civil wars. At one point, for example, they arrive during a revolution in the "little Republic of Jujuy." Violent detail is plentiful: "the signal was given and the volley sounded. Nineteen men fell with bullets in them" ("A President for Five Minutes," *Rover*, no. 122 [28 June 1924], p. 359). The fighting, though, is not caused by political upheavals but is the result of Fang's bribing of the none-too-intelligent generals of the small country in order to seize power. And once the malicious Japanese has secured that and has left Jujuy, the bogus revolution dissolves into thin air. The uprising merely adds an exotic flavor to the detectives' eternal hunt for the master crook. Indirectly, however, this and similar descriptions conveyed a notion of violence as justified by (white men's) intelligence and turned politics into a combat between goodies and baddies that always saw justice victorious in the end.

In general, the jobs rooted in urban society and its problems served as vehicles for individual accomplishments, bravery, and intelligent maneuvering. The work process itself was of no importance; it only played a part when it came to scientific details, which were singled out for minute description—much different from Charles Hamilton's vague references in the *Magnet* and the *Gem* to "the combustion engine" and other mechanical miracles. Technical accuracy yielded an extra aura of competence to the courageous characters and demonstrated that scientific skill was becoming an integral part of the male ideal also in papers for young boys that was more important than the Harry Wharton capacity for human introspection and judgment of character.

In reality, inventions were no longer primarily changing laborers' experiences in the factory and the workshop, but they were entering the everyday lives of families, of children, as never before. People living outside the area of

12. "The Wireless Tecs" first appeared in the *Rover*. no. 54, 1923. One year later, the stories were serialized, starting with no. 116, and featured at regular intervals until 1931.

production were deeply influenced by novelties such as electricity, the radio, cars, and the cinema. When this fascination with science was combined in the storypapers with the interesting options of adult occupations that lay beyond the concrete experiences of the young reader, the tales gained an element of safe strangeness—safe because the boys knew about and were interested in mechanics, strange because the technicalities were applied to types of work that many of these boys longed for. In 1932, for example, a "job top 10" competition in the *Rover* indicated that "airman" was the most coveted occupation followed by engineer, reporter, doctor, teacher, sailor, soldier, diver, jockey, and miner. Apart from the mundane tasks of teaching and perhaps mining, the readers' work choices all had mobility as a common denominator. Mobility, and its corollary of liberty, were also essential qualities in the heroes roaming around less-civilized parts of the world.

From the inception of the Dundee weeklies, the U.S. frontier and the Canadian forests made up popular venues of exciting action. This change in locale was undoubtedly spurred by the contemporary upsurge in the film western. One of the long-running series, "The Railway Kid," features the fourteen-year-old Danny Dixon, an orphan brought up by employees on the Great Canadian Railway. As with most of these heroes, Danny's connection to the line secures him a unique position between the unspoiled, but ferocious nature and a cultured, but corrupted civilization. He possesses the best from both worlds, the technological superiority of industrialized society (shotguns and dynamite) as well as the resourceful independence created by a life near animals and other powerful forces of nature.

The railway, in itself an admirable symbol of the advancement of industrial society into precapitalist areas, is personified by Danny Dixon, and thus any overt confrontation between the two social systems is avoided. The line, moreover, secures ample opportunities for plot variation. On his train, Danny meets crooks attacking the railway, villains blowing up bridges, changing signals, or tying gagged people to the rails. The boy always turns up trumps on such occasions, and his valor even includes participation in labor disputes. Alfalfa Ike and his followers want revenge when they are fired by the railway manager who claims that they have been working too slowly:

> "Where would you get yer big wages from if it weren't for the likes of us?"
> "From using my brains," answered the manager swiftly.
> "Where I've got them before." ("The Railway Kid," *Rover,* no. 17 [24 June 1922], p. 451)

The moral picture is clear and so is Danny's stand. He helps defy the workers, not because they are proletarian or poor, but because they are idle and aggressive. Conversely, the manager is right, not because he is rich or a capitalist, but because he is the more intelligent and sensible and therefore able to gauge moral right from wrong. This belief in an ultimate and general morality is the reason why Danny sides with the underdogs in later incidents. On one occasion, the railway line is to be purchased by big American financiers. "New men, new methods, new everything. Many of the old hands would be paid off and young men brought in from the States, and the sturdy British air of the line would vanish completely" ("A Railroad for Sale," *Rover*, no. 100 [26 January 1924], p. 91). The description would appeal less by its naive nationalism than its evocation of security, its playing on the young readers' experiences of neighborhood safety. Danny Dixon's unmasking of the dollar magnates was therefore unquestionably an act of bravery within the context of the tale. His fame soon traveled around the world and Danny with it, thus yielding a new foreign flavor to the setting and extra variety to the action.

Closer to home, sport offered the most prominent venue for heroic work. Tales about professional soccer or boxing would appeal to the reader, not so much because of their exotic adventures as by their affiliation to his own leisure activities with their connotations of freedom. Also, boxing and soccer were traditional means of a comet career for a working-class lad, almost the only ways to achieve material success if one stopped believing in the meritocratic possibilities of scholarship. So despite its conventional setting, sport had an air of excitement and unrestrained energy to it, and these two aspects were of primary importance in yarns such as "Cock-Eyed Casey" and "The Boxer with the Bomb-Proof Chin" in the *Wizard* as well as the *Rover's* "Bust 'Em Junior" and "Sledgehammer Steve" ("a two-fisted human thunderbolt"). These sport tales left no one in doubt about the heroes' proclivities and physical potentials. "With the ferocious growl of a mad gorilla," the Coal Box, alias Joe Jackson, attacks Sledgehammer Steve:

> With a dreadful snarl Jackson opened his mouth wide, and bit savagely at Steve's face. The young boxer jerked his head back in the nick of time, and the bared teeth of his assailant met together.
>
> The maddened nigger was not given a second chance to bare his fangs in such manner. Wrestling one arm free by a mighty effort of strength, Sledgehammer Steve smashed his fist into the horrible, grinning face before him.
>
> Once—twice he struck, with all his force. At the first punch Jackson bellowed like a bull—at the next he reeled back, blinded, cut, and torn, wild and dazed with pain. (*Rover*, no. 53 [3 March 1923], p. 229)

Whether to assure less astute readers or to add an extra touch of thrill to the tales, the young Hercules' are described as being equally swift in using their brains. When jealous opponents and greedy coaches lay their snares, mental promptness is of primary importance—houses on fire, attempted drownings, kidnappings, and long-term starvation are only some of the adversities that the

Dundee heroes have to conquer by their ideal combination of intelligence and bodily strength. In sinister cities as well as on wild frontiers, the excitement of the heroes' work is heightened through a free combination of elements from traditional narratives: sports and detective tales are mixed, adventure and western yarns are fused. In serials taking more recognizable surroundings as their point of departure, such fusion is used to a different effect.

"Invisible Dick—the boy who can vanish at will," "Phantom Fred—prince of impersonators and japer of japes," "Lanky Doodles—the Boy with the Expanding Legs," and "Whoopee Hooper—the boy who talked to himself in two different voices" are some of the famous boy jesters, completely controlling their surroundings by means of their unlimited resources of wish strings and vanishing powder, invisibility essence and magical swastikas (this was in 1924). Judging from illustrations and the pranks performed by the high-spirited juniors, they are about ten or eleven years old. They thus appeal to the youngest sections of the readership who have just outgrown, or still read, comics in which humorous incidents abound.

The "ordinary" British schoolboy characters are immediate objects of identification, and it is therefore significant that these types are the first to openly defy any ties to realism in the papers. Like the girl ventriloquists of the 1930s, the boy jesters seem compelling because they transgress their ordinariness, because they disregard everyday sanctions and adult supervision of domestic chores or tedious lessons at school. The "normal" infallibility of grown-ups is challenged when the boys ridicule them by changing clothes and identities, impersonating apes in the zoo or the wax figures at Madame Tussaud's, or perhaps disappearing when austere aunts are expected to tea, the invisible boy thereby avoiding "catty remarks about his appearance and manners, the redness of his hands, the roughness of his hair, the untidiness of his collar and tie" ("Lucky Jimmy," *Rover*, no. 110 [6 April 1924]). Over the years, many of the recurring characters in the humorous tales not only ventured further afield, they also acquired exotic animals in serials such as "Alfie and his Elephant" and "Happy and his Hippo" (the hippopotamus was later replaced by a giraffe and then an ostrich). The development reinforced the link to comics such as the *Beano* and *Dandy* in which animals appeared as characters in their own right.

The stories clearly contained elements of wish-fulfillment, but they equally demonstrated the readers' need for protest, a wish to get the upper hand, for once, if only through laughter. As the *Magnet* figure of Billy Bunter had demonstrated, the mirth caused by the boy jesters' topsy-turvy transformations of both realism and reality at once released repressed energies of aggression and reconfirmed existing power relations through that release. Stories within a home setting were the first in the boys' papers to revert to full-blown merriment, indicating not only that the family had become the locus of insoluble conflicts for all children, but also that there were few other outlets for the young to which they could direct their energies and recompense their conflicts. It is perhaps no coincidence that the humorous upheaval of reality was thereafter emulated in the school serials.

Considering that many interwar boys were dissatisfied with, or rather disinterested in, their school experiences, one might expect that school had become a completely outmoded topic in the Big Five. Their fictional schoolboys, it is true, only had the scantiest connection to irksome lessons or to the close social life displayed in the prewar *Magnets* and *Gems*. Pioneered by Wily Watkins' perennial performances in the *Rover* from 1925 on, school yarns moved toward slapstick humor and farce. "The Tricky Triplets," "Chums of the Jungle," "Peter Pain—the 7-foot Schoolboy," and "Tricky Nixon" (a nickname invented in 1933!) are among the cunning schoolboys who continue Jack Harkaway's early escapades by exercising their pranks and pugilistic supremacy in the Dundee weeklies.

From its inception in 1933, one of these weeklies, the *Hotspur*, was mainly identified through the serial about the Red Circle School. This paper perhaps offers the clearest demonstration of the way in which the prewar school serial was transformed. Although pupils at the Red Circle could grow up and disappear from the scene of action, fictional interest centers on the unrestrained inventiveness of the boarders in their power struggle with equally unrestrained but less inventive masters. The comic relief, traditionally created by foreign pupils, is fully unfolded at the Red Circle where the characters represent a variety of nationalities and a host of curious occupations. Escaped kidnappers, Mexican outlaws and deranged lumberjacks pit their wits as assistant masters against the sons of welterweights, smugglers, and African chiefs.

Over the years, the humorous incidents assume an almost surrealist grotesqueness because of the still more energetic boarders and, equally, because masters lose any pretense of authoritative aloofness and probability. This trend is most marked in minor school stories featured in the *Hotspur* as well as in other D. C. Thomson weeklies. Some yarns are set in stone-age schools in which the last vestiges of civilization (including one machine gun) are precariously preserved after a world war has destroyed most human amenities. At other times, boys gain scholarships to schools on the moon, or they are held hostages on Mars as teachers to the Martians. The "Big Stiff," or Septimus Green, is a popular figure in many of these stories. With his radical pedagogical ideas, his unchecked imagination, and his reversal of values, the strange master at some point is declared insane. "Stiff realised that as an inmate of a mental home he could try out all his educational ideas without question" (*Hotspur*, no. 188 [3 April 1937], p. 7).[13] So pedagogical specialists who visit Big Stiff's new school at the

13. Around 1960, the "Big Stiff" still appeared in the *Wizard*, as an equally imaginative super detective.

Sunnyside Rest Home are put into padded cells while rebellious boys, sent there by exasperated parents, benefit by the jolly companionship of the usual inmates and come out as scholarship winners.

This and other school stories featured in the Dundee papers gave vent to an unchecked defiance that undoubtedly seemed fascinating to British schoolboys who could not even write an obscene word in the school toilets without it being wiped off after recess (Rex n.d., p. 28). But at the same time, the absurdities of the tales and their humor secured a narrative distance that checked the evocation of aggression and boys' feelings of opposition. Subversive sensations were most readily invoked by recognizable situations, and it was no coincidence therefore that the series taking home and school conflicts as their narrative basis were the first to turn to hilarious humor. This trend was emulated in the late 1920s in other traditional types of story such as sports, detective, adventure, and western yarns. In the girls' papers, as we have seen, a similar development occurred during the 1930s only when the combined forces of decreasing employment opportunities and more glaring educational injustices made schoolgirls turn away from psychological introspection and realistic solutions in their popular reading.

Musgrave, in his study of school story books for boys, notes a decline in the popularity of this genre during the interwar years. He explains it as a result of authors' inability to rejuvenate the genre in accordance with current ideological transformations (Musgrave 1985, pp. 240–41). Analysis of the serialized school stories suggests that authors were indeed able to rejuvenate both Hughes' moralism and Kipling's self-defined jingoism. However, they could do so only by giving up what Musgrave and others define as an integral aspect of the genre—namely, the hero's psychological development. Thus, the stories in some sense return to the episodic structure found in the Jack Harkaway stories of the 1870s. The dwindling popularity of boys' school fiction after World War I seems to have social rather than literary reasons.

Unlike their sisters, only a minority of schoolboys after 1918 entertained any renewed hopes in educational meritocracy. From their fathers or older relatives, who had been enrolled into school as the prime targets of reform, many knew and expected discrepancies between home and school and between lofty ideals of equality and an unjust reality. It is not surprising, therefore, that these young schoolboys in the 1920s favored a form of reading matter that transposed their conflicts into a personalized justice operating beyond the confines of school and, later on, tales that dissolved any feelings of aggression through a liberating laugh at obtuse adults. But, as with girls, the thirties served to reinforce the real-life problems facing boys. The Dundee papers, accordingly, took their young readers to worlds that had hitherto been confined to adult or at least adolescent tastes, worlds that not even the editors of girls' weeklies dreamed of.

Two trends held this development together. One was the elimination of reality not through laughter but through excitement, and the other was the growth of the boy or adolescent hero into a superman. The idols employed their omnipotent strength and intelligence in Manichean moral combats waged between the universal forces of good and evil. The scene of action could be a culture universe, a nature universe, or the "ultimate" universe of war invalidating all other distinctions. In 1929, readers of the *Rover* got the first glimpse of a strange figure, drilling his way out of the dark earth: "Very short and slim, he was dressed entirely in black, even to a black mask over his face. His hair was black, his tight-fitting sweater was of similar hue, and his legs were encased in black tights." "The Black Sapper" emerges in his "wonder boring underground machine," the Earth Worm, which is more minutely described than its owner: "Fifteen feet long it was, not unlike a monstrous torpedo, but with one of these corrugated cones capping either end, and the strange grooves parted by shallow fins that were now coated thickly with earth . . . although the smoothness of the metal caused most of this to fall away" (*Rover*, no. 384 [24 August 1929], p. 200). With its "diamond-studded" drill nose cutting through earth, steel, and stone "as smoothly as a knife cutting through cheese," the "land submarine" gives its sinister master an almost unlimited range of mobility. Together with the Black Sapper's other ingenious inventions (including "a periscopic mirror" to see through earth), the Earth Worm endows the hero with an added aura of unpredictability, reinforcing the impression created by his mysterious attire. The epitome of calculating scientific intelligence and a never-failing self-control, the Black Sapper is a natural continuation of the adventurous detective figures. His chosen orbit of activity lies within civilized areas, though he never hesitates to travel under the Atlantic Ocean or the Alps to get there. Once arrived, he will trap anyone trying to cross his plans, whether it is a malignant international criminal or "one of those wooden-headed dolts who, luckily for us, fill so many high positions in the police force," as he tells his assistant Marot (*Rover*, no. 564 [4 February 1933], p. 116).

Unlike his predecessors, the Black Sapper only complies with law and order when it fits into his own schemes. These include a theft of the Russian crown jewels, the two-ton, twelve-foot statue of Ramses II from the British Museum, as well as involvement in numerous kidnapping affairs, the English prime minister being one of the more remunerative victims—the Earth Worm secures the success of the rescue operation by simply cutting its way right into the grounds of Parliament. Also paying a nice ransom is the multimillionaire Gregory Boulton. The money equals, says the Black Sapper, the sums that the financier has "swindled the public of since he started promoting his shaky companies." This form of retribution would find a ready response with many readers when the story appeared in 1933, a time when the Slump intensified economic inequalities and heightened people's consciousness of social injustice. But if a touch of personal indignation was permissible in order to create sympa-

The *Rover*, no. 565 (11 February 1933), front cover. The superhero takes center stage in the boys' weeklies of the 1930s.

thy with the audience, general political criticism was anathema. The Black Sapper, being no Robin Hood, kept his gold to himself, so the ultimate message of the tale was a reinforcement of individualism and an idealization of supreme intelligence irrespective of its ways and means.

By and by, the Black Sapper is endowed with a past. Born as Richard de Hyeatt into a famous British family, "a hereditary strain of wildness and a quarrel with his father" turn the young nobleman into his sinister exile. The information also turned the Black Sapper into a less mysterious and hence a less fascinating figure. His popularity was eclipsed by superhuman characters such as "The Flaming Avenger," a lone lawmaker with a "wonderful armoured suit" and an "ammonia gun" and his even more ingenious successor "The Hovering Avenger." Like Superman, his transatlantic counterpart, the Hovering Avenger, alias Smasher Loftus, first appears in 1938 when he discovers a flying metal, "heliolide." Used in a "floatation-waistcoat," the wonderful metal enables its wearer to travel at a great pace. Together with his brother, the Hovering Avenger is thereby able to capture his enemies, among whom are the Ten Tentacles, Chicago's vilest gang, whose leader turns out to be head of the city police. This and similar feats immediately attracted school-boy readers such as Maurice Kutner: "My juvenile reading matter had no place for frail humans. I wanted to read about supermen, or superboys. The strong boy, the boy who could make himself invisible, the boy ventriloquist, the boy who could fly—were my fundamental heroes, because youth is given up to day dreams, dreams in which one is the central figure" (Kutner 1964, p. 179).

The vividness of Kutner's evocation reveals that he may actually have under-estimated the importance played by his juvenile dreams. Indeed, the new super-human heroes owed their popularity to their extreme competence, their supreme mastery of their surroundings, and their disregard for any authority. In this, their function resembled that of earlier series in which boys had magically changed their identities to baffle their elders. The scene of struggle had changed, the adversaries were larger, but the superheroes still exercised their powers within a recognizable universe—the Black Sapper would emerge right outside Parliament, and the Hovering Avenger foiled a bunch of crooks from Chicago. The fascination of these tales lay exactly in the tension between the well-known and the fantastic, between identification and imagination. Contrary to fairy fantasies, whose universes were completely self-contained, and to realism, which described an explicable clash of opposites, the super-series offered an imagina-tive compromise: "it could happen like this!" These stories, too, modulated the readers' role conflicts, but under less painful circumstances.

The superhero need not necessarily confine himself to an urban radius of action (a sphere which most readers identified with). He might also operate within the framework of nature where he personfied its positive potentials.

"Logan the Mountie" in the *Wizard* and his correlative in the *Rover*, "Morgyn the Mighty," both begin their careers in 1928—fourteen years after Edgar Rice Bourroughs had presented *Tarzan of the Apes* to the American public (he wrote twenty-six Tarzan books in all) and one year before Harold Foster's comic-strip version conquered the African Jungle and Jane as well as the imagination of millions of young readers.

Thirteen years on a desert island in the South Pacific forces Morgyn to develop his boyish agility into a super-manly strength—but without losing the personal marks of British civilization. He "kept his hair trimmed and his face comparatively smooth. He had a marked objection to turning into a bearded creature, though there was every excuse for it" (*Rover*, no. 304 [11 February 1928], p. 151). Together, the best aspects of nature and culture, brawn and brains, create an ideal masculinity that secures the survival of the matchless Morgyn regardless of the dangers he encounters. These come thick and fast once he escapes Beach Island and starts to catch up with life ("I've got thirteen years to make up"). In Canada, he joins the mounted police and fights "half-breeds and indians"; in the Wild West he has a thirty-minute struggle with a buffalo. He then proceeds to New York where he escapes the electric chair by bending the iron bars of his prison cell. Weary of civilized injustice, the omnipotent giant becomes the lawmaker of Africa ("Leo the Lion was King of the Jungle—till Morgyn came"). In Africa his days are enlivened by ferocious carnivores and insubordinate natives. Once, when the natives wrongfully attack him, Morgyn the Mighty has to teach them a lesson:

> Biff! Bash! Someone had pierced the fleshy part of his thigh with a spear, but a second later had gone down as though dead beneath the impact of a left hook to the stomach. The next man leapt high into the air to bring his club down on Morgyn's head. Morgyn the Mighty caught him with one hand in mid-air by his throat, swung him like a flail, and knocked down four others.
>
> One of the fallen clutched at his leg, and tried to sink a knife in him. Morgy kicked the man in the face with his other foot, and that man moved no more.
>
> Two men he caught as they tried to duck behind a tree, and he brought their heads together so violently that they dropped unconsciously at his feet. Three more got direct punches from his clenched fists, and lay in the grass like corpses. (*Rover*, no. 390 [5 October 1929], p. 24)

Morgyn refrains from actually killing his opponents, for, as he notes with Christian forbearance, "they only acted through ignorance." The remark, however, was merely a token consolation after the detailed description of the battle. Despite this Goliath's alleged superiority of intelligence, he did not exactly rule through the power of the word. The stories centered on the process of fighting itself with only the scantiest references to its causes and possible effects. While the Black Sapper's hyperintelligence was idealized, Morgyn's paramount strength formed the basis of his appeal. His African adventures, which were perhaps prolonged because of the contemporary popularity of the Tarzan figure, were later replaced by exotic exploits in other parts of the world where the hero's ever-growing potency was needed. "The strongest man alive" had become established as a type, and he was in fact one of the characters in the boys' papers to survive World War II.

The emphasis in the new series upon a single savior's superhuman powers and the dissolution of former rules of authority, law, and order indirectly denoted a cultural pessimism and indicated that the readers' real-life conflicts were increasingly difficult to solve in a "realistic" manner. [14] As portents of a new war began to loom larger on the horizon and gradually overshadowed national unrest, the notions of pessimism became more pronounced. Prefiguring the war hero, a new type of protagonist emerged: the spy. Combining paramount strength and superior reasoning, the spy was the urban Superman and nature's Tarzan figure rolled into one. Among the earliest and most successful in a sequence of Dundee super aces was "The Wolf of Kabul." Bill Samson—the Wolf's mundane name—started his extraordinary career as Britain's master spy on what was then the northwestern frontier of India in the *Wizard* in 1930; he still roamed the "savage border lands" north of the Khyber Pass during the early 1960s in the final volumes of that paper as one of the only prewar heroes to retain currency with the boy readership growing to magazine maturity after 1945.

Together with his Himalayan helper and bodyguard, Chung, the Wolf controls the half-mad "warrior-tribes" that constantly conspire to overthrow British supremacy and civilized common sense. In "The War Gong of Kashgar," a group of deaf Cossacks, led by the ferocious Gan, steal a magic gong whose terrible sound incites people to battle. One of the ploys used by the Wolf to destroy the gong and its evil possessors is to turn their own live weapons against them. Five hundred starved rats, kept by Gan as instruments of torture, are let loose on his own men: "Yelps of human pain mingled with the sharp squeals of the rats" as these "hurled themselves at the stampeding Killers . . . to get at their faces and their hands." In particular, the Wolf enjoys seeing "thirty or forty of the monster rats attacking Gan at once, and he gloried in the scoundrel's howls of pain" (*Wizard*, no. 559 [1933], p. 207). Moral right, it seems, not only justifies violence, but it also legitimates its enjoyment. In a final desperate fight on the parapets of Gan's castle, the evil-doer, clutching the dreaded gong, is hurled over the edge by the Wolf's "good honest punch on the jaw." The British ace, "the man who makes peace by starting wars," embodies old-fashioned physical strength and scheming intelligence. Living on the out-

14. In an expression of the trend in the boys' papers to emphasize wicked, but forceful, heroes, the *Rover* in the mid-thirties resuscitated nineteenth-century characters such as Dick Turpin, Ned Kelly, Claude Duval, and others, whose hazardous, but successful, deceptions of the law were recounted with loving detail but with little historical specification. The series was called "The World's Famous Outlaws."

skirts of civilization where nature meets culture, he uses evil for the sake of good and thus paves the way psychologically for the approaching war.

Subtle editorial underpinnings indicate that the spy theme became extremely popular with readers from the mid-thirties on. "Spy Leagues" and "Secret Circles" were launched. Their participants could be recognized by their little blue badges, their individual membership number, and a warrant card ("keep it in a SECRET, SAFE place"). All received a copy of the indispensable code whereby the would-be spies were able to decipher strange messages and thus obtain a chance of winning footballs, boxing equipment, or athletes' outfits. More devoted and well-off readers could follow the numerous advertisements and buy the special "Boy Detective Marvel Packet," which contained "fingerprint, invisible ink, radio ink and mystic fire ink powders." Or they might opt for one of the more mundane versions, either a "Boy Detective Domino Outfit" comprising among its interesting items "handicuffs, revolver, bullets, S.S. badge, call-whistle and black mask," or perhaps one of the "World-Famous Boy Detective Outfits" that offered "German, Chaplin and Sgt. Major Moustaches, Unbreakable Monocle, Grease Paints, Sallow or Chinese, Sunburn or Red Indian."

In the tales, total destruction ceased being a danger that threatened only master-spies in Afghanistan, native tribes in Africa, or explorers in the Antarctic when they were attacked by mammoth beetles, monster rats, or giant water snakes. The turn had come to Britain herself. The movement of evil toward home was a development that reiterated a trend in the Edwardian boys' papers. Alfred Harmsworth's anti-German feeling was notorious, and it had been fiercely promoted in both dailies and weeklies from the Amalgamated Press. One of the firm's most popular war sequels for adolescent boys had been "Britain Invaded" followed by "Britain at Bay" and "Britain's Revenge." Written by the prolific "John Tregellis" (pen name for Sidney Gowing), the series follows two adolescent brothers, Sam and Stephen Villiers, and their heroic struggles against the German foe when they are appointed as special scouts to the British army and become the informal leaders of the resistance movement. The tales were first serialized in the *Boys' Friend* in 1906, and like their counterparts for adults they became extremely popular.[15]

15. Sidney Gowing's war sequel, which was reissued first in the *Gem*, starting in vol. 2, no. 41 (1908), and later in the *Marvel*, was undoubtedly inspired by the enormous success enjoyed by Erskine Childers' and William Le Queux' books for adults. Childers' book *The Riddle of the Sands* (1903) describes the devastating effects of British unpreparedness in case of a German attack, and its cheap edition sold several hundred thousand copies (Roberts 1977, p. 180). Le Queux' *The Invasion of 1910*, which was first serialized in the *Daily Mail* in 1906, brought about a considerable boost in the sales of the paper by having the German invaders sent through the major British towns (Cadogan and Craig 1978, p. 27).

Beginning in 1933, when two new serials called "Britain Invaded" and "Britain at Bay" were issued in the *Rover*, a spate of fictional invasions of Britain was published in the Big Five. Initially, native safety is threatened by "bloodthirsty mongols" led by the "War Lord Wu Fang" whose brute power is soon reinforced by the devastating technology brought by the "Chans" or Japanese. Extraterrestrial forces operate in other serials such as "Raiders from the Red World" in which readers of the *Wizard* could follow a group of Martians from their landing in the Congo until they enter Britain. Tusker Gordon's single-handed struggle to combat the raiders even takes him to Mars in a later follow-up called "The Blood Trail on Mars." As in other serials, D. C. Thomson authors freely mixed genres and themes that had been developed in late-Victorian and Edwardian periodicals for adolescent and adult readers. In the thirties, an interest in science fiction and war was no longer confined to maturer tastes.[16]

In the final years before the outbreak of World War II, Nazi Germany's rearmament provided a fertile source of fictional interest and offered British master spies new fields of action. As early as 1936, "Britain Attacked" describes Commander Silver, "Britain's Secret Service man number one," and his lonely fight against the Germans. His first undertaking is to destroy the newly invented "Henkel Robots." These remote-controlled machines with their "blunt noses, single-structure wings, and peculiar undercarriages" have been constructed to drop bombs on Britain—very similar, indeed, to the V-1 bombers used by Germany eight years later. Despite Commander Silver's success in averting the initial German air raid on his native country, London is flooded from the coast by ten thousand Nazi soldiers and their "modern monsters of destruction." Some of the vile invaders are burned, though, when the British suspend "electrified wires" across the ground. And as if air and land warfare combined is not enough, the caption concluding one installment promises expectant readers that "enemy submarines lay a thick band of chemical 'fog' right round Britain next week" (*Rover*, no. 756 [10 October 1936], p. 41).

Contrary to the Edwardian Amalgamated Press series in which the war heroes were usually found in the thick of action busily defending the empire, Commander Silver's main function is to mastermind that action. He predicts and prevents further disaster by going to the Sudan to discuss tactics with the British forces there or by disguising himself as a traitor or a German army doctor to obtain their formula for a dangerous "truth drug" or a new poison gas. His master stroke, however, is his single-handed capture of the enemy general who "believed in the power of speeches," and who is so engrossed in his oratory

16. For a detailed description of Edwardian science-fiction and invention serials, see Turner 1976, pp. 181–90, 203–16.

rehearsals that he hardly notices his own defeat. The stock-in-trade conclusion follows: the prisoner shoots himself, thus mercifully avoiding any drastic British measures. Bereft of their master, his forces completely disintegrate, and peace is restored with Britain back at her imperial pinnacle.

Warfare had become an integral part of the schoolboy papers. The war series of the late 1930s took the cultural pessimism, implicit in the spy and superhero trend, to its logical conclusion. Life was basically a battle between good and evil. War was therefore a necessary but, in the papers, also a manageable affair in which moral justice, personified by the hyperintelligent spy or soldier, came out victorious in the end. The tales highlighted the general function of leisure reading, the modeling of the reader's latent anxieties and unrecognized conflicts. War invoked a real, though vague, fear. Encompassing the more pressing everyday problems and the disillusions about the immediate future, it was a total and therefore an ideal universe for fictional mediation. The thrills of battle absorbed the boy's concrete apprehensions and concerns, made them conscious but at the same time tangible as malleable moral conflicts, and provided a strong man to control the happy solution, the restoration of order.

After 1939, the war accounts developed in two directions. On the one hand, dramatic skirmishes and military offensives were often removed to more distant locations, like Egypt, Libya, or Canada, where warfare was spiced by elements from traditional adventure stories and westerns. Hard-neck heroes further developed their omnipotent strength and masterly independence—features that characterized the good spy of the 1930s. Their insurrection occasionally went as far as to defy incompetent and bureaucratic R.A.F. officials, but never the British defense per se. The recognition of certain military idiosyncrasies served to reinforce in the readers a subtle sense of patriotism, but never the kind of unquestioned jingoism found in war tales from before World War II.

On the other hand, there was a boost to humor in the tales set in Britain, and here young boys gained a prominent place. In the *Rover* of 1941, the "Blitz Kids" set up a Bicycle Brigade whose members rescue cats from blazing buildings, round up Nazi spies, and deliver vital messages when the telephone network breaks down. The resourceful schoolboys always manage to deceive any inept adult trying to oppose their dangerous but well-organized plans, and the readers' enjoyment of the yarns would be as much a result of this clever circumvention of authority as of the stirring events themselves. Similarly, a *Hotspur* series "The War Time Wonder" features Alf Coppin, an "unkempt youngster" and dunce at Rope Street Council School, who coincidentally reveals his magic capabilities of decoding German messages at a mere glance. Keeping his usual schoolboy routine as a perfect alibi, Alf becomes a trusted member of the Secret Service, thus at once foiling obtuse masters and the dangerous German foe. At the Red Circle School, now a center of juvenile intelligence activities, German

The *Hotspur*, no. 355 (15 June 1940), front cover. War is the ultimate theme of boys' papers. In 1940, real danger may temporarily be transformed into fictional laughter.

spies disguise themselves as British masters only to be ridiculed and have their true identities revealed by clever schoolboys.

Conversely, British Secret Service men enter German training academies somewhat more successfully in order to disclose the cruel tactics employed there in the brainwashing of the recruits. Some of these keep their wits about them so that when Herr Hitler himself at one stage inspects one of the schools, the dais is made to break under his weight during the obligatory speech. Enraged by the ensuing laughter, the führer "threw himself unto the floor and began to bite the boarding like a dog, hammering the floor with fists and feet as though in a fit" ("School of the Gestapo," *Hotspur,* no. 355 [15 June 1940], p. 281). If juvenile readers could not actively combat the outer enemy of danger or its inner corollary of fear, they could at least momentarily invalidate both through a good laugh.

Unlike girls' papers, boys' weeklies during the war years already possessed a narrative framework within which the notions of fear and apprehension could be treated. But when the threat of air raids and German invasions became realities, it ceased being possible, apparently, to treat that threat in a manner that was at once probable and pleasing. So the seriousness of battle was turned into a matter of laughter and merriment, or the center of action was transposed to exotic areas a safe distance from the British shores. World War II epitomized the social dependence felt by the young, a main characteristic of modern childhood, and it equally radicalized the psychological conflicts attached to that existence. Not surprisingly, then, the developments in the theme of war, the "ultimate" theme engulfing all former narrative trends, highlight what this book reveals to be the main catalyst of fictional change operating in the commercial papers in different ways and with varying speed.

The magazines, in order to retain a continuous appeal with their readers, took reality as their narrative point of departure but not necessarily as their end limit. If the role conflicts and the anxieties engendered within one social area became too difficult to reconcile in an entertaining fashion, the problems were either dissolved through humor, or they were removed to a less concrete, and hence a safer, area of solution. The development of the sinister superman, the omnipotent boy japer, and finally the disillusioned war hero—all completely mastering their real and recognizable surroundings—yielded no proof that schoolboys' leisure reading was becoming increasingly improbable or that it had turned into complete wishfulfillment bearing no relation to the readers' lives and thoughts. Rather, the emergence of these characters denoted that the real conflicts of childhood had become too painful to be pleasingly resolved within the tradition of realism, not to mention didacticism. Viewed from the historical perspective of juvenile consumerism, it was necessary and in a sense "realistic" to expand the fictional universe in the weeklies. D. C. Thomson and Company was most successful in doing so, war or no war.

PART SIX

Conclusion

14

More Next Week?

IN THE course of this book, we have followed two related histories, namely, the gradual inclusion of all British children into what we today understand as a real childhood and the concomitant development of the commercial juvenile magazines. The two histories have been held together by the market mechanism and its weekly or monthly adjustments of the balance to be kept between continued moral or economic profitability to the publisher and continued pleasure to the purchasers whether these were the parents or juveniles themselves.

Although the periodicals were read not only by "real" children, we have seen how magazine developments were spurred by specific reorganizations within childhood and especially by the inclusion into that childhood of new juvenile groups. From their inception as general periodicals, the magazines have gradually been diversified—initially according to class, then to age and gender—as first the middle-class boy, then his sister and his working-class peers, and finally working-class girls were introduced to full-time schooling and a future-oriented upbringing.

This book began by asking why so many children and adolescents prefer popular literature to what adults term quality books and what causes literary changes within popular reading. The history of British juvenile magazines first demonstrates that children of various age groups have favored periodicals because the market sensibility of the papers often made them more topical and generally more sensitive to changes in the readers' needs than were books. Thus, the religious magazines display a more secular social awareness in their "street arab" stories before Hesba Stretton attains fame with her books. The *Girl's Own Paper* and similar ventures portray independent-minded schoolgirl heroines ahead of Angela Brazil, while D. C. Thomson's interwar boys' papers take their readers into orbits that are only seriously pursued in boys' books after World War II.

But if magazine publishers have had to be sensitive to the desires of their public, they are also responsible for the molding of those desires. We have seen that as the regulation of juvenile sexuality is established as natural within the frameworks of the family and school, the need for overt inculcation of morality

237

disappears in favor of an indirect safeguarding of existing power relations. Children and adolescents gain more independence but within stricter limits. This social development sets new demands for the magazine publisher and also creates new fictional possibilities. The overt didacticism inculcated by the religious periodicals is gradually replaced by secular norms displayed first by the narrator and then through the fictional account itself, through character development and then through the fictional structure.

The secondary aim of this book is to explain the literary change over time in juvenile periodicals. As leisure became an increasingly important area for juveniles in which they could establish a sense of independence and power, their minute consumer consciousness added to the publishers' awareness of their papers' entertainment value. This awareness in turn propelled fictional change. We have seen how the modern—that is, the commercial—juvenile periodicals took their point of departure in actual experiences of juvenile conflict and also how their sustained commercial survival depended on their successful molding of those conflicts into acceptable—that is, entertaining—resolutions.

What can be called the commercialization of popular reading for the young has two important implications. First, the process through which the fictional resolution is attained becomes blurred over time. As the papers become more fun to read, the audience loses awareness of why they laugh. Second, when real-life conflicts become too difficult to mold in an entertaining manner, they simply disappear from the magazines and are replaced by less painful, but still pertinent, themes. This process of conflict transformation forms the motor of fictional change in the papers.

Along with the gradual concealment of textual conflict, the viable existence of conflict transformation as a catalyst to fictional change constitutes the main finding of this investigation. While the adolescent boy of the 1860s, on the threshold of a secure middle-class career, accepted the firm promotion of restrained manliness in the *Boy's Own Magazine,* such adamant advocacy was rather less palatable to the working-class schoolboy of the 1930s saving his Saturday pennies for the *Wizard* or the *Rover.* Equally, the adolescent reader, delving into the *Girl's Own Paper* articles on work or cookery with the awareness of a newly educated girl who is about to confront adult choices, is a far cry from the twelve-year-old schoolgirl reading her *Girls' Crystal* before World War II with the knowledge that her adult choices are limited and her school life not all that eventful.

The persistent silences in the papers on sexual matters and the transformation of parents into nonexistent or inept details hiding in the background only serve to confirm this conclusion. The regulation of sexuality, which we initially described as being at the core of childrearing, is simply too painful an experience for writers, publishers, and children alike (if with different explanations) to be treated openly in the papers. So much more significant is the strong vein of violence that from early on runs through the boys' papers: the disregard for, even hatred of, foreigners and, less explicitly, of women. In the girls' magazines, the correlative to violence seems to be romance and later humor. This distinctive difference between boys' and girls' papers can help to explain another result that has been brought to light by this book. While the commercial demand for expanding markets and a broad reader appeal of the papers gradually undermine former class differences between juvenile periodicals, gender differences persist, and they can even be said to have been reinforced in the twentieth century. As children's lives formally become more alike, it seems easier to find common social denominators rather than common sexual denominators in the weeklies. The gender differences of sexual regulation seem insurmountable even for inventive magazine publishers.

Those findings are borne out by the developments in popular reading after World War II. The juvenile magazines, which survived the war despite paper shortage and irregular publication, were gradually superseded by the more popular comics or they were transformed into picture storypapers carrying an assortment of humorous strips and picture stories. In the storypapers, the sharp gender differences continued. For girls, only the *Schoolgirls' Own Library* and a refashioned *Girls' Crystal* made it into the 1960s. In 1950, the Amalgamated Press issued a new *School Friend* that bore the marks of a comic, just as the *Girls' Crystal* was to do three years later, and Cliff House was not among the *School Friend*'s attractions. The paper lasted until 1965 when it was incorporated with *June* as *June and School Friend*.

The demise of the old-style weeklies, however, did not mean an end to girls' popular reading. In 1951, the Hulton Press brought out *Girl* (1951–64). Edited by the Reverend Marcus Morris and printed in brightly colored photogravure, the weekly found a large following with schoolgirls in the 1950s. In 1953, 94 percent of 11 to 13-year-olds read either *Girl, Girls' Crystal*, or the new *School Friend*—the last being the most popular (Fenwick 1953, p. 33). For although *Girl* still printed 310,000 weekly copies by 1962, the output of *School Friend* was then 414,000 (Campbell and Campbell 1962, p. 25). The heroines in *Girl* seemed more familiar with the altruistic notions governing fictional characters of the 1920s than with the magical properties that supergirls displayed in the *School Friend*, which a host of picture storypapers from the late 1950s were to develop. In 1958, D. C. Thomson and Co. brought out *Bunty*, which rapidly outdistanced the other girls' papers. By the early 1960s it came out in 500,000 copies a week (Campbell and Campbell 1962), and it was soon followed by *Judy* (1960–), *Mandy* (1967–), and *Debbie* (1973–83). In the meantime, Amalgamated Press had been taken over by the International Publishing Corporation (IPC) in 1960. During the 1970s, IPC rivaled Thomson with weeklies such as *Tammy* (1971–84) and *Jinty* (1974–81). *Bunty* set the fictional pace: in twenty-eight pages it had ten picture stories and the comic

"Toots" ("you'll never feel glum with this yummy new chum"). From the outset girl ballet dancers held a prominent position in the papers. In *Bunty*, "Moira Kent—the famous British ballerina" roamed round the world in perennial assistance of blind, deaf, or orphaned colleagues. She was followed by "Sandra of the Secret Ballet" in the companion paper *Judy* that also in one of its early issues gave away "glossy photo-cards of lovely young dancers." In general, the girls' picture storypapers of the 1960s and 1970s featured unrestrained characters—trapeze artists, riders, or swimming champions—whose common characteristic is supreme control of body and mind. Significantly, Bessie Bunter, who had her own strip in *Tammy and Misty* of the early 1980s, was replaced by Bella, a top gymnast who resolved mysteries and other problems in between her numerous public shows: in 1983, for example, she visits the "Shah of Ramaski" whom she assists in securing "the freedom of women" against the scheming queen and her brother.

D. C. Thomson comics such as the prewar *Beano* and *Dandy* continued to form a fictional mainstay for children of both sexes—in the mid-seventies the two comics were read by 62.7 percent of girls and 76.4 percent of boys aged ten (Whitehead 1977, p. 259). In 1968, the Scottish firm started *Twinkle*, "the picture paper specially for little girls," as it says in the subtitle. Thus, the ongoing trends of age and gender diversification continued after the war. But an interesting reversal of sex roles has taken place. While boys of various ages formed the core readership well into the present century, girls today seem to offer the most profitable magazine potential. This is evident not so much perhaps from the publication of girls' comics for the very young, but more strikingly from the developments in publications for adolescents.

In 1955, one year before the final demise of the *Girl's Own Paper*, the first weekly for teenagers (as adolescent girls were now called) appeared. Taking into consideration the boom in commercial youth culture during the 1950s, the new paper bore the timely title *Marilyn*. In its ten-year run it was followed by *Valentine* (1957–74), *Roxy* (1958–63), and about a dozen similar weeklies. Printed on cheap newsprint like other juvenile storypapers, the teenage magazines initially focused on emotional problems both in their picture and straight text stories. These were touched up with fashion and beauty hints and the indispensable problem page. Then, as today, difficulties around "going all the way" formed a main preoccupation of the readers, although editors were rather more circumscribed in their advice: "Look him straight in the eyes and have it out with him—preferably with a table between you. . . . Say that the man you give your heart to isn't going to get anything shop-soiled" (*Marilyn* 1, no. 39 [1955], p. 9).

Influenced by the booming music industry, the teenage weeklies around 1960 began to assume the features of today's music papers with fan clubs, pop gossip, and pull-out centerspreads of male idols (always in full color). *Valentine*, the most popular of the magazines, offered articles to train British adolescents in "American slanguage." By 1962, when the papers had a weekly output of about three million copies, they were deemed "one of the most remarkable journalistic phenomena of the last ten years" (Campbell and Campbell 1962, p. 24).

True to the infallible workings of the market mechanism, the early all-round teenage magazines were graded into different types: in 1960, IPC brought out *Honey*, the first glossy monthly, catering to an older, fashion- and career-conscious clientele. In the first issue, the editor struck the youthful optimism of the early 1960s with the Beatles and Swinging London getting underway: "What fun lies ahead of us! Discs and dancing. Old friends and new. Adventure. In fact, all manner of exciting interesting, simply shattering things" (No. 1 [April 1960], p. 3). To the standard fashion and beauty hints, *Honey* added entries on books and music (Doris Lessing and Josephine Baker were among the names readers were introduced to in 1960). In 1964, D. C. Thomson's *Jackie* came to light as a pop and romance paper for the adolescent schoolgirl (McRobbie 1978); and in 1976 and 1978, respectively, IPC launched *Oh Boy!* and *My Guy*. In these two papers, as their titles indicate, a more sexualized idolization of boys became evident, while at the same time photo-strip stories replaced the usual picture strips, giving the magazines a harder, more realistic edge (Harron 1983, p. 22). Greater realism was evident also in the regular advice columns. From the outset, the companion papers featured a special page on body problems in addition to their agony columns. In *My Guy*'s "You and Your Body," "Chris" gives repeated advice to readers on the different size of breasts, discharge between periods, and the use of tampons ("can one still be a virgin when using them?"). In *Oh Boy!*, a similar page, clinically termed "Medical File," was conducted by a carefree young man and woman, if one may judge from accompanying photos. "Medicus" of the late-Victorian *Girl's Own Paper* would hardly have fulfilled that role. *Oh Boy!* and *My Guy*'s contradictory mixture of idolized sexuality and bodily consciousness struck a new, popular note in teenage publishing. In 1981, three years before *Oh Boy!* merged with *My Guy*, all teenage weeklies had a total output of about two million copies, and in 1986 *My Guy* covered just under ten percent of these sales (Griggs 1981, p. 36; *Willing's Press Guide 1987*, p. 403).

In the early 1980s, that volatile market underwent yet another turn. In 1981, IPC launched *Girl*, a photostory weekly for the preteenage schoolgirl. Two years later, *Just Seventeen* was brought out fortnightly by the East-Midland Allied Press. In this paper, the nice girl is less prominent than in other teenage weeklies—the front cover of the first issue showed the face of a pert-looking young woman sporting an outsize boxing helmet and boxing gloves. Inside the covers, realism is blended with a good deal of irony (Winship 1985), and the unconventional layout of the paper clearly owes much to the punk fanzines of the 1970s. In 1985, the tycoons D. C. Thomson and IPC both launched similar

Just Seventeen, no. 1 (20 October 1983), front cover. The paper inaugurates a new trend in girls' publications with its mixture of ironic contents and a layout emulating the cut-up technique of punk fanzines.

magazines (*Etcetera* and *Mizz*), a clear indication that their dominance can still be shattered by publishers who manage to strike the right tone with the right readership at the right time. Thus, by 1984 *Jackie's* weekly sales had dropped to 384,000 from over a million in 1973 (Winship 1985, p. 31). Conversely, *Just Seventeen*, which is now a weekly, has managed to reach a circulation of 247,000 copies in just three years (*Willing's Press Guide 1987*, p. 331).

Girls today are catered to from nursery to school to bedroom and disco by a plethora of finely graded publications. By contrast, the postwar years have seen no similar developments in boys' papers. As our study has demonstrated, the old-style boys' weeklies before World War II went further than the girls' periodicals in their fictional transformations. They were also rather successful in holding out against the influx of so-called horror comics that were initially brought to England during the war years by American G.I.'s and later printed from stereotypes in Britain. The 1950s fostered an ideal climate for renewed debates on the vicious influence of comics. These debates deeply influenced the cultural politics that shaped the postwar world for juveniles in most Western countries. In England, import of American comics was banned in 1954 through the Children's and Young Persons (Harmful Publications) Act, but the embargo proved only partially effective. In 1950, the Reverend Marcus Morris continued the tradition staked out by numerous of his professional predecessors by editing a better-class magazine, *Eagle*, in an attempt to oust not chapbooks or penny dreadfuls but hardhitting horror comics. Like its female companion, *Girl*, which Morris also edited, *Eagle* was published by the Hulton Press. With its bright colors and good quality paper, the new weekly became a successful rejuvenation of the manly ideals that the *Boy's Own Paper* had found it increasingly hard to uphold. During the 1950s, *Eagle* sold about a million weekly copies (Ellis 1969, p. 202), thanks not least to its main attraction, the space hero Dan Dare, "pilot of the future." The paper lasted until 1970 when it merged with IPC's *Lion*. Among the prewar weeklies, the most thrilling papers, the *Wizard*, the *Rover*, *Adventure*, and the *Hotspur* managed to hold their own against the joint competition from *Eagle* and the horror comics. They featured some of the most successful prewar characters such as "Big Stiff" and "The Wolf of Kabul."

While the new picture storypapers for girls have reinforced the use of slapstick humor and magic much as boys' weeklies did in the 1920s, the new picture storypapers for boys, published during the 1960s and 1970s, have continued the most powerful theme of the interwar boys' weeklies—war. Papers such as D. C. Thomson's *Victor* (1961–), *Commando* (1961–78), and *Warlord* (1974–) have competed for the schoolboys' pennies with *Valiant* (1963–76) and *Battle Picture Weekly* (1975–) brought out by IPC. World War II is the basic distant scenario. Its variations in battle grounds, equipment, and methods of killing were most effectively recounted by *Warlord* in the 1970s when it sold over 235,000 copies a week (Rosie 1977, p. 34). In the 1980s, *Battle Action*

Force, as *Battle Picture Weekly* is now called, has taken over *Warlord*'s position, priding itself to be "today's top tough comic" ([8 October 1983], p. 1). In 1983, George Orwell's dystopia loomed in the immediate future. In *Battle Action Force*, the usual run of war stories is touched up with a series "Invasion 1984." Here, the well-known theme is replayed as the last remnants of British defense, the "Storm Squad," defies a horde of extraterrestrials. The British retrieve their enemy's deadly bacteria ZX–17 and use it against the aliens, having inoculated themselves first, of course. The final installment appears in the Christmas number when two civilian survivors, father and son, emerge from their underground bunker to face masses of distorted corpses: "Gosh dad! Are we the only people left alive in the whole world?" "I hope not, Mikey! But it's a possibility we have to face." The series ends with a candid editorial statement: "This has been a work of fiction but remember . . . invasion 1984 could happen tomorrow!" ([31 December 1983], p. 21).

Unlike girls, boys seem to graduate directly from these action-packed comics and storypapers to hobby and music magazines or soft-porn novels and thrillers that are read also by adults. There are no simple reasons for this persistent gender difference. Even if girls in general seem to be more avid magazine readers than boys, the sheer number of action storypapers and their weekly output amply demonstrate that popular fiction is by no means a female prerogative, nor is the female consumer market as such more lucrative—surveys since the 1950s have clearly shown that boys have more leisure time and more spending money than their sisters (Abrams 1959, p. 9). One reason why we have seen an upsurge in papers for teenage girls in the last thirty years can be that before the war the fictional concoctions cooked up in the boys' papers could appeal to, and hence be used for, a wider readership than the fiction found in the girls' papers. For adolescent girls to be interested, publishers simply had to come up with untried fictional mixtures. That these, unlike the boys' papers and adult thrillers, have changed so rapidly in both style and substance is clearly related to the fact that the lives and future perspectives of adolescent girls have been altered more dramat-ically over the last decades relative to the lives of boys. Today, young women compete with men for the scarce educational and occupational opportunities. The pressures in female adolescence are as great as ever. Papers such as *Just Seventeen*, which tackle these pressures head on but with tongue in cheek, must seem some of the more appealing answers for adolescent girls to their unrelieved problems.

Why could such problems not be treated by the old-style magazines? Why have these periodicals been replaced by more visual forms of fiction? Far from being created by inventive British publishers or unscrupulous competitors from overseas, the development after World War II confirms what was already evident before the war, namely, that the magazines in which text matters more than pictures have exhausted their fictional possibilities. They gradually became capitalist answers to real needs. It is no surprise that comics and picture story-papers have proved more successful in answering these needs. Their visual appeal is a perfection of trends that the juvenile magazines initiated but that their emphasis on the written word made it difficult to develop any further. The interwar weeklies toned down character development in favor of rapid changes in fate and scenery. The papers were composed as an emotional jigsaw puzzle, an assortment of intense thrills and laughs that could be enjoyed without reading through the entire paper to complete one's mental image. Indeed, such an image seemed irrelevant to the readers' enjoyment. But unless the written word turns into lyric, it nevertheless adheres to narrative progression and mental cognition to a degree that pictures do not. In the development of popular reading toward emotional intensities rather than intellectual enlightenment, pictures must be the inevitable winners. Naturally, the postwar decline of the juvenile magazines has been hastened by the enormous influence of television. Since the 1950s, visual storytelling has become the order of the day for all children and is so before they are introduced to the wonders of the cinema. Far from seeing television as the sole cause of fictional changes, however, we should remember that the foundations for the pictorial victory were laid in the interwar periodicals themselves. These periodicals went pictorial not as a matter of form but because the visual appeal seemed to serve the readers' needs better. Far from creating new needs, then, the visualization of juvenile fiction after the war gives a more effective, that is a more entertaining, answer to persistent problems.

This book and its conclusions does not endorse either of the conventional views upheld since the nineteenth century about popular reading matter for the young. Those views have perhaps been most eloquently expressed in a dispute carried out in *Horizon* in 1940 between George Orwell and Charles Hamilton. Taking as his point of departure a comparison between the old-style *Magnet* and *Gem* stories and the interwar brand of boys' papers, Orwell argues with much wit that despite internal differences in style, through their reading of such weeklies the young absorb:

> a set of beliefs which would be regarded as hopelessly out of date in the Central Office of the Conservative Party. All the better because it is being done indirectly, there is being pumped into them the conviction that the major problems of our time do not exist, that there is nothing wrong with *laissez-faire* capitalism, that foreigners are unimportant comics and that the British Empire is a sort of charity-concern which will last forever. Considering who owns these papers, it is difficult to believe that this is unintentional. (Orwell 1976, p. 528)

Without disregarding the readers' enjoyment, Orwell levels his attack at the publishers' moral brainwashing of the young, at the snob appeal of the papers, their racial and social biases and unalloyed patriotism. This form of ideological seduction, according to Orwell, is deliberately encouraged by the publishing giants, D. C. Thomson and the Amalgamated Press. Hardly surprising, such blanket hostility hurt the professional pride of Charles Hamilton, the pioneer of school story perennials. Not only did Orwell erroneously assume that the stories about Greyfriars and St. Jim's were written by several authors, his ideological revelations equally undermined the tenets on which Hamilton's self-image relied. Cogently pointing to Orwell's misconceptions about fictional realism as a guarantee of political objectivity, Hamilton in his reply states that the aims of any author should be "to entertain his readers, make them as happy as possible, give them a feeling of cheerful security, turn their thoughts to healthy pursuits, and above all to keep them away from unhealthy introspection, which in early youth can do only harm" (Richards 1976, p. 540).

Against Orwell's theory of ideological seduction, Hamilton sets up his defense of innocent entertainment. Hamilton counters Orwell's denunciation of popular reading with an idealized image of his beloved magazines. The two contestants thus represent what we have found to be the two most consistent attitudes to popular literature. Despite their stated differences of opinion, however, both writers share a normative approach to juvenile reading. In the 1870s and 1880s this approach found expression in, for example, James Greenwood's and Edward Salmon's adamant proposals for censorship of the penny dreadfuls. In recent years, children's librarians and teachers concerned with their pupils' social and cultural outlook have advocated increased selection and literary choice from the assumption that if quality is available then quality will ultimately prevail. Although this approach grants the young readers some integrity, it nevertheless shares with most other forms of critique a division of literature that often seems irrelevant to the readers themselves.

In the past, just as today, the reading of popular magazines did not necessarily preclude an enjoyment of juvenile books or other forms of so-called quality literature. To the young, the use value of their reading matter was of greater importance than differences in form and style. And as for use value, the weeklies could easily compete with books, as already noted. Indeed, formal differences have undergone drastic revaluations over time. The penny dreadfuls, for example, which in the mid-Victorian decades were banned by right-minded parents and clergymen, are today reprinted and read as examples of good old stories. In more recent times, the advent of videotapes has all but silenced former debates over the impact of ordinary television on youthful minds. By taking the readers' own choices seriously as a basis of research, we do not only have to revaluate our normative preconceptions of culture, however. We can also see the infelicity in separating cultural production from historical circumstances. Children and adolesents have been active in shaping the mass-produced expressions of culture, and those expressions are also more complex than is revealed at first glance. While the history of the juvenile magazines on the surface can be a history of increasing commercialization and exploitation of youthful minds and pockets, that surface hides a covert history of resistance, revealing strong wishes for independence and personal control, sexual curiosity and social power.

The hidden needs of juveniles have been formed in different ways and given different outlets through time. But the continued viability of these needs and the persistence of their expression point to juvenile resources that are often overlooked. By remembering that we do not start participating in the formation of our own lives only when we leave school, get jobs, or have babies, we can avoid the latent elitism that guides so much research on juveniles and their cultures. Equally, by combining the aspects of both literary production and reception we can reach beyond one-sided notions of popular reading as either pure entertainment or a clever form of moral or commercial exploitation. The magazines, as we have seen, generally did reinforce existing power relations, and they often strengthened social, sexual, and ethnic biases. But their very purchase also conveyed a sense of freedom to the young, a space of independence, just as the reading process itself created a momentary balancing of conflicts, a unity of emotion and intellect that was divided in many other areas of life.

Seen from the readers' point of view, the chief limitation of the periodicals lies not so much in their moral corruption or commercial exploitation as in the fact that they provide only momentary satisfaction: in order to reenact one's sense of relief, psychological balance, and sheer enjoyment, one has to buy another issue, and yet another. And there is always more next week. The use value of the commercial magazines invariably depends on the market mechanism and its economic rationale. Juvenile magazines were, indeed, genuine expressions of the historical predicaments facing the young, but they never formed ideal solutions to their problems.

REFERENCES

PRIMARY SOURCES

Only periodicals analyzed are listed here. For other magazines mentioned in the text, please see the Index.

Adventure (1921–61).

Aunt Judy's Magazine (1866–85).

Battle Picture Weekly (1975–77), then *Battle Action* (1977–81), then *Battle* (1981–83), then *Battle Action Force* (1983–).

Boy's Own Magazine; An Illustrated Journal of Fact, Fiction, History and Adventure (1855–74).

Boy's Own Paper (1879–1967).

Boys of England; A Magazine of Sport, Sensation, Fun, and Instruction (1866–99). Incorporated with *Up-to-date Boys*.

Boys' and Girls' Penny Magazine (1832–33).

Boys' Friend (1895–1927). Incorporated with *Triumph*.

Brett, Edwin J. *Jack Harkaway's Schooldays.* "Boys of England Edition." London: Brett, ca. 1880.

Bunty (1958–).

Chatterbox (1866–1948).

Child's Companion; or, Sunday Scholar's Reward (1824–44), then *Child's Companion and Juvenile Instructor* (1846–1921), then *Child's Companion* (1922–23), then *Children's Companion* (1924–28), then *Every Girl's Paper* (1928–32).

Children's Friend (1824–69), new ser. (1861–1930).

Children's Magazine; or Monthly Repository of Instruction & Delight (1798–99).

Crystal (nos. 1–9 1935), then *Girls' Crystal* (1935–53), then a picture-story weekly (1953–63).

Commando (1961–78).

Debbie (1973–83). Incorporated with *Mandy*.

Eagle (1950–70). Incorporated with *Lion*.

English Girls' Journal, and Ladies' Magazine, the Ladies' Favourite Companion (1863–65?).

Every Boy's Magazine (1862–64), then *Routledge's Magazine for Boys* (1865–68), then *Young Gentleman's Magazine* (1869–73), then *Every Boy's Magazine* (1874–88).

Gem Library (1907–29), then *Gem* (1929–39). Incorporated with *Triumph*.

Girl (1951–64).

Girl of the Period Miscellany (1869).

Girl's Own Paper (1880–1908), then *Girl's Own Paper and Woman's Magazine* (1908–27), then *Woman's Magazine and Girl's Own Paper* (1928–30), then separation as *Girl's Own Paper* (1931–41), then *Girl's Own Paper Heiress* (1941–50), then *Heiress* (1950–56).

Girl's Realm (1898–1915).

Girls' and Boys' Penny Magazine; Consisting of Light, Moral and Amusing Tales, calculated to Improve and Instruct the Rising Generation (1832–33).

Girls' Best Friend (1898–99), then *Girls' Friend* (1899–1931). Incorporated with *Poppy's Paper*.

Girls' Home (1910–15). Incorporated with *Our Girls*.

Girls' Reader (1908–15). Incorporated with *Our Girls*.

Good Words for the Young (1868–72), then *Good Things for the Young of All Ages* (1872–77).

Halfpenny Marvel Library (nos. 1–3 1893), then *Halfpenny Marvel* (1893–98), then *Marvel* (1898–1922). Incorporated with *Sport and Adventure*.

Honey (1960–85).

Hotspur (1933–59).

Jackie (1964–).

Jinty (1974–75), then *Jinty and Lindy* (1975–77), then *Jinty* (1977–80), then *Jinty and Penny* (1980–81), then *Jinty* (1981). Incorporated with *Tammy*.

Judy (1960–).

Just Seventeen (1983–).

Juvenile Magazine; or, an Instructive and Entertaining Miscellany for Youth of Both Sexes (1788).

Lilliputian Magazine (1751–52).

Magnet (1908–40). Incorporated with *Knockout*.

Mandy (1967–).

Marilyn (1955–65).

Monthly Packet of Evening Readings for Younger Members of the English Church (1851–98).

My Guy (1978–).

Oh Boy! (1976–84). Incorporated with *My Guy*.

Peter Parley's Magazine (1839–63).

Rover (1922–61).

Roxy (1958–63).

School Friend (1919–29), then *Schoolgirl* (1929–40).

School Friend (1950–65). Incorporated with *June*.

Schoolgirls' Own (1921–36). Incorporated with *Schoolgirl*.

Schoolgirls' Weekly (1922–39). Incorporated with *Girls' Crystal*.

Tammy (6 February–27 March 1971), then *Tammy and Sally* (1971–72), then *Tammy* (1972–73), then *Tammy and Sandie* (1973–74), then *Tammy and June* (1974–75), then *Tammy* (1975–80), then *Tammy and Misty* (1980–82), then *Tammy* (1983–84).

Twinkle (1968–79), then *Twinkle and Magic* (1979–80), then *Twinkle* (1980–).
Valentine (1957–74).
Valiant (1963–76).
Victor (1961–).
Warlord (1974–).
Youth's Magazine; or, Evangelical Miscellany (1805–67). Incorporated with *Bible Class Magazine*.
Youth's Monthly Visitor (1822–23).
Wizard (1922–63).

SECONDARY SOURCES

Abrams, Mark. *The Teenage Consumer*. London: London Press Exchange, 1959.
Adorno, Theodor. *Aesthetic Theory*. 1970. Reprint. Tr. by C. Lenhardt, eds. Gretel Adorno and Rolf Tiedemann. Boston: Routledge & Kegan Paul, 1984.
Altick, Richard D. *The English Common Reader: A Social History of the Mass-Reading Public, 1800–1900*. 1957. Reprint. Chicago: Univ. of Chicago Press, 1967.
Ariès, Philippe. *Centuries of Childhood*. 1960. Tr. 1962. Reprint. Harmondsworth: Penguin, 1973. New York: Random, 1965.
Arnold, Matthew. *Culture and Anarchy: An Essay in Social and Political Criticism*. London: Smith, Elder, 1869. Reprint. Ann Arbor: Univ. of Michigan Press, 1965.
Ashby, M. K. *Joseph Ashby of Tysoe, 1859–1919: A Study of English Village Life*. Cambridge: Cambridge Univ. Press, 1961.
Avery, Gillian. *Childhood's Pattern: A Study of the Heroes and Heroines of Children's Fiction, 1770–1950*. London: Hodder & Stoughton, 1975.
Bailey, Peter. "Custom, Capital and Culture in the Victorian Music Hall." In Robert D. Storch, ed. *Popular Culture and Custom in Nineteenth-Century England*. London: Croom Helm, 1982, pp. 180–208.
Banks, Joseph A. *Prosperity and Parenthood: A Study of Family Planning among the Victorian Middle Classes*. London: Routledge & Kegan Paul, 1954.
Barker, Theo, ed. *The Long March of Everyman*. Harmondsworth: Penguin, 1978.
Beal, George, ed. *The Magnet Companion '77*. London: Baker, 1976.
Bennett, Tony. "Popular Culture: a 'Teaching Object.'" *Screen Education*, no. 34 (1980): 17–29.
Best, Geoffrey. *Mid-Victorian Britain, 1851–1875*. London: Weidenfeld & Nicolson, 1971.
Blanch, Michael. "Imperialism, Nationalism and Organized Youth." In John Clarke et al., eds. *Working-Class Culture: Studies in History and Theory*. London: Hutchinson, 1979.
Branca, Patricia. "Image and Reality: The Myth of the Idle Victorian Woman." In Mary Hartman and Lois W. Banner, eds. *Clio's Consciousness Raised: New Perspectives on the History of Women*. New York: Harper, 1974, pp. 179–91.
———. *Silent Sisterhood: Middle-Class Women in the Victorian Home*. London: Croom Helm, 1975.

Branson, Noreen, and Margot Heinemann. *Britain in the Nineteen Thirties*. St. Albans: Panther, 1973.

Bratton, Jacqueline S. *The Impact of Victorian Children's Fiction*. London: Croom Helm, 1981.

Briggs, Asa. *Mass Entertainment: The Origins of a Modern Industry*. Adelaide: Griffin, 1960.

———. *The Golden Age of Wireless: The History of Broadcasting in the United Kingdom*. Vol. 2. London: Oxford Univ. Press, 1965.

———. "The Language of Class in Early Nineteenth-Century England." In Asa Briggs and John Saville, eds. *Essays in Labour History*. London: Macmillan, 1967, pp. 43–73.

Browne, Phillis [Sarah Sharp Hamer]. *What Girls Can Do: A Book for Mothers and Daughters*. London: Cassell, Petter, Galpin & Co., 1880.

Burnett, John. *Plenty and Want: A Social History of Diet in England from 1815 to the Present Day*. London: Nelson, 1966.

Burnett, John, ed. *Useful Toil: Autobiographies of Working People from the 1820s to the 1920s*. Harmondsworth: Penguin, 1977.

———. *Destiny Obscure: Autobiographies of Childhood, Education and Family from the 1820s to the 1920s*. 1982. Reprint. Harmondsworth: Penguin, 1984.

Burstyn, Joan N. *Victorian Education and the Ideal of Womanhood*. London: Croom Helm, 1980.

Cadogan, Mary, and Patricia Craig. *You're a Brick, Angela! A New Look at Girls' Fiction from 1839 to 1975*. London: Gollancz, 1976.

———. *Women and Children First: The Fiction of Two World Wars*. London: Gollancz, 1978.

Cadogan, Mary, and John Wernham. *The Greyfriars Characters: The Charles Hamilton Companion*. Vol. 2. Maidstone: Museum Press, 1976.

Cadogan, Mary. "How I Became a Collector." *Collectors' Digest Annual* (1974).

Campbell, Mary, and Flann. "Comic Love." *New Society* 14 (1962): 24–25.

Carpenter, Kevin. *Vom Penny Dreadful zum Comic: Englische Jugendzeitschriften, Heften und Comics von 1855 bis zur Gegenwart*. Oldenburg: Biblioteks- und Informationssystem der Universität Oldenburg, 1981. Rev. ed. tr. as *Penny Dreadfuls and Comics: English Periodicals for Children from Victorian Times to the Present Day*. London: Victoria and Albert Museum, 1983.

Census of England and Wales, 1911. London: HMSO, 1915.

Census of England and Wales: General Report. London: HMSO, 1950.

Census of England and Wales, 1931: General Report. London: HMSO, 1951.

Clay, Norman L., ed. *I Remember: An Anthology of Childhood Reminiscences*. London: Heinemann, 1964.

Cobbe, Frances Power. *Life of Frances Power Cobbe as Told by Herself*. 1894. Reprint. London: Swan Sonnenschein, 1904.

Cole, George D. H., and Raymond Postgate. *The Common People, 1746–1946*. 1938. 4th rev. ed. 1956. Reprint. London: Methuen, 1976.

Comfort, Alex. *The Anxiety Makers: Some Curious Preoccupations of the Medical Profession*. London: Nelson, 1967.

Cominos, Peter T. "Late-Victorian Sexual Respectability and the Social System." *International Review of Social History* 8, nos. 1, 2 (1963): 18–48, 216–50.

Creighton, Ellen R. C., ed. *Ellen Buxton's Journals, 1860–1864*. London: Bles, 1967.

Crossick, Geoffrey. "The Emergence of the Lower-Middle Class in Britain: A Discussion." In Geoffrey Crossick, ed. *The Lower-Middle Class in Britain, 1870–1914*. London: Croom Helm, 1977, pp. 11–60.

Cruse, Amy. *The Victorians and Their Books*. London: Allen & Unwin, 1935.

Cudlipp, Hugh. *At Your Peril*. London: Weidenfeld & Nicolson, 1962.

Cutt, Margaret N. *Ministering Angels: A Study of Nineteenth-Century Evangelical Writing for Children*. Wormley: Five Owls, 1979.

Darton, F. J. Harvey. *Children's Books in England: Five Centuries of Social Life*. 3d rev. ed., ed. by Brian Alderson. 1932. Reprint. New York: Cambridge Univ. Press, 1982.

Davidoff, Leonore. "Mastered for Life: Servant and Wife in Victorian and Edwardian England." *Journal of Social History* 7, no. 4 (1974): 406–28.

Davies, Margaret Llewelyn, ed. *Life as We Have Known It: By Co-Operative Working Women*. New intro. by Anna Davin. 1931. Reprint. London: Virago, 1977.

Davin, Anna. "Imperialism and Motherhood." *History Workshop* 5 (1978): 9–65.

Delamont, Sara. "The Contradictions in Ladies' Education." In Sara Delamont and Lorna Duffin, eds. *The Nineteenth-Century Woman: Her Cultural and Physical World*. London: Croom Helm, 1978, pp. 134–63.

Doyle, Brian, ed. and comp. *Who's Who of Boys' Writers and Illustrators 1964*. London: Brian Doyle, 1964.

Drotner, Kirsten. *Drengemagasiner—magasindrenge: masselitteratur for drenge i det 19. århundredes England*. Grenaa: GMT, 1977.

———. "Schoolgirls, Madcaps, and Air Aces: English Girls and Their Magazine Reading Between the Wars." *Feminist Studies* 9, no. 1 (1983): 33–52.

Dunae, Patrick A. "*Boy's Own Paper:* Origins and Editorial Policies." *Private Library* 2d ser., 9, no. 4 (1976): 122–58.

———. "Penny Dreadfuls: Late Nineteenth-Century Boys' Literature and Crime." *Victorian Studies* 22, no. 2 (1979): 133–50.

Dyhouse, Carol. "Social-Darwinistic Ideas and the Development of Women's Education in England, 1880–1920." *History of Education* 5, no. 1 (1976): 41–58.

———. "Good Wives and Little Mothers: Social Anxieties and the Schoolgirl's Curriculum, 1890–1920." *Oxford Review of Education* 3, no. 1 (1977): 21–35.

———. *Girls Growing Up in Late-Victorian and Edwardian England*. London: Routledge & Kegan Paul, 1981.

Egoff, Sheila A. *Children's Periodicals of the Nineteenth Century: A Survey and Bibliography. Library Association Pamphlet No. 8*. London: Library Association, 1951.

Ellis, Alex. *A History of Children's Reading and Literature*. Oxford: Pergamon, 1969.

Engledow, J. H., and William Farr. *The Reading and Other Interests of School*

Children in St. Pancras. London: Passmore Edwards Research Series, no. 2, 1933.

Esdaile, Arundell. *The British Museum Library: A Short History and Survey.* London: Allen & Unwin, 1946.

Eyken, William van der, ed. *Education, the Child and Society: A Documentary History, 1900–1973.* Harmondsworth: Penguin, 1973.

Fayne, Eric. "Editorial." *Collectors' Digest* 16, no. 182 (1962a): 2–3.

Fayne, Eric. "Ave Atque Vale." *Collectors' Digest* 16, no. 182 (1962b): 3–8.

Fee, Elizabeth. "Psychology, Sexuality, and Social Control in Victorian England." *Social Science Quarterly* 58, no. 4 (1978): 632–46.

Fenwick, L. "Periodicals and Adolescent Girls." *Studies in Education* 2, no. 2 (1953): 27–45.

Fleming, Marjory. *The Complete Marjory Fleming: Her Journals, Letters and Verses.* Transcr. and ed. by Frank Sidgwick. London: Sidgwick & Jackson, 1934.

Foot, Percy W. R. *The Child in the Twentieth Century.* London: Cassell, 1968.

Forrester, Wendy. *Great-Grandmama's Weekly: A Celebration of the Girl's Own Paper, 1880–1901.* Guildford, London: Lutterworth, 1980.

Foucault, Michel. *The History of Sexuality.* Vol. 1, *An Introduction.* 1976. Tr. London: Lane, 1979. New York: Pantheon, 1978.

Fox, Geoff, and Graham Hammond, eds. *Responses to Children's Literature: Proceedings of the Fourth Symposium of the International Research Society for Children's Literature.* New York: Saur, 1980.

Fraser, W. Hamish. *The Coming of the Mass Market, 1850–1914.* London: Macmillan, 1981.

Frith, Gill. " 'The Time of Your Life': The Meaning of the School Story." In Carolyn Steedman et al., eds. *Language, Gender, and Childhood.* London: Routledge & Kegan Paul, 1985.

Gathorne-Hardy, Jonathan. *The Rise and Fall of the British Nanny.* London: Hodder & Stoughton, 1972.

Gibson, Ian. *The English Vice: Beating, Sex and Shame in Victorian England and After.* London: Duckworth, 1978.

Gifford, Denis. *The British Comic Catalogue, 1874–1974.* London: Mansell, 1975.

Gilbert, Alan D. *Religion and Society in Industrial England: Church, Chapel and Social Change, 1740–1914.* London: Longman, 1976.

Gillis, John R. *Youth and History: Tradition and Change in European Age Relations, 1700–Present.* New York: Academic Press, 1974.

———. *For Better, for Worse: British Marriages, 1600 to the Present.* New York: Oxford Univ. Press, 1985.

Gittins, Diana G. "Married Life and Birth Control Between the Wars." *Oral History* 3, no. 2 (1975): 53–64.

Gorham, Deborah. "The 'Maiden Tribute of Modern Babylon' Reexamined: Child Prostitution and the Idea of Childhood in Late-Victorian England." *Victorian Studies* 21, no. 3 (1978): 353–79.

———. *The Victorian Girl and the Feminine Ideal.* Bloomington: Indiana Univ. Press, 1982.

Gosden, Peter H. J. H. *Education in the Second World War: A Study in Policy and Administration.* London: Methuen, 1977.

Graves, Robert, and Alan Hodge. *The Long Week-End: A Social History of Great Britain, 1918–1939.* London: Faber & Faber, 1940.

Grey, Jill E. "The Lilliputian Magazine—a Pioneering Periodical?" *Journal of Librarianship* 2, no. 2 (1970): 107–15.

Griggs, Barbara. "Today's Thrills." *Sunday Times* (28 June 1981): 36.

Groom, Arthur. *Writing for Children: A Manual for Writers of Juvenile Fiction.* London: Black, 1929.

Haining, Peter. *The Penny Dreadful: Or, Strange, Horrid and Sensational Tales.* London: Gollancz, 1975.

Hall, Catherine. "Married Women at Home in Birmingham in the 1920s and 1930s." *Oral History* 5, no. 2 (1977): 62–83.

———. "The Early Formation of Victorian Domestic Ideology." In Sandra Burman, ed. *Fit Work for Women.* London: Croom Helm, 1979, pp. 15–32.

Hammerton, A. James. *Emigrant Gentlewomen: Genteel Poverty and Female Emigration, 1830–1914.* London: Croom Helm, 1979.

Hare, Augustus J. C. *The Years with Mother: Being an Abridgement of the First Three Volumes of the Story of My Life.* Ed. with notes and intro. by Malcolm Barnes. London: Allen & Unwin, 1952.

Hare, E. H. "Masturbatory Insanity: The History of an Idea." *Journal of Mental Science* 108, no. 452 (1962): 1–25.

Harron, Mary. "Oh Boy! My Guy." *Times Educational Supplement* (1 July 1983): 22.

Harvey, Robert W. *A Bristol Childhood.* Bristol: Workers' Educational Association, 1976.

Hazeltine, Alice I. "Aunt Judy: Mrs. Gatty and Mrs. Ewing." *Horn Book* 16, nos. 5, 6 (1940): 323–30, 457–66.

Henriques, Ursula R. Q. *The Early Factory Acts and Their Enforcement.* London: Historical Association, 1971.

Hobsbawm, Eric J. *Labouring Men: Studies in the History of Labour.* London: Weidenfeld & Nicolson, 1964.

Hoggart, Richard. *The Uses of Literacy: Aspects of Working-Class Life with Special Reference to Publications and Entertainments.* 1957. Reprint. Harmondsworth: Penguin, 1977.

Holcombe, Lee. *Victorian Ladies at Work: Middle-Class Working Women in England and Wales, 1850–1914.* Newton Abbot: David & Charles, 1973.

Holub, Robert C. *Reception Theory: A Critical Introduction.* New York: Methuen, 1984.

Hopperton, Tom. "Victorian King-Pin." *Story Paper Collector* 4, no. 78 (1962): 31–37.

Houghton, Walter E. *The Victorian Frame of Mind, 1830–1870.* New Haven: Yale Univ. Press, 1957.

Hughes, Molly V. *A London Girl of the 1880s.* 1946. Reprint. Oxford: Oxford Univ. Press, 1978.

Humphries, Stephen. *Hooligans or Rebels? An Oral History of Working-Class Childhood and Youth, 1889–1939.* Oxford: Blackwell, 1981.

Hurt, John S. "Drill, Discipline and the Elementary School Ethos." In Phillip McCann, ed. *Popular Education and Socialization in the Nineteenth Century.* London: Methuen, 1977, pp. 167–91.

———. *Elementary Schooling and the Working Classes, 1860–1918.* London: Routledge & Kegan Paul, 1979.

Hyde, Harford M. *Mr. and Mrs. Beeton.* London: Harrap, 1951.

James, Louis. *Fiction for the Working Man, 1830–1850: A Study of the Literature Produced for the Working Classes in Early Victorian Urban England.* London: Oxford Univ. Press, 1963.

———. "Aspects of Victorian Juvenile Fiction." *International Library Review* 2, no. 2 (1970): 125–33.

———. "Tom Brown's Imperialist Sons." *Victorian Studies* 18, no. 1 (1973): 89–99.

Jauss, Hans R. "Literaturgeschichte als Provokation der Literaturwissenschaft." In Hans R. Jauss, *Literaturgeschichte als Provokation.* Frankfurt am Main: Suhrkamp, 1970, pp. 144–207. A shortened version was tr. by Elizabeth Benzinger as "Literary History as a Challenge to Literary Theory." *New Literary History* 2, no. 1 (1970): 7–37. Reprinted in Hans R. Jauss, *Toward an Aesthetic of Reception.* Minneapolis: Univ. of Minnesota Press, 1982. Tr. Timothy Bahti.

———. "Levels of Identification of Hero and Audience." *New Literary History* 5, no. 2 (1974): 283–317. Tr. by Helga and Benjamin Bennett. Reprinted in Hans R. Jauss, *Aesthetic Experience and Literary Hermeneutics.* Minneapolis: Univ. of Minnesota Press, 1982. Tr. Michael Shore. A longer version, "Negativität und Identifikation: Versuch zur Theorie der ästhetischen Erfahrung," appears in Harald Weinrich, ed., *Positionen der Negativität: Poetik und Hermeneutik, Bd. 6.,* Munich: Fink, 1975, pp. 263–339.

Jay, Frank. "Peeps into the Past." *London Journal* (18 January 1919): 49–50; (29 March 1919): 89–90; (9 October 1920): 164; (23 October 1920): 172; (30 October 1920): 176; (13 November 1920): 184.

Jenkinson, Augustus J. *What Do Boys and Girls Read?* 1940. Reprint. London: Methuen, 1946.

Jephcott, Agnes P. *Girls Growing Up.* London: Faber & Faber, 1942.

Johansson, Sheila R. "Sex and Death in Victorian England: An Examination of Age- and Sex-Specific Death Rates, 1840–1910." In Martha Vicinus, ed. *A Widening Sphere: Changing Roles of Victorian Women.* Bloomington: Indiana Univ. Press, 1977, pp. 163–81.

Jones, Gareth S. *Outcast London: A Study in the Relationship Between Classes in Victorian Society.* Harmondsworth: Penguin, 1976.

Kamm, Josephine. *Hope Deferred: Girls' Education in English History.* London: Methuen, 1965.

Kern, Stephen. "Freud and the Discovery of Child Sexuality." *History of Childhood Quarterly* 1, no. 1 (1973): 117–41.

———. "Explosive Intimacy: Psychodynamics of the Victorian Family." *History of Childhood Quarterly* 1, no. 3 (1974): 437–61.

Kirk, Edward B. *A Talk with Boys about Themselves.* London: Simpkin Marshall Hamilton Kent & Coy, 1895a.

————. *A Talk with Girls about Themselves*. London: Simpkin Marshall Hamilton Kent & Coy, 1895b.

Kleinbaum, Abby R. "Women in the Age of Light." In Renata Bridenthal and Claudia Koonz, eds. *Becoming Visible: Women in European History*. Boston: Houghton Mifflin, 1977, pp. 217–35.

Kutner, Maurice. "Hero Worship when Young." *Story Paper Collector* 4, no. 85 (January, 1964): 179–80.

Lamb, Geoffrey F. *The Happiest Days*. London: Joseph, 1959.

Lang, Majory. "Childhood's Champions: Mid-Victorian Children's Periodicals and the Critics." *Victorian Periodicals Review* 13 (1980): 17–31.

Laqueur, Thomas W. *Religion and Respectability: Sunday Schools and Working-Class Culture, 1780–1850*. New Haven: Yale Univ. Press, 1976.

Laslett, Peter. *The World We Have Lost*. New York: Scribners, 1965.

Lawson, John, and Harold Silver. *A Social History of Education in England*. London: Methuen, 1973.

Lofts, William O. G. "The Circulation Mystery." *Story Paper Collector* 3, no. 73 (1960): 322–26.

————. "We Beg to Disagree." *Story Paper Collector* 4, no. 76 (1961): 3–10.

Lofts, William O. G., and Derek J. Adley. *Old Boys' Books: A Complete Catalogue*. London: n.p., 1969.

————. *The Men Behind Boys' Fiction*. London: Baker, 1970.

Low, Florence B. "The Reading of the Modern Girl." *Nineteenth Century and After* 59 (1906): 278–88.

Lowe, Rose. *Daddy Burtt's for Dinner: Growing Up in Hoxton Between the Wars*. London: Centerprise, 1976.

Lynd, S. *English Children*. London: Collins, 1942.

Lyttelton, Edward. *Training of the Young in Laws of Sex*. London: Longmans, Green & Co., 1900.

McBride, Theresa. *The Domestic Revolution: The Modernisation of Household Service in England and France*. London: Croom Helm, 1976.

————. "'As the Twig is Bent': The Victorian Nanny." In Anthony S. Wohl, ed. *The Victorian Family: Structure and Stresses*. London: Croom Helm, 1978, pp. 44–58.

MacCabe, Colin. "Defining Popular Culture." In Colin MacCabe, ed. *High Theory, Low Culture: Analysing Popular Television and Film*. Manchester: Manchester Univ. Press, 1986, pp. 1–10.

McCann, Phillip. "Popular Education, Socialization and Social Control: Spitalfields 1812–1824." In Phillip McCann, ed. *Popular Education and Socialization in the Nineteenth Century*. London: Methuen, 1977, pp. 1–40.

McCrindle, Jean, and Sheila Rowbotham, eds. *Dutiful Daughters: Women Talk about Their Lives*. London: Lane, 1977.

McLaren, Angus. *Birth-Control in Nineteenth-Century England*. London: Croom Helm, 1978.

Mack, Edward C. *Public Schools and British Opinion, 1780–1860: An Examination of the Relationship Between Contemporary Ideas and the Evolution of an English Institution*. London: Methuen, 1938.

————. *Public Schools and British Opinion since 1860: The Relationship Between Contemporary Ideas and the Evolution of an English Institution.* New York: Columbia Univ. Press, 1941.

McRobbie, Angela. *Jackie: An Ideology of Adolescent Femininity.* Stencilled Occasional Paper, no. 53. Birmingham: Centre for Contemporary Cultural Studies, 1978.

Melly, George. *School Experiences of a Fag at a Private and a Public School.* London: Smith, Elder & Co., 1854.

Ministry of Reconstruction. *Juvenile Employment During the War—and After: The Report of an Enquiry.* London: HMSO, 1919.

Mitchell, Sally. *The Fallen Angel: Chastity, Class and Women's Reading, 1835–1880.* Ohio: Bowling Green Univ. Popular Press, 1981.

Musgrave, Peter W. *From Brown to Bunter: The Life and Death of the School Story.* London: Routledge & Kegan Paul, 1985.

Musgrove, Frank. *Youth and the Social Order.* Bloomington: Indiana Univ. Press, 1965.

Neuburg, Victor E. *Popular Literature: A History and Guide, from the Beginning of Printing to the Year 1897.* Harmondsworth: Penguin, 1977.

Neuman, R. P. "Masturbation, Madness, and the Modern Concepts of Childhood and Adolescence." *Journal of Social History* 8 (1975): 1–27.

Newsome, David. *Godliness and Good Learning: Four Studies on a Victorian Ideal.* London: Murray, 1961.

Newton, Arthur. *Years of Change: Autobiography of a Hackney Shoemaker.* London: Centerprise, 1974.

Opie, Iona, and Peter, eds. *The Oxford Dictionary of Nursery Rhymes.* New York: Oxford Univ. Press, 1951.

————. *The Lore and Language of Schoolchildren.* 1959; St. Albans: Paladin, 1977.

Orwell, George. "Boys' Weeklies." *Horizon* (March 1940). Reprint. Sonia Orwell and Ian Angus, eds. *The Collected Essays, Journalism and Letters of George Orwell.* Vol. 1, *An Age Like This, 1920–1940.* 1968. Reprint. Harmondsworth: Penguin, 1976, pp. 505–31.

Pearsall, Ronald. *The Worm in the Bud: The World of Victorian Sexuality.* Harmondsworth: Penguin, 1971.

Pedersen, Joyce Senders. "Schoolmistresses and Headmistresses: Elites and Education in Nineteenth-Century England." *Journal of British Studies* 15, no. 1 (1975): 135–62.

————. "The Reform of Women's Secondary and Higher Education: Institutional Change and Social Values in Mid- and Late-Victorian England." *History of Education Quarterly* 19, no. 1 (1979): 61–91.

Peterson, M. Jeanne. "The Victorian Governess: Status Incongruence in Family and Society." In Martha Vicinus, ed. *Suffer and Be Still: Women in the Victorian Age.* Bloomington: Indiana Univ. Press, 1972, pp. 3–19.

Pike, E. Royston. *Human Documents of the Industrial Revolution in Britain.* 1966. Reprint. London: Allen & Unwin, 1978.

————. *Human Documents of the Victorian Golden Age, 1850–1875.* London: Allen & Unwin, 1967.

Pinchbeck, Ivy, and Margaret Hewitt. *Children in English Society.* Vol. 1, *From Tudor Times to the Eighteenth Century.* Vol. 2, *From the Eighteenth Century to the Children Act 1948.* London: Routledge & Kegan Paul, 1969, 1973.

Pocock, John Thomas. *The Diary of a London Schoolboy, 1826–1830.* Ed. by Marjorie Holder and Christina Gee. London: Camden History Society, 1980.

Pollock, Alice. *Portrait of My Victorian Youth.* London: Johnson, 1971.

Pollock, Linda A. *Forgotten Children: Parent-Child Relations from 1500 to 1900.* New York: Cambridge Univ. Press, 1983.

Prochaska, F. K. "Charity Bazaars in Nineteenth-Century England." *Journal of British Studies* 16, no. 2 (1977): 62–84.

———. "Little Vessels: Children in the Nineteenth-Century English Missionary Movement." *Journal of Imperial and Commonwealth History* 6, no. 2 (1978): 99–118.

Protherough, Robert. *Developing Response to Fiction.* Milton Keynes: Open Univ. Press, 1983.

Quinlan, Maurice J. *Victorian Prelude: A History of English Manners, 1700–1830.* New York: Columbia Univ. Press, 1941.

Reed, John R. *Old School Ties: The Public School in British Literature.* Syracuse: Syracuse Univ. Press, 1964.

Renier, Anne. *Friendship's Offering: An Essay on the Annals and Gift Books of the Nineteenth Century.* London: Private Libraries Association, 1964.

Rex, Ida. "Schoolteacher." In Richard Gray, intro. *Working Lives.* Vol. 1, *1905–45.* London: Hackney WEA/Centerprise, n.d.

Richards, Frank [Charles Harold St. John Hamilton]. "Frank Richards Replies to George Orwell." *Horizon* (May 1940). Reprint. Sonia Orwell and Ian Augus, eds. *The Collected Essays, Journalism and Letters of George Orwell.* Vol. 1, *An Age Like This, 1920–1940.* 1968. Reprint. Harmondsworth: Penguin, 1976, pp. 531–40.

———. *The Autobiography of Frank Richards.* London: Skilton, 1952.

Roberts, Robert. *The Classic Slum: Salford Life in the First Quarter of the Century.* 1971. Reprint. Harmondsworth: Penguin, 1977.

Robertson, Priscilla. "Home As a Nest: Middle-Class Childhood in Nineteenth-Century Europe." In Lloyd de Mause, ed. *The History of Childhood.* New York: Harper, 1974, pp. 407–31.

Rollington, Ralph [H. J. Allingham]. *A Brief History of Boys' Journals: With Interesting Facts about the Writers of Boys' Stories.* Leicester: Simpson, 1913.

Rosie, George. "The Private Life of Lord Snooty." *Sunday Times Magazine* (29 July 1973): 8–16.

———. "The Warlocks of British Publishing." In Paul Harris, publ. *The D. C. Thomson Bumper Fun Book.* Edinburgh: Harris, 1977, pp. 9–49.

Rowntree, B. Seebohm. *Poverty and Progress: A Second Social Study of York.* London: Longmans, Green & Co., 1941.

Ruskin, John. "Letter L: Agnes' Book." In *Fors Clavigera: Letters to the Workmen and Labourers of Britain.* London, 1875. Reprinted in *The Works of John Ruskin,* eds. E. T. Cook and Alexander Wedderburn. London: Allen & Unwin, 1907.

Salmon, Edward. *Juvenile Literature as It Is.* London: Drane, 1888.

Sangster, Paul. *Pity My Simplicity: The Evangelical Revival and the Religious Educa-tion of Children, 1739–1800*. London: Epworth, 1963.

Seaman, Lewis C. B. *Life in Britain Between the Wars*. London: Batsford, 1970.

Selleck, Richard J. W. *English Primary Education and the Progressives, 1914–1939*. London: Routledge & Kegan Paul, 1972.

[Shaw, Charles]. *When I Was a Child: By an Old Potter*. London: Methuen, 1903.

Sherrard, Owen A. *Two Victorian Girls: With Extracts from the Hall Diaries*. Ed. by A. R. Mills. London: Muller, 1966.

Shore, Emily. *Journal of Emily Shore*. London: Kegan Paul, Trench, Trabner, 1898.

Simon, Brian. *The Two Nations and the Educational Structure, 1780–1870*. London: Lawrence & Wishart, 1974a.

———. *Education and the Labour Movement, 1870–1920*. London: Lawrence & Wishart, 1974b.

———. *The Politics of Educational Reform, 1920–1940*. London: Lawrence & Wishart, 1974c.

Smith, F. Barry. "Sexuality in Britain, 1800–1900: Some Suggested Revisions." In Martha Vicinus, ed. *A Widening Sphere: Changing Roles of Victorian Women*. Bloomington: Indiana Univ. Press, 1977, pp. 182–98.

Smith, Frances B. *The People's Health, 1830–1910*. London: Croom Helm, 1979.

Smith, Hubert Llewellyn, dir. *The New Survey of London Life and Labour*. Vol. 1, *Forty Years of Change*. London: King, 1930.

Smith, Lil. *The Good Old Bad Old Days*. London: Centerprise, 1975.

Spain, Nancy B. *The Beeton Story*. London: Ward, Lock & Co., 1956.

Spinney, G. H. "Cheap Repository Tracts: Hazard and Marshall Edition." *Library*, 4th ser., 20, no. 3 (1939): 295–340.

Spitz, René A. "Authority and Masturbation: Some Remarks on a Bibliographical Investigation." *Psychoanalytic Quarterly* 21 (1952): 490–527.

Springhall, John. *Youth, Empire and Society: British Youth Movements, 1883–1940*. London: Croom Helm, 1977.

———. *Coming of Age: Adolescence in Britain, 1860–1960*. Dublin: Gill & Macmillan, 1986.

Stevenson, John. *Social Conditions in Britain Between the Wars*. Harmondsworth: Penguin, 1977.

Stewart, Mary. *The Leisure Activities of School Children*. London: Workers Educational Association, 1948.

Stickland, Irina, comp. *The Voices of Children, 1700–1914*. Oxford: Blackwell, 1973.

Stone, Lawrence. "Literacy and Education in England, 1640–1900." *Past and Present* 42 (1969): 69–139.

———. *The Family, Sex and Marriage in England, 1500–1800*. Rev. and abridged ed. Harmondsworth: Penguin, 1979. New York: Harper and Row, 1985.

Suleiman, Susan R., and Inge Crosman, eds. *The Reader in the Text: Essays on Audience and Interpretation*. Princeton: Princeton Univ. Press, 1980.

Summerfield, Geoffrey. *Fantasy and Reason: Children's Literature in the Eighteenth Century*. London: Methuen, 1984.

Taylor, Gordon R. *The Angel-Makers: A Study in the Psychological Origins of Historical Change, 1750–1850*. London: Heinemann, 1958.

Temple, Nigel, select. and intro. *Seen and Not Heard: A Garland of Fancies for Victorian Children*. London: Hutchinson, 1970.

Thompson, David N., ed. *Nonconformity in the Nineteenth Century*. London: Routledge & Kegan Paul, 1972.

Thompson, Edward P. and Eileen Yeo, eds. *The Unknown Mayhew: Selections from the Morning Chronicle, 1849–50*. Harmondsworth: Penguin, 1973.

Thompson, Edward P. *The Making of the English Working Class*. 1963. Reprint. Harmondsworth: Penguin, 1975.

Thompson, Flora. *Lark Rise to Candleford*. 1939. Reprint. Harmondsworth: Penguin, 1973.

Thompson, Paul. *The Edwardians: The Remaking of British Society*. St. Albans: Paladin, 1977.

Thompson, Thea. *Edwardian Childhoods*. London: Routledge & Kegan Paul, 1981.

Tompkins, Jane P., ed. *Reader-Response Criticism: From Formalism to Post-Structuralism*. Baltimore: John Hopkins Univ. Press, 1980.

Trudgill, Eric. *Madonnas and Magdalens: The Origins and Development of Victorian Sexual Attitudes*. London: Heinemann, 1976.

Turner, Barry. *Equality for Some: The Story of Girls' Education*. London: Lock, 1974.

Turner, Ernest S. *Boys Will be Boys: The Story of Sweeney Todd, Deadwood Dick, Sexton Blake, Billy Bunter, Dick Barton, et al.* 1948. Reprint. Harmondsworth: Penguin, 1976.

Urwick, Edward J., ed. *Studies of Boy Life in Our Cities*. London: Dent, 1904.

Vance, Norman. "The Ideal of Manliness." In Brian Simon and Ian Bradley, eds. *The Victorian Public School: Studies in the Development of an Educational Institution*. Dublin: Gill & Macmillan, 1975.

Vincent, David. *Bread, Knowledge and Freedom: A Study of Nineteenth-Century Working-Class Autobiography*. London: Methuen, 1982.

———. "Reading in the Working-Class Home." In John K. Walton and James Walvin, eds. *Leisure in Britain, 1780–1939*. Manchester: Manchester Univ. Press, 1983, pp. 206–26.

Walvin, James. *Leisure and Society, 1830–1950*. London: Longman, 1978.

———. *A Child's World: A Social History of English Childhood, 1800–1914*. Harmondsworth: Penguin, 1982.

———. "Children's Pleasures." In John K. Walton and James Walvin, eds. *Leisure in Britain, 1780–1939*. Manchester: Manchester Univ. Press, 1983, pp. 227–41.

Warner, Philip, ed. and intro. *The Best of British Pluck: The Boy's Own Paper*. London: Macdonald & Jane, 1976.

Webb, Robert Kiefer. *The British Working-Class Reader, 1790–1848: Literacy and Social Tension*. London: Allen & Unwin, 1955.

Weeks, Jeffrey. *Sex, Politics and Society: The Regulation of Sexuality Since 1800*. London: Longman, 1981.

Wells, Herbert G. *Ann Veronica*. 1909. Reprint. Harmondsworth: Penguin, 1968.

————. *Experiment in Autobiography: Discoveries and Conclusions of a Very Ordinary Brain (Since 1866)*. Vol. 1. London: Gollancz, 1934.

Wertham, Frederic. *The Seduction of the Innocent*. New York: Rinehart, 1954.

West, Edwin G. *Education and the Industrial Revolution*. London: Batsford, 1975.

White, Cynthia L. *Women's Magazines, 1693–1968*. London: Joseph, 1970.

Whitehead, Frank. *Children and Their Books*. London: Macmillan, 1977.

Willing's Press Guide 1987. East Grinstead: British Media Publications, 1987.

Willis, Frederick. *101 Jubilee Road: A Book of London Yesterdays*. London: Phoenix, 1948.

Wilson, John J. "Penny Dreadfuls and Penny Bloods." *Connoisseur* 89 (1932): 226–33.

Winship, Janice. "'A Girl Needs to Get Street-Wise': Magazines for the 1980s." *Feminist Review* 20 (1985): 25–46.

Wohl, Anthony S. *The Eternal Slum: Housing and Social Policy in Victorian London*. London: Arnold, 1977.

Wolveridge, Jim. *"Ain't It Grand"* (or *"This Was Stepney"*). London: Stepney, 1976.

Yglesias, Roy. "Education and Publishing in Transition." In Asa Briggs, ed. *Essays in the History of Publishing*. London: Longman, 1974, pp. 358–88.

INDEX

Abortion, 95; abortifacients, 165n
Adams, Harriet S., 207
Adolescence: definition of, 12, 116–17;
  and sexuality, 80, 136–38; female,
  116, 117. *See also* Labor, child; Mar-
  riage, and work; Youth
Adventure, 187–88, 190n, 216, 217, 243
Adventure story: in books, 68; in *Boys' of
  England*, 103–04; in Edwardian boys'
  papers, 179 and n; in schoolgirl week-
  lies, 209–10; in schoolboy weeklies,
  218–20; in girls' picture stories, 239–
  40
Advertisements: 67, 125, 165, 165n,
  179–80, 230; illustration, 69. *See also*
  Consumerism
Age of consent, 131
Alice's Adventures in Wonderland (Carroll),
  68
Ally Sloper's Half Holiday, 125
Andersen, Hans Christian, 70
Annuals, 13, 64n
Answers to Correspondents, 125
Arabian Nights, The, 40, 67n
Argus, 187
Arnold, Matthew, 5, 125
Ascott, Adelie. *See* Bobin, John W.
Ashby, Joseph, 94, 94n
A Token for Children (Janeway), 22
"At the Back of the North Wind" (Mac-
  Donald), 70
Aunt Judy's Magazine, 70, 70n, 118; il-
  lustration, 82
Authors, earnings, 75n, 128n, 188

Baden-Powell, Lord, 147, 179
Ballantyne, Robert M., 68, 124

Band of Hope, 91
Battle Action Force, 243–44. See also *Bat-
  tle Picture Weekly*
Battle Picture Weekly, 243
Beano, 189, 222, 240
Beauty. *See* Health
Beeton, Samuel O., 65, 67, 98, 119
Beeton's Boy's Own Magazine, 68
Bezer, John James, 56
Bible Class Magazine, 25
Big Stiff. See *Hotspur*
Birth: registration, 30n; children's atti-
  tudes to, 55n; control, 135, 194
Black Bess (Viles). *See* Turpin, Dick
"Black Sapper, The": 225, 227; illustra-
  tion, 226. See also *Rover*
Blake, Sexton. *See* Detective stories
Bobin, John W., 206, 207
Book of Household Management, The
  (Beeton), 65
Boys, 123
Boys' and Girls' Penny Magazine, 66n
Boys' Brigade, 147
Boy's Cinema, 208n
Boy Scouts, 147, 198, 198n; in maga-
  zines, 176
Boys' Friend, 125n, 127, 129, 179n, 230
Boys' Herald, 127
Boys' Magazine, 190n
Boy's Monthly Magazine, 68
Boys of England, 127, 129; origin, 73–76;
  illustrations, 74, 110; circulation, 75;
  contents, 103–11; foreigners in, 171n;
  and *Magnet* and *Gem*, 178–79. See also
  Harkaway, Jack
Boys of the World, 126
Boy's Own Annual, 123

263